Al McGuire
The Colorful Warrior

Roger Jaynes

Forewords by Hank Raymonds
and
Rick Majerus

Sports Publishing L.L.C.
www.SportsPublishingLLC.com

Director of production: Susan M. Moyer
Acquisitions editor: Mike Pearson
Developmental editor: Regina D. Sabbia
Project manager: Alicia D. Wentworth
Copy editor: Cynthia L. McNew
Photo editor: Erin Linden-Levy
Dust jacket design: Christine Mohrbacher
Imaging: Christine Mohrbacher
Marketing Manager: Scott Rauguth

ISBN: 1-58261-842-9

Printed in the United States of America.

Sports Publishing L.L.C.
www.SportsPublishingLLC.com

For Mary, with love

(And remembering all those lunches, Al,
and how you let me pay)

Contents

Foreword
By Hank Raymonds

I first met Al McGuire during the 1960-61 college basketball season, when I was coaching at Christian Brothers College in Memphis, Tennessee. At that time, Al was coaching at Belmont Abbey in Belmont, North Carolina, where he had attracted some national attention because of his winning teams. What few people knew was that all his games had to be played on the road (the college had no gymnasium), and so I thought, what the heck, and called him about playing us in Memphis. He quickly agreed, and we scheduled a game for the following season.

Funny thing was, I never got to coach that game against Al because in the interim I had left Christian Brothers to come to Marquette University, as an assistant to my former college coach, Ed Hickey.

After the 1963-64 season, Marquette let Ed go, and naturally I applied for the position and—ironically enough—found I was a finalist along with a guy named Al McGuire. Well, as we all know, Al got the job. And the same day he got it, he called me and asked if I would stay on as his assistant, assuring me I could do anything I wanted. "They tell me you're the Adolph Rupp of Memphis," Al insisted. "Stay with me, and we'll knock 'em dead."

I was flabbergasted. Remember, this was from a guy who I'd never met and only talked to on the phone a couple of times. And yet, right then, I felt for him to put that kind of trust in me was pretty gratifying. Al went on to tell me that when his Belmont Abbey team played Christian Brothers in Memphis, we'd beaten him pretty good. "Where the hell did you get those guys?" he asked me.

To this day, I don't know how much a factor that was in Al's deciding he wanted me to stay on as his assistant. (But I do know the fact that "my" team had beaten Belmont Abbey was something I never let him forget. It was that little ace I always liked to have on hand, when we were kidding around over the years.)

A week after that phone call, Al and I finally met face to face in Milwaukee, and I immediately sensed that he wasn't kidding, when he talked about giving me my head. Right from the start, I learned two things about Al—he never liked long meetings, and he almost always trusted my judgment and suggestions. I was especially astonished when, after he and his lovely wife Pat had looked at homes in the Milwaukee area, he handed me a signed blank check to buy the house before he left to go back to North Carolina. It was just another indication, right up front, of how much trust he had in me, and that always meant a lot to me.

Our relationship was mostly a professional one. Al and I seldom socialized. I didn't mind that. I think it's why we were able to accomplish all we did together. To this day, I feel, for two people who had never met and only spoken twice over the phone, for Al and I to end up with the very special 13-year relationship we had was nothing short of a miracle.

One thing I found, this guy was a real maverick. But what most people didn't realize was that everything he did had a purpose, no matter how off the wall he sounded. Al was the type of guy who didn't want to stand still. He always wanted the next level in a conversation and, I noticed, was usually two steps ahead in his thinking. And contrary to his public appearance, Al was most often a loner away from the court. While he loved the limelight, he also liked to go on his motorcycle. He liked to take walks. He liked to think. So there was a big contrast between Al on the court and off. I remember once how I joked about how Al was "a legend in his own mind," but I really do think, all his life, he danced to a different tune than you and I.

One thing I noticed was that when things were going well, Al needed a little pinprick sometimes, when complacency entered in. So I would remind him, and he would catch himself and once again become the fierce competitor, which was his trademark. That was Al. He was always at his best when he felt his back was against the wall. It was just the way he was.

I remember one of my jobs was to make all the travel arrangements for our trips. And I would always check with Al first, to get his thoughts about the basics—departure times, practice times, and so on—and then go ahead and schedule the details. After which, he would suddenly want to make changes at the last minute, and I would explode. It was only after this happened a few times, I sensed he was doing it just to calm me down and take my mind off the game. So after that, I just said OK, and you know what? He never made any last-minute changes again.

On the court, Al was always the show. He knew that; we all knew that. But what a lot of people probably don't realize was that he was one of our big strengths. When things got tight, Al would purposely get up and do his stuff—taking the heat from the opposing team and fans on his shoulders so that our guys could just go out there and play.

When it came to basketball philosophy, everything was simple, just like the game. Like I said, Al gave me my head in that area. He asked me to devise an offense where everyone touched leather, with one option for each play. But our game was really defense.

Maybe it was because of his street-smart background, but Al was strictly a percentage person. The key to our success was that we had our "patterns" and we ran them, again and again if necessary, until we were so good at them that nobody could stop us. Execution was the key.

One thing I always respected about Al: When he talked to his players, he talked about life. Treat people like you want to be treated. Work hard. As he put it, always try to "Be a Hertz, don't be an Avis." It will pay off in the end. Another thing he preached to them about was to "put something back into the pot." In other words, don't just take all your lives, but give as well. It was something he did when he started Al's Run for Children's Hospital in Milwaukee, back in 1978. And look what a run that has had!

The only thing Al and I didn't discuss was when he was considering leaving Marquette to coach the Milwaukee Bucks, back in 1968. Personally, I'm glad he didn't, or I probably wouldn't be writing this today. On the other hand, if Al had talked to me at the time, things might have turned out differently. Where Al made his mistake, I feel, was that he went to the wrong person to obtain a release from his contract, certainly not the person I would have suggested. But that's another story.

Al was noted for his antics during the games and getting nailed with a "T"—sometimes at the worst possible times. I generally knew when he wanted a technical for an advantage, but I have to admit, I lost a couple of sport coats (trying to hold him back) when I knew he would get in trouble.

At one game, I'll never forget, I tossed my program up about a foot in the air and the official called a "T" on me. I was scared to death about what Al would do, but all he did was look at me and laugh. "That'll teach you to go to church every day," he said.

I only visited Al once at the end, after he had entered the hospice. He handled his end like a pro. He said, "Hank, I got about two months left. I've had a good run. That's all she wrote." As we talked, I realized that his main concern was for his grandchildren, who might not understand. At one point, I thanked him for being so good to me and for keeping his word. He looked at me and said, "No, Hank. Thank you for helping me."

I have to say, too, I'm happy Roger called me, and asked if I'd do this foreword. And I'm happy he's doing this book. Because he was there, like all of us, and he knows so well the type of person Al really was. As I told him, I think he's got a winner. Because his book reveals many of the things I experienced firsthand in my years with Al. After reading it, I'm sure you will agree with me, there will never be another Al McGuire.

Hank Raymonds
Assistant Basketball Coach Marquette University (1961-1977)
Head Basketball Coach Marquette University (1977-1983)
Athletic Director Marquette University (1977-1987)
Written May, 2001

Foreword

By Rick Majerus

I was very pleased to have been asked by Roger to do this foreword for his book about Coach McGuire. It was an honor and a privilege to have coached under him, but even more so, to have been his friend. I was privy to most of what went on in Coach's life, a confidant of sorts, particularly so after his career ended. I would also like to think that I was a good friend to him until his untimely passing in January of 2001.

This book chronicles and recapitulates numerous stories and has many anecdotal meanderings that will amuse and entertain the reader. It conveys a sense of who McGuire was as a coach and also portrays the compassion inside him as a person. His tenacious, competitive spirit seemed to belie the kind, caring, and concerned man that he was regarding the well-being of his players.

Coach McGuire always used to say, "If I didn't know you, I wouldn't give you a straw hat in a blizzard." I believe like all coaches, he mellowed out as the years went by. His reference to coaches as the "last cowboys" was a very telling and intuitive look at the man himself. Coach had an independent spirit of adventure that most parallels those who settled the American West and those who entered into the combative nature that is the essence of what goes on in the game.

I've found the book to be factual, and it accurately portrayed Coach, certainly as a consummate competitor and somewhat as the clown prince of basketball. It gives a more humane insight into the Solomon-like qualities of the man who would not know the Ignatian discernment principles from an anthology of Mark Twain's works, but who in the course of everyday life imparted wisdom and spirit to his players unlike that of any other professor on a campus that contained some academic giants.

Roger's book is written with integrity, so as to present to you the man who so captivated the press. Unfortunately, his career as a coach does not leave as great a legacy as a Hall of Famer probably should, because it was so overshadowed by the brilliance of a broadcasting career unparalleled in the profession.

Roger Jaynes does a wonderful job of delving into the inner workings of a man, chronicling events, recalling stories, and relaying information in such a manner that you are able to look into the inner sanctum, so to speak, of Warrior basketball and what made it special for a relatively obscure campus overshadowed in almost every way by the prestigious Big Ten institutions that surrounded it.

Coach's was a life well lived in service to others, whether that service be to entertain and engage or to teach and mentor. The man's engaging charm becomes evident as you read through the pages of this book. There is no way you can't like what it is that has made him so special and endeared him to the heart of so many basketball aficionados at all levels. His common sense, Will Rogers approach, and self-deprecating sense of humor are all presented here. You will enjoy the observations that Roger notes as to the diverse cast of characters, all of whom play on the pages of this book.

If you like it, I hope that you'll consider a contribution to Marquette University and to the Al McGuire Center. It would be a fitting tribute to someone whose love of the game and passion for life have been played out before you via Roger's poignant perspectives. Regardless of what your feelings are, you won't regret this look into the world of college basketball, the heart and soul of a man who wore it all on his sleeve for good or bad, entertaining us to the end with a dignity and class for which he is revered by coaches, players, and fans everywhere and anywhere.

Rick Majerus
Assistant Basketball Coach Marquette University (1971-83)
Head Basketball Coach Marquette University (1983-86)
Assistant Basketball Coach Milwaukee Bucks (1986-87)
Head Basketball Coach Ball State University (1987-89)
Head Basketball Coach University of Utah (1989-2004)
Written August 1, 2001

Introduction
The Ultimate "Keeper"

The amazing thing I found out, over the years, was that Al McGuire sometimes surprised even himself. Most people who came in contact with him—players, alumni, reporters, announcers, fans—were almost always amused and often astonished by the nonstop retinue of funny lines and fascinating stories this street-smart Irishman had to tell. Where does he come up with that all stuff? I was asked, again and again.

Well, believe it or not, Alfred E. McGuire—one of the greatest quipsters God ever put on earth—more than once asked himself that same question.

The scene varied over the years, when I was covering Marquette University for the *Milwaukee Journal* in the mid-1970s. We might be doing an interview in Al's quiet, softly lit office, or sitting on those old, hard wooden benches that lined the walls of the Warriors' dreary practice gym, conversing while the players pounded up and down the floor. Later, after Al quit the coaching ranks—to become a vice president for Medalist Industries and a commentator on NBC—our talks took place in quite different surroundings, usually a George Webb's or some side-of-the-road chili and hot dog place in Milwaukee's western suburbs, near his home in Brookfield.

No matter. Every so often, the same thing would happen. All of a sudden, as Al was rattling along, he'd utter a line and then momentarily pause, thinking over a bit what he'd just said, then giving me a smile and a glint of satisfaction in his eye.

"Hey, that's a pretty good line, isn't it?" he'd say, amused. "Be sure you write that down, Rog. That's a 75-dollar line."

Al McGuire's life was full of 75-dollar lines.

Whether Al was coaching on the basketball court, speaking in a corporate board room, delivering an after-dinner talk, or commenting on national TV, there was no such thing as a prepared speech. "Roger, I'm strictly off the cuff," he told me so many times. "I always have been. I play to the moment. A stream of consciousness sort of thing. I don't know where it all comes from. All I know is, it's me."

"Me" was what made Al totally different from any other college basketball coach—or person, for that matter—that I ever met. Never, in my 33-year involvement in the world of sports, both in writing and public relations, did I ever know a sports personality who was so vibrant, so colorful, so full of the joy of the moment, on stage and off, and frankly, just so much darned fun to be around.

He could be flamboyant, of course. And egotistical, and angry, and arrogant, and loud when he chose. But that was what made it so much fun. Because Al McGuire was, all his life, first and foremost, a colorful scrapper from the streets of New York, who spent most of his life fighting to make it to what he called "the white cuff" areas—even if, at times, the ride got more than a little bumpy along the way. The element of the unexpected was always there in Al McGuire, on court and off, and that—combined with his Irish wit and fierce spirit—was what made him so charismatic and exciting.

Ah yes, those 75-dollar lines. Those unique quips that went beyond the world of college basketball and applied to life itself. "The Tenets of Professor Al" I once called them, because not only were they things that he believed in, but they reflected both the dreams of life we all grow up with—and the truths of that life we all must face.

"Dream big," he used to tell his players. "Don't be just another guy going down the street and going nowhere."

"Who says life is fair?" he once questioned. "If it was, nobody would be in wheelchairs."

Some things he said sounded like contradictions. But it depended on what he was talking about—sports or life in general. About college basketball, Al said, "If winning weren't important, nobody would keep score." But in other, more reflective moments, he often ventured: "Winning is only important in war and in surgery."

My two favorites? How better to sum up what William Saroyan called "the human condition" than by saying: "We rush for the stars as we crawl to our graves." And, of course, the words that, over the years came to be his credo: "I like seashells and balloons. Ribbons and medals. Bare feet and wet grass." That was Al's wish for all his friends, that they, like him, could step back and enjoy the moment. Let life come to them and try to understand what the at times crazy-quilt game of life all of us must play is all about.

A maudlin phrase? Perhaps. But do not mistake the sincerity. For there were, as I saw over the years, two Al McGuires, and just as surely as Hyde harangued officials by night, so did Jekyll talk philosophy by day in low whispers. But Hyde performed before packed houses, remember, and so that image remains. Best leave it that Al McGuire was more complex than any of us knows, a maniac perhaps, an egotist surely, but also the possessor of a mind that staked out huge claims.

He even had a language of his own, and if you wanted to understand and savor the world of Al McGuire to the fullest, you had to learn the lingo along the way. A "thoroughbred" was a gifted athlete who was "dynamite," a "nose-bleeder" a super jumper. An "aircraft carrier" a dominant big man, a "dance-hall player" one who was short on talent, but big on effort. "Curtain time" was game time. "Park Avenue" was anything first class. "Tenth Avenue" was the opposite of "Park Avenue." And a "cupcake" was an easy opponent. "Dunkirk" was how he described a poor team performance, and, of course, "uptown" was where he wanted to go every year—to a postseason tournament with an invitation in hand. He even had terms that were combinations of other terms, like "three o'clocker." That was a "thoroughbred" who was "dynamite" in practice and mediocre at "curtain time."

But the descriptive phrase that comes to mind most now, when I think about my friend Al McGuire, is what he called "a keeper." It was his way of describing something he felt was truly special and that had great worth. Perhaps it was a player who had true talent, and a golden future. Or an award or title, like the NCAA championship, that was truly worth the winning. It related, of course, to fishing, and what part of the catch that you threw back and what was good enough to keep.

During the years I was associated with Al, I was fortunate enough to meet a whole school of "keepers"—people who made my life richer and fuller for the knowing. Al's wife Pat, God bless her. Could anyone be more considerate, polite or kind? His two assistants, Hank Raymonds and Rick Majerus, who went on to become winners in their own right. Kevin Byrne, MU's SID, a consummate professional who never lost the human touch (and now wears a Baltimore Ravens Super Bowl ring). Big Bob Weingart (now deceased), MU's hard-working and long-suffering trainer, who had a hearty laugh and a heart of gold. Leo Flynn, Marquette's director of admissions (sincerity should be his middle name), and his lovely wife, Nancy. And who could forget the marvelous bunch of TV and radio guys who traveled with us—Merle Harmon, Bob Uecker, Tom Collins, Bob Bach…and Al's son Allie, who played a cutthroat game of gin rummy on the plane. And, of course, the players— the super talents like Bo Ellis, Butch Lee, and Earl Tatum; a real gentleman named Ulice Payne; soft-spoken Jerome Whitehead, son of a preacher man; Gary Rosenberger, who made the longest shots imaginable, and Jerry Homan, whose heart and desire, even when hurt, could not be denied.

Al, of course, was the ultimate keeper. If you were lucky enough to earn his friendship, his respect, it was something you cherished for the rest of your life. I always wanted to write a book with Al McGuire during his lifetime. Sad to say, I never got the chance. I always felt that there should be a living record of this man, warts and all, who accomplished so much and affected so many people so deeply. I hope this book, at least to a certain extent, can do that.

It has been written that a man does not truly die, so long as he lives on in the hearts of those who knew him best. Others, like Hank and Rick, and Kevin, probably knew Al better than I did. All I know is that it was a privilege to know him well. And I hope that, after reading this book, you'll understand why.

Sign on Al McGuire's Door:
"Busy, but if you can look over the
transom, enter"

Chapter 1

Showman and Philosopher

"Hey! What the hell's going on here?"

This was Al McGuire like I'd never heard him before. The voice was raspy and irate. An Irish bartender's voice that cut through crowd noise like a buzzsaw, sending out shockwaves all the way up to the cheap seats way on high.

At courtside, the tension and excitement hit me smack in the gut, like an unexpected right. Suddenly, like that traffic accident you never expect, it was happening—what I, the new beat reporter for the *Milwaukee Journal*—had been told about, and what, it was suddenly crystal clear to me, the Marquette diehards who sold out the Arena night after night had paid their money to see.

Al McGuire was up and pacing, an angry, brooding storm before the Marquette bench. Five fouls had been called on his Warriors in less than eight minutes' time (against a cupcake like St. Mary's of California, no less!), and it was more than he could stand. Back and forth he went, like a caged lion, hands on his hips, frowning, furious. Black hair flowing he marched off those mincing steps, searching out the officials, his dark eyes flashing.

New guy on the block, I had been lulled by two previous Marquette routs in which Al hadn't done more than yell a few instructions to his players along the way. Come on. And they called this guy a wild man? Now, as I looked around me, I was about to find out why.

The storm, the Arena aficionados knew, was about to break. Unlike me, they had heard McGuire's "What the hell?" call-to-arms cue line many times before, and they knew what was sure to follow. Eagerly now, they leaned forward in their seats to savor the coming chaos, screaming their support. For the uninitiated like me, however, experiencing a McGuire tirade for the first time was all a little bit frightening. A circus and a four-alarm fire all in one. Like the keepers had opened the cages at the zoo, but the outside doors were locked.

My heart pounded. Surely, I thought, this was how Custer must have felt when he saw all those Indians...and had no place to hide.

The MU faithful were not disappointed. Arms flailing, McGuire first grabbed the timekeeper's cards off the scorer's table, ripped them to shreds, and tossed them into the air. And then, as his homemade confetti floated down about him, he turned and kicked his chair, threw back his coat with indignation...and rushed out onto the court!

"Hey? Where the hell are we?" he screamed at the official, the veins in his neck bulging. "California? What the hell do we do to get a foul called?"

The official, his honor on the line, immediately obliged, slamming one hand down on the other in the form of a T, slapping McGuire with a technical foul. The crowd erupted, and McGuire, like a bull who has seen the cape, charged again, lacing the official with words good Irish Catholic boys aren't supposed to know. The Arena was pandemonium now, boos drowning out all else, with crumpled programs sailing down onto the court. McGuire, screaming into the maelstrom, was all over the official like a farmer's dog on a corncrib rat.

At this point, the student section at one end began to chant, raising the noise level another hundred decibels. "Give 'em hell, Al!" they roared. "Give 'em hell, Al! Give 'em hell, Al! Give 'em hell, Al!"

Can a building really shake from noise? At that moment, I was sure of it.

Unbowed, the official again raised his hands, slamming them again into a T. Another technical! Two for the price of one. And again the crowd erupted, really behind Al now, loving it, getting more than their money's worth. They were with this street-smart showman, a veteran practitioner who had his act down pat, who continued to gesture wildly and spew a barrage of words at the evil guy in the striped shirt even as he retreated grudgingly into his team's huddle on the sidelines. Inside the circle of blue and yellow uniforms, Al didn't let up, still yelling between the shoulders of his players, and the fans didn't let up, either. Now I knew what they had come to see. Yes, Al's Marquette teams were good. But there was a lot more to it than that. The real lure was McGuire. The legendary Ref Baiter. Doctor Al and His Traveling Road Show. The coach of scrappy dance-hall teams that would just as soon ask you to step outside as look at you. This was a vicarious thrill those 10,938 strong could savor, of telling off not just an official, but their boss, the doctor who overcharges, the guy who sold them the car with that bad engine. There is, of course, that needed release for all of us, and I realized at that moment that Al, because of his blue-collar background, could play to it quite handily.

As I walked across the street to *The Journal* that night, to write my story after the game, one thought kept coming back to me: Man, who is the guy? And what kind of a Barnum & Bailey show does he run?

Jekyll, I soon found out, had another side. I had called to set up an interview, and Al had invited me to stop by his office. When I showed up, I was escorted by his secretary into a softly lit, tastefully furnished room, to find Al sitting behind his desk in the semi-darkness, sipping tea. I noticed, when he got up to shake my hand, that he was in his stocking feet. Had soft music been playing in the background, or incense burning, the atmosphere could not have been more relaxed.

What I immediately noticed, hanging on the walls, were pictures of clowns. A Bozo here, an Emmett Kelly there, some standing, sitting, sprawled across chairs, all looking down on us with faces of melancholy or downright sadness. So of course, I had to ask.

"I relate to them a little bit, I guess," Al said, loosening his tie. His gaze fell upon a court jester, pensive in ceramic, one of many that filled a tall, lighted glass case against the wall. "What was it Shakespeare said in one of his plays? 'What does the jester do when he finds out his court is full of fools?' He leaned back, putting his black stocking feet up on the desk. "But, um, they're all sad-eyed clowns. They're painted that way. To suggest the laughing on the outside, crying on the inside, that sort of thing. I don't know whether I relate to them or not." He smiled wanly. "I guess it's just the mystery of the clowns."

As we continued talking, I began to realize that the mystery of the clowns was also the mystery of Al McGuire. Like the clowns, he wore many faces, and somewhere behind one of them was a person who always tried hard to camouflage his true being, whose psychological makeup was much thicker than any coat of colored greasepaint. The more you were around him, the less you were able to gauge the true depth of the man. His psyche, like a shadow, was hard to pin down.

For in spite of his outside displays of bravado and showmanship, there was also an inner side to the man, a psychological side that questioned his place in the whole scheme of things, who he was, and why he was the way he was. In spite of his success, the question continued to haunt him: Was he, when he walked out on that court, really the king? Or was he fooling himself—merely the prancing court jester, who was only there to entertain the people while he pretended to be king?

And so I showered him with questions: Which was the real Al McGuire? What image strikes true? Coaching genius, or overrated showman? Cocky, carefree con man, or groping, introspective intellectual? Mere psych artist, or true psychologist? Egomanic or calculating performer? What I was trying to find out was what was real and what was show. How much truth, and how much play-acting.

What spoke volumes was that Al had no ready answers to those questions, and to this day, I don't know that he ever found them, at least not to his troubled satisfaction. But at times, as he tried to explain things that day, I saw some doors momentarily slide open and got a peek at what he was all about and how he felt about himself.

"I don't think you can draw lines around me," he explained, a pensive frown upon his face. "You see, what happens is that you've created something, an image over the years, one that you can't let down. And for me to get a message across, many times I have to allow myself to be what someone wants me to be. To let them put me in a certain niche.

"Different people have different conceptions of me, and whatever they want to think of me, fine. You know, Rog, they read a lot of different things into things I do. I have a lot of peculiar habits, and if we ever start losing, they'll say I'm doing them because we're losing and forget I've been doing them all these years we were winning. Like getting off the bus to walk a bit, not coming on the floor until just before the game starts. You see? For years, I was a nut. Now, now that we're winning, I'm eccentric." He laughed, and in a heartbeat the psychologist vanished and the clown reappeared. "The only difference between a nut and an eccentric is finer threads and a bigger car."

The feet slipped off the desk, and as he leaned forward in the gloom to make a point, another door momentarily opened and closed, revealing what it concealed. "I do things that seem irrational," he told me, "but I do them because they serve my purpose, the end result, and that is success, whatever that might be."

All the while he talked, I was scribbling furiously. This, I knew, was *good stuff.*

Al was off and running now, feet back up, gazing moodily at the ceiling as he talked on. For whatever reason, he had suddenly decided to open the door just a little bit more, and I was not about to interrupt.

"I prefer winning," he said. "I guess it's like being rich or poor. If you've been both, you prefer to be rich. What really matters to me? Repetition. Repetition. Showing by repetition. Being successful year after year. That's what brings happiness."

He put on a shy face now, this man who so actively sought publicity, exposure, fame. Who, once the curtain went up, not only liked to win, but to do it in his own flamboyant style—by entertaining, at times shocking, by making heads turn.

"I don't think the news media really know me," he continued. "They just catch me in a half hour, or 45 minutes, catch a couple of glib lines. It's just a job. They're working and I'm working with them. You really get to know someone in the off hours, talking about off subjects. Really, Rog, I don't think I have that type of ego drive. What everyone sees of me is not what they see on TV, or in the Arena."

So it's all an act? I asked. Al frowned.

"No, it's not all an act. Just a bit of one-upsmanship. I'll take what you throw at me, but if the dice come up seven, you take what I have to give out. That sort of thing." His eyes were fierce now. "I'm realistic that way. I don't believe in tipping blackjack dealers."

That afternoon I realized just how complex a man Al McGuire really was. He could be charming and gentle, sarcastic and screaming, warm and generous, cold and ruthless. His moods were many and stark contrasts—hills and valleys, starbursts and shadows, always the extremes. With Al, there was no in between.

When I showed up for practice the day after my story about the clowns appeared, Al saw me coming into the gym, got up off the bench where he was sitting, and walked over to meet me halfway. He put his hands on my shoulders.

"Roger," he said, looking me dead in the eye. "You know me better than I know me." It was the beginning of a friendship I have always treasured.

Oh, the things that he did and the things that he said. If Al McGuire's life was an inner struggle between showman and philosopher, in the public eye at least, the showman always prevailed. Because he was, after all, not only a truly great college basketball coach, but a first-class entertainer. And it can never be said that Al McGuire—win or lose—couldn't bring down the house.

"Sometimes," he admitted once, "I say things that I shouldn't. I go berserk. If I were a university, I wouldn't hire me.

"Let's face it, I'm a ham. I enjoy standing-room-only situations. Hey, if you're a piano player, you go to a bar that has a band. Most of what I do is off the top of my head, but a lot of times I'm not sure myself if I'm acting. But what I hate worse than anything is a dead crowd. I sent our manager over to the PA system once and had him ask the crowd to vote on whether I should get my hair cut. The season ticket holders said yes, but the student body overwhelmed them and voted no." McGuire laughed. "Actually, I should get my hair cut," he told me. " My mother's been threatening to disown me."

McGuire's zany exploits, controversial actions, and wild remarks were the heart of his legend. During his years at Marquette, he once bought ice cream for the crowd, sent MU T-shirts to members of the press, got crowned with a shillelagh, was presented with 100 pounds of baloney, was charged with assault and battery by a policeman in Detroit, got decked by one of his players in practice, and as a PR stunt, had one of them throw a basketball into Lake Michigan.

Who else but Al McGuire—son of an Irish bar owner in Rockaway Beach, New York who said he learned all about life from listening to the clientele—would pack beer and salami sandwiches into a catamaran and make his own attempt to row home to Ireland, only to be thwarted by a Coast Guard cutter just as he passed the Statue of Liberty?

Who else, angered at some adverse calls during a game with archrival DePaul University, would slide out onto the court on his knees in front of the offending referee and scream, "Take my car, take my house, take my job! Take whatever you want! But don't take this game from me!"

Who else but Al McGuire—when his team was competing in the Mideast Regional in Baton Rouge, Louisiana, in 1976—would casually wile away his off hours that weekend trying to get nothing more than a good picture of the LSU Tiger, shooting away at the big cat with his camera from this angle and that, while it lounged in the sunshine in its purple and gold cage next to the Assembly Center?

"Rog, stay back, would you please?" he cautioned me in almost whispered tones, when I walked up to see what he was doing. "You'll disturb him, and I need him calm. And the light's just right, right now."

And yes, he did have trouble remembering names...even those of his own players. Guard Dave Delsman was always "Dousman." Jerome

Whitehead, the center on his 1977 NCAA championship team, was always "Whitehorse"—even though we all kept reminding him that was a scotch. And there was one player—Mark Ostrand—whose name Al never did learn. He just called him "the white blond."

McGuire's last two sports information directors, Mike Gonring and Kevin Byrne, fared just as badly. Gonring was always introduced as "Goring," and Kevin was called "Keith." Bryne got his revenge at the Marquette Awards Dinner in March of '76, however, when Al slipped him a note as he was speaking that read, "Keith—be sure to introduce the players."

Byrne paused what he was doing and replied, "Okay, Dick," referring to McGuire's brother.

In Atlanta one year, he sat with Furman Bisher, then sports editor for the *Atlanta Journal*, for a half-hour doing an interview. When it was over, Al got up, shook hands, and left. "Thanks, Burman," he said.

I was lucky, I guess. Not once, in 26 years, did Al ever mess up or forget my name. (Not that anyone told me about, that is.)

When it came to words, Al was never hesitant about expressing his opinion on anything, a trait that caused some to love him and some to hate him, but that kept reporters like me at his elbow wherever he went, pencil and notebook at the ready, the safety catch on our recorders flipped off, waiting for McGuire to suddenly fire away. The point was, you never knew when he would unload those "75-dollar lines"—at practice, at the airport, in a car, watching television in his room, sitting in a bar, grabbing lunch at a greasy spoon restaurant, in the bleachers watching practice on the road, or just walking from home to his bank to make a quick deposit. From the time he was born, until the day he died, the world was Al McGuire's podium. Only he knew the subject, times and places.

He was great, of course, at dinners. For the right price, Al would speak to any group at any time, any place. The one constant—he must always be paid.

"My father told me two things before he died," Al said to me once. "One, never co-sign. Two, always get paid."

He was infuriated one winter when a group asked him to travel to Atlanta to speak at their convention, but when Al asked the fee, he was told, "Oh, well, we never pay coaches to speak. Just expenses."

"I said to the guy, 'What do you mean you don't pay?'" Al told me after. "Do you ask Frank Sinatra to sing, and not pay? Do you ask a carpenter to fix the front stoop, and then say, 'Thanks, see you later.' What do you mean, you don't pay?"

Over the years, his audiences varied greatly. He spoke to coaching groups, college and high school groups, at father-son breakfasts, the Lions Club, the Elks Club, the Rotary Club, women's groups, insurance companies, doctors' and lawyers' organizations, and even one night to a plumbers' convention.

Not that it mattered. Because all Al had to talk about was what he knew best—Al McGuire. That's what the people came to hear—his priceless, groping, stream-of-consciousness delivery that wandered from subject to subject while the audience laughed along.

Here's an example of one such speech, circa 1976.

After being introduced, Al stepped to the microphone, thanked the president of the organization, the people on the dais, and the guy who drove him in from the airport. Then he said how glad he was to be here, and how good the food was.

That was the extent of his planned remarks. After that, Al was off and running, touching on different subjects like a baseball player rounding the bases.

"First of all, I'm glad to see so many women here. You know, guys, we, um, try to get women very involved in our program at Marquette. We have Ladies' Day luncheons every year and special clinics. The last thing you want is a woman who thinks a double dribble is a set of twins with a cold.

"Things are going great now, but I don't know how long it will last. I've always said the bubble has to burst sometime. Coaching is a funny profession. The longer you stay, the closer you are to being fired…I, uh, personally don't think I'll be coaching too much longer. I've always said you leave nothing behind you, that it doesn't add up to anything. I mean, can you imagine being in your fifties and still worrying if some cheerleader is pregnant?"

He paused for the laughs to die down.

"I've always said," he added quickly, "that the ideal coach has a mother with money and a wife fully employed in a civil service job."

Then on to the next stop, recruiting: "I've always said, I'll go anywhere once, make one trip to see a kid. I'll go, I'll kiss your mother, but then I want your name on the dotted line.

"You know, it's a funny thing. Any time anyone takes me into the kitchen, I figure I got 'em locked up. If they take me into the living room, then I'm worried…I guess it's my Irish background. When I grew up, we spent all the time in the kitchen. The time we got into the living room was when somebody died.

"Hey? How the hell can I get to a player? I'm 47—45 for the papers—and so how can I rap with a young kid? I can't. But I can put some moves on his family.

"I think, um, Lefty Driesell, at Maryland, is probably the toughest guy to recruit against. Oh, he's tough. Lefty will get a kid in his office, lock the door, put the key in his desk drawer and say, 'I won't let you out again until you sign.'" A quick pause. "But he'll do it in a nice way."

Another standard was his relationship with the media. "I think my relations with the press have been good over the years," he'd always say. "But I will say this—I have never been misquoted. But I have been misunderstood."

Usually, he concluded by telling the people why he never made appointments.

"I don't like to make appointments. When I drive to work each morning, I get to Capitol Drive. If I turn left, I go the office. If I turn right, I go to Kenosha, Oconomowoc, all the little towns out west, right down the line. And I always like to have that prerogative, to be able to turn right if I want to, drive up the road to a little bar where I can have a beer and a sandwich. Oh, I don't do it more than once every 10 or 12 times, but I like to know I can do it. So I don't make appointments.

"I leave the appointments, the clock stuff, to Hank Raymonds, my assistant. Hank is the guy who makes me look good. He's our Xs and Os guy, our nuts and bolts man. He does the work and I go to the cocktail parties. Hank's a perfectionist. I've always said, if he were married to Raquel Welch, he'd expect her to cook."

Like any good performer, Al loved nothing better than to play before a packed house. 10,938. That was his magic number at the Milwaukee Arena, a sellout, the number of seats he always wanted to fill. Many were the nights I waited, then followed him out as he made his entrance on court, just minutes before the game began. And every time, as Al walked out to a growing crescendo of cheers, I noticed his eyes were glancing skyward, toward the cheap seats in the corners, way up top, where the rows were only two chairs wide. If those were filled, he was satisfied. He had sold out the place again.

Al also kept track of who was in the seats, and depending on what he saw, he used that information as a barometer to forecast the strength of his opponent. After drubbing little St. Leo's of Florida, 80-39, in the Warriors' home opener one year, Al admitted to me that he knew when he stepped on the court that it was going to be a rout. "Roger, I could tell by who was in the seats," he said. "It was a young crowd tonight, so that means the adults have given their tickets to the kids and stayed at home."

When it came to dialogue, Al had a repertoire that varied somewhere between William Gillette and William Faulkner...and he was never afraid to play things to the max. Over the years, I heard him use no less than five different phrases to describe Marquette's season opener in pregame interviews—"The Real Thing," "The Moment of Truth," "The Tide's Up" ("time to jump in with both feet"), "Pop Time," and "The Point of No Return." And one year, he used all of them in the same interview...in no less than five minutes' time!

If you were around Al long enough, you also noticed that certain lines always came back. Normally, at least once a year (and especially if his team had lost a couple games early on), I knew I was about to hear what I always called his "pretty boys" speech—his way of signaling to his players, through the press, that it was time they got more physical, that he didn't think they were playing aggressively enough.

Example: In a 1974 pregame interview prior to a road game against Portland University (following a poorly played 58-54 victory over San Diego State two nights before), Al stunned the local reporters when he told them he had ordered Bob Weingart, the Marquette trainer, to break out an extra box of bandages that night.

"I think it's time we had some guys get some cut eyes, or a tooth knocked out, or a broken nose," Al insisted, the tenor of voice raising as he spoke. "And I'm not a sadist. But I think it's time. That's what I've got Bob Weingart for. It's time for us to get some physical marks on us."

The result? Marquette outscored Portland by 16 points the first half and buried them, 87-57.

Fast-forward now to December of 1975, after Marquette had beaten Northern Michigan at the Arena, 56-45, in totally unimpressive style. Little wonder, then, that Al felt the time was right and was steaming in the postgame interview, when the "pretty boys" speech—this time a diatribe—surfaced once again.

"The trouble with these guys is that they're a bunch of pretty boys!" he declared. "Nobody wants to get physical. Nobody wants to get hurt.

Everybody wants to shoot; nobody wants to go underneath and play defense." He paused and glared around the room for effect. "Isn't anybody going to get hit in the eye, sooner or later? This is a contact sport, isn't it? But nobody wants to get hurt! I don't need a trainer. It's not possible for anybody to get hurt on this team! We got too many mirrors in our locker room. Everybody's busy looking at themselves in the mirror.

"Hey, I was embarrassed by these guys tonight! We don't have to clean our uniforms because nobody touches the ground. Everybody wants to be a star, stand out and shoot. But nobody is underneath to rebound."

This time, Al backed up his words with action. When I walked into the gym that following Tuesday, I could see by the grim look on his face that something was coming. "I'm gonna run 'em," he said to me, then turned away to conduct practice himself, because both Hank and Rick were gone scouting. And for one breakneck, exhausting hour, he did just that—ran his players without mercy. Running drills, passing drills, jumping back and forth over benches, around chairs. Ran them until they were gasping, and one player threw up in the corner.

Not even that was enough. On and on, up and down the creaky old Marquette gym floor, he ran them, feet pounding, as they gasped for breath, and all the while, Al kept pacing back and forth, yelling, "Faster, faster! Come on, faster! Push! Move it, dammit! Move!"

I had to admit, I was a little shocked. It was something I had never seen Al do. Something, he admitted to me after the exhausted players had left to shower, that he hadn't done in three years. Because he felt they not only were physically not up to par, but psychologically down as well. "Maybe it's my fault," he admitted. "Maybe I've let things slide. After all, what is it they say? That the dead fish stinks from the head."

Whatever it was, it worked. Marquette drubbed Drake in its next game, 80-58, and followed it up by pummeling its archrival, the University of Wisconsin, 78-54. The showman, by backing his words up with action, had turned things around once again.

Al, of course, always knew what he was doing, and why. He had a code of performance he lived by, whether in victory or defeat, and if he felt his players weren't playing up to that, the score on the board didn't matter. I remember one night, when Marquette was winning handily, but playing sloppily, and Al spent most of the first half on his feet before the bench, this time berating his own players for their poor performance. I understood where he was coming from, because he had told me once,

"I don't accept anything in victory that I would accept in defeat." But the Arena faithful, who didn't understand, threw some uncharacteristic boos his way that night, when they felt he was being too rough on his own team.

Not that it bothered Al. He knew the role he had to play. Turning to the scorer's table during one chorus of boos, he simply shrugged his shoulders and said to them, "Nice, gentle profession, isn't it?"

Then, too, there was the McGuire ego. Like the tirades, like the clowns, it was the third ingredient, I always felt, of what made up the psyche of this truly remarkable man. Make no mistake. Al McGuire's ego was a Hindenburg ego, always hovering silently overhead—huge, volatile, and thinly skinned—and when pricked it caused his Irish temper to explode into flames in the night. Nothing, opposing coaches found out over the years, set Al off quicker than a public affront, real or otherwise.

Hal Wissel, then the coach at Fordham University, made the mistake of rousing Al's ire in February of 1975, just before ninth-ranked Marquette was to play Fordham at The Garden in New York City. Al, in spite of a bad cold and the flu, had tried to help Wissel out, flying to New York two days early, then carrying off a headline-making press conference he hoped would help hype what he had been told were slow pregame ticket sales. Wissel, perhaps jealous of Al's headlines in all the New York dailies, called his own press conference the next day and told the press that Al's teams always played a patsy schedule, and that, had they played Fordham's schedule, they would have had four defeats by that time of the season as well.

"That," guard Lloyd Walton told me later, "was the worst thing that man could have done."

Al was so incensed he refused to shake hands with Wissel before the game and left the first team in nearly the whole way. The result was an embarrassing 101-64 defeat for Fordham—a wild game in which Marquette led by as much as 47 points in the second half, causing irate Fordham fans to throw a dead fish and varieties of fruit down onto the court, and one bookie (who had seen the point spread shattered) to walk up behind McGuire and hurl a stream of truly inventive "Big Apple" obscenities in his direction.

With eight minutes left in the game, Al suddenly stood up, put his hands on his hips, and turned to the Fordham bench, glaring over at

Wissel, who refused to return his withering gaze, instead sitting almost frozen in his chair, staring dejectedly at the floor.

"Hey!" Al yelled. "What's that about that patsy schedule we play?" Wissel didn't answer, still staring at the floor. Al moved a few steps closer, then pointed at the giant scoreboard overhead. "Come on, pal! Tell us about your schedule! Welcome to the big time, you jerk!"

Carl Tacy, the coach of Marshall University, also made a big mistake in December of 1971, when he ordered his players not to shake hands with McGuire or his players prior to their game for the annual Milwaukee Classic tournament title. What was obviously an attempt at a psych job also spurned what had been an MU tradition at the Arena for years, and Al felt it was Tacy's way of insinuating that the only place Marquette could win was at home, with hometown officials.

So when Tacy refused to shake hands after Marquette had beaten Marshall, 74-72, for the championship, McGuire exploded with a string of abuse in his best four-letter street vernacular. Once in the locker room, he seemed in control again, until a West Virginia reporter asked him what he'd said to Tacy.

"That question belongs back in the hills of West Virginia," Al snapped. "You think I don't know what's going on here? Hey, every coach comes in here and screams about what's happening to him. Hey, we've won 23 of our last 24 games on the road, and the one we lost was by one point down at Athens, Ohio, against Ohio State. And the last one we lost before that was in double overtime. When somebody goes out and wins 23 of 24 on the road, then they can come in here and scream, and I'll listen. There's too much emphasis on coming in here and getting gypped."

The reporter started to ask another question, but Al cut him off. "Don't try to con a con man," he said coldly, his face decorated with scorn. "I've been through this with Marshall before. I played them a couple years ago. Why do you think I'm trying to bite my tongue? Go back to the hills, fella."

And with that, he turned on his heel and walked away.

Even Adolph Rupp, the legendary coach at Kentucky, felt the bite of McGuire's tongue when they met during the NCAA tournament a number of times over the years.

In March, 1968, Marquette drew Kentucky in the first round of the Mideast Regional, which was being played (believe it or not!) in Rupp's hometown of Lexington, Kentucky. Al had a whole week to stew over the injustice of that situation, and the night before the game, at the coaches' dinner, he boiled over.

Rupp, after he had given his speech, told the other coaches in his Southern drawl, "All right, y'all, come on. Y'all gonna be on mah television show."

McGuire, who felt he was being patronized by the "Baron," stood up, stuck out his Irish chin and told Rupp in a loud voice just what he could do with his TV show, and the microphone, too. Later on, during the question-and-answer part of Rupp's show, when he and the other coaches were seated before the cameras, somebody called in and pointedly asked Rupp about the propriety of allowing Kentucky a home-court advantage in the NCAA regionals.

Recognizing the voice, Rupp turned crimson. "I know you're out there somewhere, McGuire," he snapped bitterly into the cameras.

Three years later, the Mideast Regional was in Athens, Georgia, and this time Rupp and McGuire were talking peaceably enough at a press conference—until Rupp turned to Al and said, "Now, son…"

"If you're going to call me son, you better put me in your will," Al shot back.

And then there was the time Rupp, reportedly urged by friends to try and make up with Al, called him and tried to soft-soap him. But given Al's ego, it was no-go. "Al," Rupp said, "I know we've had our differences in the past, but I just can't begin to tell you how great a coach you are."

"Well, then why don't you hang up and let someone call who can?" Al replied.

"I think everyone should go to college and get a degree, and then spend six months as a bartender and six months as a cab driver. Then they would really be educated."

Chapter 2

The Family

Rockaway Beach was where the McGuire legend began. Rockaway, just south of Brooklyn, 15 minutes from Kennedy Airport. A narrow, straight finger of land at the southern tip of Long Island, in some places only two blocks wide, pinched between Jamaica Bay on one side and the Atlantic Ocean on the other.

Today, it's as built up, noisy and crowded as any other New York City suburb. There are too many cars, too many buses, rundown houses, graffiti-sprayed walls…and only the rumbling subways—the "Downtown Trains" that Rod Stewart has made famous—connect the peninsula with Brooklyn and Manhattan.

But back in 1938, when John McGuire sold his bar in the Bronx and moved his family there, Rockaway Beach was a flourishing resort community. Inhabited by typical middle-income workers and their families, firemen, policemen, some white-collar workers, the merchants in the area predominantly Jewish. It was hotels, bungalows on the sand, tent cities, old and new boardwalks, a place where you woke up in the morning to the clapping sound of waves smacking the wooden jetties, flocks of white seagulls crying, and the taste of salt in the strong sea breeze.

"In the winter, it was a ghost town," Al told me once. "But in the summer it was like 42nd and Broadway. At that time, I think there were some 50-odd bars in the area...all Irish. O'Reilly's. The Shillelagh House, Hennessey's, McNulty's." He paused and smiled, "And of course the best of all...McGuire's."

It was Pep McGuire's, actually (Pep was the shortened nickname of McGuire's co-owner, Norton Peppas). Best way to describe it was that it was a sort of high-class bar and grill, with rooms to rent to vacationers upstairs, the family living in the basement during the summer when the rooms were all rented out. The family was John, his wife Winifred, and the four children—Johnny, Dick, Al and Kathleen. Everybody worked, and money was tight.

Johnny, a policeman who later went on to own his own place, Pat McGuire's, in New York City, recalled how seasonal the family's income was and how "during the season" he, Al, and the other kids slept in the basement below the bar.

"What you have to realize is that you lived all year on what you made during the summer," John explained. "So we slept in the cellar. But we kids loved it down there. Sleeping next to the beer boxes, stealing soda from the crates, playing hide and seek. When you're young, you don't realize how bad things really are. We were a close family, but not lovey-dovey close, you know, just close in a clannish sort of way."

The Family. That was the source of many of Al McGuire's best stories and "75-dollar lines" that I heard him use during our years together. From little hustlers do great con men grow, and Al's philosophy of life (which would later impact mightily on his philosophy of coaching) was already taking root back then, during his formative years growing up on Rockaway Beach.

Al's world was that of the scrapper, the underdog, the little guy from the streets who takes on the world with a slingshot. Always looking for an angle, an edge. To keep 'em guessing, confused, unsure, until he could find a way to win. It was basketball played like the old shell game, with Al playing the role of crafty riverboat gambler, and the opposition never sure whether he really had a pea.

Hustling for a buck as well as a basket, Al got a bartender's education long before he went to St. John's University and—thanks to basketball—got his degree. Like the other brothers, he helped out his father behind the bar from time to time (when, he admitted, he couldn't get out of it), and because of his razor-sharp intellect, he learned the ropes quickly. "Don't try to con me," I heard him say so many times, when someone tried to sell a line, or pull a fast one. "You can't fool a bartender. If you've ever been one, you've heard every story in the world."

And, believe me, the Al McGuire stories from that era that I heard—told by Al, John, and their mother, Winifred—are priceless. "Mother was a big woman," John recalled. "She was 260-280 pounds, tremendously strong, and a hard worker. I remember her bottling beer by hand in the old days in the Bronx. A real tough old broad. We'd never answer her back.

"My father? I remember the first time I saw him get mad. It was at the supper table, and he got so mad he picked up his plate and bit it. Bit it so hard he broke off one of his teeth and it fell out on the plate. I knew where I stood with him then. He never had to lay a hand on us, though. He just gave you that look…"

Al listened hard, and learned, at his father's elbow behind the bar.

"My job," Al explained, "was to get the bar stools out of the place before the customers got there. We always did that on weekends to keep the clientele moving.

"One night, this lady came in, who was a real good customer," he told me, "and she asked for a stool. She told my dad, 'Look, I'm on my feet all week at my job, and I don't want to have to stand up when I have a drink.'

"Dad paused a second, then told her, 'Then there's only one thing you can do. You'd better quit your job.'"

Another time, Al was working behind the bar when a guy named Brennan (he said), who was a regular, came in and wanted to borrow some money from the till. "He told me he wanted to borrow four dollars," Al said, "and I said, 'You'll have to wait a minute, I'll ask my Dad.' So I go down to the end of the bar where my dad was standing, and I ask, and Dad says, 'Give him two.' So back I go to Brennan and give him two dollars. He looked at me, insulted. 'Al, I asked for four dollars,' he said. 'Go see my dad,' I said. So he goes down to my dad and says, very dignified, 'Mr. McGuire, I asked your son for four dollars. How come he only gave me two?'

"'That way,' my dad told him, 'we split even. You lose two and I lose two.'" Al smiled, then added, "And he was right. We never saw the two bucks again."

Al admitted to me that his first real hustle was a flop, that summer when he was growing up when he and John came up with the idea of trying get into their Aunt Kate's will.

"Aunt Kate must have been in her 70s then," Al said. "She had gray hair and wore high lace collars and an ivory broach. Anyway, one day Johnny says to me, 'Al, how long do you think Aunt Kate can live?' And I said, 'I don't know.' So he said, 'Well, she can't live forever.' And he devised this plan. All summer long we waited on her hand and foot. We ran to the delicatessen to get her tea biscuits for her. We ran across the street to get the papers. Anything she asked, we did. And we'd always kiss her on the cheek and tell how sweet she looked, and she'd pat us on the heads and say what good boys we were.

"So anyway, to make a long story short, Aunt Kate died. And at the wake, Johnny gives me this big wink, you know, like 'We're in.' Well, the day finally comes, and they read the will. So Dick and Kathleen each get $10,000, and Johnny and I each got $250." Al couldn't help but laugh. "Johnny was crushed. She'd known all along, of course, what we were doing. I'll never forget, Johnny sat there for a while, looking like a dog his master had kicked, and then he finally sighed and said, 'You know, Al, when you work it all out, it breaks down to about a penny a kiss.'"

At the time I covered Marquette, of course, things hadn't changed all that much. Only by then, it was Winifred who was getting up in years, and now it was Al and Johnny carrying on a constant game of one-upsmanship in an attempt to curry her favor.

And according to Al (this was in 1976), the cost of kisses had gone up considerably. "I have to go back to New York every six months or so, just to make sure I'm still in Mom's will," he'd tell people from time to time. "Every time Johnny kisses her, it's $500 on his side."

John, always the optimist, at that time figured he already had a lock on the estate.

"I've been way ahead of the rest of 'em for years," he told me. "I was always one up on 'em. Come Mother's Day, they'd show up with the same old things, flowers or candy. I'd give her a broach, or a diamond ring. You see? They got no imagination. For years, I knocked 'em out of the box."

A story I heard Al tell often occurred in the late 1970s, when Winifred was hospitalized and things looked deadly serious. The two arrived at the hospital, and John, thinking this might be his last pitch, grabbed some flowers out of a vase in the hospital lobby to gain an edge as they headed for the elevator. Al, playing defense as always, grabbed John and insisted on a brief con-fab, supposedly to plot their strategy.

"Listen," he told John, "she may not last too long. So we got to get her to sign over the hotel rights to us. The inheritance taxes would kill us."

"Right," John agreed. And up they went.

There lay Winifred, quiet, no expression, eyes half-closed. Another woman lay in the other bed, but appeared to be sound asleep. The lights were low, a television set was on, but barely audible, since it was hanging on the other side of the room.

As the brothers approached her bed, Winifred suddenly opened her eyes and beckoned with a feeble hand for Al to come closer. Al, fearing the worst, glanced at his brother, then leaned over the bed, close to his mother's face.

"What is it, Mom?" he asked.

"Al," she whispered back, "who's paying for the TV? Me or Mrs. Ochs?"

Al turned and looked at Johnny. "Don't worry," he said in a low voice, so Winifred couldn't hear. "She's good for another 10 years."

The story John liked to tell best happened when Al was six or seven, before they moved out to Rockaway.

"We used to live in this railroad flat, on the fifth floor of a five-story apartment house in the Bronx," he recalled. "Well, a railroad flat runs straight, in case you don't know, with a long hall down the middle and a door every few yards or so leading to another room. The kitchen and living room are up front, the bedrooms in the back.

"Well, anyway, my folks were in a business where they dealt with cash a lot, and so Mother would keep this big jar with quarters and change and bills in it, hidden in the dresser. Well, I found out about it, where it was, and I thought I was the only one dipping into the half-dollars. But one day, I hear footsteps, so I hide under the bed, and in comes Dick. I watch him start to dig in, and suddenly we hear more footsteps and he slides under the bed. He looks at me, and I look at him, and then in comes Al. And no more did he get the jar open than in comes Mother.

"Oooh, was she mad! She grabbed Al by the ear and let him have it, and then she opened the window and hung him out there, shakin' him, holding him by just one leg. We're five floors up, remember, and he's screaming bloody murder for her not to drop him. And so Mother shouts at him, 'Don't you ever do that again, or I'll let you go!'"

John laughed. "Dick looked at me, and I looked at him, and we both gulped. And we never went near that money jar again."

Years later, when Winifred was in town, and we were talking, I couldn't help but ask: Would she have really dropped Al?

Her face split open wide with an Irish grin. "No," she assured me. "I just shook him to let the money fall out of his pants."

You must realize, of course, that Winifred is where Al inherited his gift of gab. She was a big, hearty woman, with twinkling eyes and a crackling laugh that would have made a cigar store Indian drop its panatela and laugh right back. I didn't have the good fortune to meet

Winifred until she was 79 and in Milwaukee to do her bit to help "Al's Run"—an annual event he and the *Milwaukee Journal* hosted to raise funds for Milwaukee Children's Hospital. She was sitting in the *Journal* lobby, along with Al's wife Pat, folding orange T-shirts that were presented to the runners who participated. Even though "Al's Run" was only in it second year then (1979), by the time I caught up with Winifred, the first-year total of 4,101 runners had already been surpassed—which meant that she and Pat were looking at folding between 6,000 and 7,000 T-shirts. Not that Winifred minded.

"It's fine with me," she said with a wink. "I told Al, no matter what the count, that I'd charge him a quarter each."

In the blink of an eye, she laid her hand upon my arm. "No, really, I'm very happy to do it for him. I don't know much about the Run, but it's great, because he's doing something for children."

Winifred smiled, and then like Al, knowing she was on center stage, continued on. "Besides, it gives me something to do," she said, mischievous look in her eye. "I really don't like just sitting around. And nobody wants me to smoke cigarettes any more. I only smoke four a day, anyway. That's not enough to hurt you.

"It's like brandy. Al always told me, 'Mother, always keep a bottle of brandy in your room, and every night take a drink of brandy before you go to bed.' Well, the doctor said, 'No. When you're taking high blood pressure pills, don't take brandy.' So I told Al, and you know what he said? He said, 'Forget the pills.'"

I asked Winifred if the T-shirts were permanent press or if they had to be ironed. That reminded her of another story, she said, and about the dangers of ironing.

"I was at a wedding recently," she said, "and I met this fella I knew many years ago named John. I noticed one of his ears was gone. So I said, 'John, what happened to your ear?

"And he said, 'You know, I was pressing my pants and the phone rang. Instead of answering the phone, I put the iron up to my ear.'

"So I said, 'But John, your other ear is gone, too.'

"And he said, 'Yeah, wouldn't you know. The son of a gun called back.'"

Winifred chuckled, a deep belly laugh that shook her. She clearly was enjoying this.

"I've got another one," she said. "There were two brothers who were killed in a car accident. One went to heaven, the other went to hell.

"Well, the one in hell was having a real good time, drinking beer and all. So he called his brother and said, 'John, come on down. I'm having a great time. There's plenty of beer. Bring all your friends and come on down.'

"And John said, 'Friends? What do you mean? I'm the only one up here.'"

Like Al, Winifred also had a string of one-liners. When I asked her about the wages of shirt folding in particular, and the economy in general, she replied: "This job doesn't pay very well. But look, a dollar's only worth 20 cents these days. No job pays good any more."

And on how to grow old gracefully: "Me, I'm not looking back. I'm still looking for a man. But I can't find one at my age."

And on her grandchildren, "I've got lovely grandchildren. But it's funny with grandchildren. On their birthday, they don't even look at the card. They just shake it to see what drops out."

Al was not the only son Winifred talked about, of course. I remember one time, after telling me a particularly funny Al story, she suddenly shifted topics to her eldest son, John. "Have you met my son, John?" she asked me. No, I told her, but I had talked to him on the phone for almost an hour, gathering material for what I hoped someday would be a book on Al, and came away quite impressed. Winifred beamed and gave me a nod and a wave of her arm to back it up. "Oh, you've never met anybody until you've met John," she said.

Oh man, I thought. Al's slipped up somewhere here. Johnny's got the edge in the will once again.

"I remember the time he bought a race horse," Winfred told me. "He said, 'Mother, I want you to see my race horse.' I think we spent a whole Sunday driving to Jersey to look at that horse. I thought once, maybe I should make him stop off at a church somewhere and get a little holy water to sprinkle on that horse—but I didn't.

"So anyway, we're all waiting for the horse's first race, so we can all get down a bet, and wouldn't you know? The horse dropped dead on the track, and John had to pay $300 to have it hauled off." Her sides shook with laughter. "Can you imagine?"

Once, I heard Al relate to someone that his mother was probably more responsible than his father for the financial success of the family's bar. "My father chased the customers out," Al said. "My mother brought them back in."

One story he liked to tell was about a rival hotel owner named Mrs. Sullivan (though I always suspected this had happened to Winifred instead), who, as Al put it, "had had a good summer and was going into New York to get a mink coat.

"So she's standing by the corner waiting for a bus," Al said, "when the priest drives past in his long, black Cadillac. 'Can I give you a lift?' he asked. She said, 'No, Father, I'm going into the city.' He said, 'Me, too.' So she got in.

"Now they're driving along, and the priest asked, 'Why are you going into the city, Mrs. Sullivan?' And she replied, 'I had a good summer this year, Father. So I'm getting myself a mink stole.'

"'You know, Mrs. Sullivan,' the priest said, 'the Blessed Virgin never had a mink stole.'

"'That's right Father,' she shot back. 'And Jesus Christ never drove a Cadillac.'"

Winifred died in September of 1986. Her death was not unexpected; she had been in a coma since May. Al flew into New York for the funeral, and when he got back, he was both reflective and philosophical, as I had expected. He had passed another watershed in his life, after all, now faced with his own mortality, with both his parents gone. And yet, he said, the wake had not been a sad affair, but rather "a celebration" of Winifred's life, a chance to remember fondly that robust, no-nonsense person who made her way through life with a great sense of humor and good old-fashioned common sense.

"It was not an unpleasant time," Al said, some distance in his eyes, as we talked over a beer at a table outside a small Milwaukee restaurant, enjoying the warmth of the afternoon sun. "Mother was in her 80s; she'd had a nice long run. Now she was having her 'last hurrah,' overseeing things even though she'd cashed in.

"You see, after this, that thread, that nation of our family, now breaks into our own city-states. The next time my brothers and sister and I will all meet again, there will be one less of us, because one of us will have died.

"Mother went down in May, for all practical purposes. But she wanted one more summer. She slept through the summer, in a room overlooking the beach. She had her last July 4, last Labor Day, summer storms, and when the summer ended, that was it."

At the wake, Al said, he had seen what he called "a kaleidoscope of life, right there" made up of the four distinct groups of people who were there.

"The first group were mother's chums," he said, "the Edgar Allen Poe group, last leaf of the tree thing, predominantly women. They wore comfortable clothes, no jewelry, the golden-age type. They know there's not too many bake sales left, and everything was priest-oriented. They talked about how mother sold the most chances at the raffle, made a matinee appearance and checked out early.

"The second group was our sphere, the three brothers and sister. Their dress was more conservative, shirt and tie, nothing flashy. It seemed to be Middle America, the fireman, policeman, civil service, union guys. That group was the tidal wave, everybody saying, 'You look so young,' even though the hair was gone and there were lots of facial road maps. It was a last hurrah-type thing, the last time you'd see most of the people you grew up with, had fights with, tore your clothes.

"The next group was the grandchildren. The women wore Green Bay Packer shoulder pads-type clothes, and the hair was completely dry. It was a group trying to identify, discussing their economic levels.

"The last group, the great-grandchildren, always seemed to wear clothes on top of clothes, the layers, the baggy pants; that's the style that's in. This is the group that has no realization that they're ever going to die. Which is nice to see. They came in as pious as the blue-haired ladies, because they think that's the way they're supposed to be."

I gathered some background on Winifred for my story—where she was born, her family history, where the wake, funeral services and burial took place. Al grinned when he told me the wake was at O'Connor's in Rockaway Beach. "That's the one thing I knew before I got there," he quipped, "that the place had to have an O' something in front of it."

When I asked how old Winifred was, Al smiled again. "It's all according to who you talk to," he replied. "Mother always had three ages, all according to who she was trying to impress. She was anywhere from 84 to 87; we're not too sure." He chuckled, then added, "She had one age put in there to beat Social Security. All I know is that she had about 27 grandchildren, and for the great-grandchildren, you need a computer."

Winifred had been born in Herefordshire, England, and come to that tiny finger of Long Island nearly 60 years before, after marrying John McGuire in the 1920s. From 1937 to 1970, the McGuire family operated their popular bar and restaurant on the beach, with Winifred taking over after John's death in the 1950s. Al told me it was then, during those years his mother performed the dual roles of parent and bar owner, that she had passed on to him much of the simplistic philosophy for which he had later become famous.

"She had a great sense of humor," Al recalled. "What I tried to do, when I was listening to her, was to pick up words, thoughts, ideas. I don't think I ever came away that I didn't have a Will Rogers or Einstein thought that was done in a very simple, common-sense way. She had a 'two plus two is four' philosophy. She'd never use words a shoe-shine boy couldn't understand.

"Mother's background was people. She was always touching people; there was a singleness in her approach. She always used to say, 'The best manners in the world are to be natural.' And that a liar could ruin a regiment."

Who could have known it then? That just 15 years later we would all be saying goodbye to Al as well, at Gesu Church, on the Marquette campus in downtown Milwaukee. Unfortunately for all of us, his "run" was not so long as Winifred's...but one thing is certain. He learned his mother's lessons well.

"A team should be an extension of a coach's personality. My teams are arrogant and obnoxious."

Chapter 3

From Kid to Coach

A scrapper. That's the term that best describes Al McGuire as an athlete, both when he was growing up and competing in high school sports in Rockaway Beach and later when he played college ball at St. John's University and briefly for the New York Knicks in the National Basketball Association.

Al was a skinny kid, brash, short on talent, but long on hustle. A guy who beat you with his mouth, if not his jump shot. Which was not to say that he didn't have a fair degree of talent. He was an All-City football and basketball player at St. John's Prep in Brooklyn and ran the 440 and 880 events in track. He also ran three meets as a freshman at St. John's University, before school officials made him choose one sport. He had nowhere near the natural ability of his older brother Dick, but both starred (Dick for his scoring and passing, Al for his hard-nosed defense) at St. John's in 1950-51 when the school was third in the National Invitation Tournament and finished with a 26-5 record under Coach Frank McGuire (no relation, who later went on to coach at both North and South Carolina).

"Al was competitive, but clumsy," brother Johnny recalled. "Everything came hard for him. But everything for Dick came easy. Dick would beat you at checkers the second time he played you. Al would go off to school and figure out a way. I gotta believe that if Al had had Dick's talent to go with his mouth, and Dick had had Al's mouth to go with his talent, those two would have been unbeatable." During Al's last six years at Marquette, South Carolina was a regular home-and-home opponent on the Warriors' schedule, and one of the things I personally enjoyed was spending some time with Frank McGuire (who was always a class act, not only as a coach, but as a person as well)—be it at the Arena once he'd arrived in town, or in his office in Columbia, South Carolina, when Marquette traveled there. Because invariably, he would start talking about his "scrapper" who had played for him 25 years before.

"Al was aggressive as a player, just like he is now in coaching," Frank recalled once in the mid-1970s. "He was an excellent rebounder. He'd go to the basket, hustle underneath, and beat your brains out if he had to, to make sure he got the ball. His game was guts and blood. Now Dick was a finesse player, like [Bob] Cousy. And that was something Al had to always live with, guys saying, 'You'll never be as good as your brother Dick.'"

Frank leaned back in his chair and smiled thoughtfully as he put the fingertips of his hands together in the shape of a steeple. "I remember later, when Al was with the Knicks, I told his folks, 'Get him out of the pros. He's going to get killed.' With Al, it was all guts. The greatest thing he had going for him was his temperament." Frank laughed. "Dick, they called 'Mumbles,' cause he never said much. Al, they called a lot of things."

The size of an opponent never worried Al, who was all of 150-160 pounds in those days. During the 1949-50 season, when St. John's and Long Island University were scheduled to play at Madison Square Garden, Frank McGuire and Long Island coach Clair Bee agreed to share a practice session...with certain provisos.

"Clair and I had agreed to do this, but there was to be no elbows, no rough stuff," Frank recalled. The problem was, Al hadn't agreed, and no sooner did the "practice" start than he tore into Long Island's Clyde Biggers, a strapping 225-pounder.

Frank McGuire chuckled. "The ball went up in the air," he said, "and about four minutes later, Al had Biggers on the ground. Everybody backed away, and I walked out kind of slow, cause I figured it would be broken up by the time I got there, but when I got up close, I see Al still has the guy all wrapped up.

"So I said, 'Come on, Al, let him up.' And Al says, 'Not til he says he gives up.' So I look down, and the guy is turning blue. Al is choking him. He couldn't open his mouth, much less say anything if he'd wanted to. I looked at Clair, and he looked at me, and I said, 'What can I do?'"

After graduating from St. John's, Al once again was brother Dick's teammate, this time with the New York Knicks in the NBA, where he played three seasons before being traded to the Baltimore Bullets, who folded just 14 games into the 1954-55 season. A sixth-round draft choice, Al's rep as a pro was the same as it had been in college—a tenacious, hard-playing defender who was long on heart and hustle, short on pure talent.

The most publicized story about Al's brief NBA career was the time when the Knicks were playing the Boston Celtics at the Garden, and Al called a press conference where he vowed he would hold Bob Cousy, the Celtics' star guard, to less than double figures that night. "I own Cousy!" Al proclaimed after the game. "And I did," he insisted to me, when I asked about that night years later over a beer. Al smiled and slapped my hand. "He only had six points when I fouled out early in the first quarter."

Johnny McGuire, however, told me the incident he remembers most concerning Al and the Celtics involved Bob Brannum, a six-foot, six-inch 240-pounder...and this time all three McGuire brothers got into the fight.

"It was in the 69th Regiment Armory, and the Knicks were playing the Celtics," Johnny recalled. "Well, like I've said, Al couldn't hit the rim with a shotgun, but it seemed like he was always punching somebody. Anyway, he and Cousy had had some run-ins, so this time, [Celtics coach] Red Auerbach figures he'll save Cousy by getting Al out of the game right away.

"Auerbach goes up to Brannum in the locker room just before the game and says, 'I want you to get Al McGuire. As soon as he comes in, we'll run a pick into him, and you let him have it right away.' So Harry Day, a Celtics scout who's a friend of ours, slips out the door and comes upstairs and tells me, 'Hey, they're going to get Al.' Well, I was a policeman then, but I had a brown coat on over my uniform, and I slip over to Al and grab him where he's warming up.

"'Watch out, Al,' I said, 'they're looking to get you. Harry Day just told me.'

"So Al comes into the game, Auerbach nods to Brannum, and the first time into the pivot, Al runs into the guy. And it's a free-for-all. Al throws a punch, Dick tackles Brannum, and I go over the scorer's table, gun and all, after the guy! Well, there I am on Al's back, and the guy is so tall I still can't reach him to throw a punch. And then they're taking me away—gun, badge, the works. I thought for a while they were going to have me committed."

And what was Al's opinion of his years as a player?

"Really, Rog? I was just a dance-hall player," he told me once, when I asked. "Strictly a ham an' egger."

When the Baltimore Bullets disbanded, most of the players were picked up by other teams in the league, but Al wasn't. So he went back to work behind the bar at McGuire's in Rockaway Beach, and it was during that summer of 1955 that Winifred brought up the idea (and nearly convinced her son) that he should become a New York City cop.

"Mother kept telling me I should take the test," Al recalled. "She'd always say, 'Al, it'll give you security. It's like the Post Office. It's steady work and they pay a pension.' And I kept thinking, 'If there's so much security, why am I always seeing stories about big funerals in the paper, with lots of flowers and a motorcycle parade, every time one of those guys gets killed?'"

Instead, thanks to a recommendation by Walter Brown, the owner of the Boston Celtics, Al took a job as an assistant coach under Alvin (Doggie) Julian at Dartmouth University that fall. Frank McGuire, watching his former player from afar, told me Al was looking hard to leave the Ivy League school after just one season. "I knew fairly soon that it was only temporary," Frank McGuire said years later. "Al was good, and he wanted to coach. But he didn't like it there."

Years later, when we were talking, Al told me the Dartmouth campus was so drab that the only week he'd dare bring kids he was trying to recruit to visit was during Carnival Weekend, during the winter. "You had to take a train ride to get there," Al recalled, "but on Carnival Weekend it was like 42nd and Broadway. Lights and music, people running around in the snow. People jumping off mountains. But the other 50 weeks of the year—blah!"

Thankfully, Al's career at Dartmouth was short-lived. In 1957, Belmont Abbey College—a small school of 450 students located in Belmont, North Carolina— was looking for a head basketball coach. And luckily for Al, Frank McGuire (then coaching at the nearby University of North Carolina), put in a good word and recommended Al for the job.

"They asked me who I thought would be a good coach, and I told them there was only one guy for the job," Frank recalled years later. "That was Al."

It didn't take long for Frank McGuire to see that Al hadn't changed a bit since his days as a player at St. John's.

"We were scrimmaging Belmont Abbey," Frank explained, "and Al had this one kid, I think Doyle was his name, and one of my guys fouled him, and the kid takes it. And Al is right after him. 'Hey, you,' he yells to Doyle. 'If you let that guy do that to you again, I'm gonna kick you right in the ass.'" Frank slapped his hand on his desk and laughed. "So what happens? The kid takes it again, and Al did it! He kicked him right in the ass."

But for all of Al's antics on-court, Frank was always quick to point out that off court, he was different. "Don't get Al wrong," he told me more than once. "Yes, he was a wildcat, but no roughneck, you know what I mean? He had a good home life, was good to his mother. But he's an Irishman, and he could only take so much."

Frank McGuire's faith in Al was justified. Al guided his first Belmont Abbey team to a 24-3 record and was 109-64 for a .630 winning percentage for seven seasons, in five of which his team received postseason tournament invitations. And so, when Frank McGuire was asked to visit the Marquette University campus in early 1964, he remembered Al again.

"The chancellor there called and asked if I'd like to help them set up a program," Frank recalled. "And they wanted to know, what do we have to do to be competitive? How many scholarships? All that. And they asked if I'd like the job. I said, 'I hate to do this, but I'll tell you: If you can get Al McGuire, get him.'"

And so, on April 11, 1964, the *Milwaukee Journal* reported the formal announcement. "Al McGuire, 35, coach at Belmont Abbey College in Belmont, NC, was named basketball coach at Marquette University Saturday night. The nomination climaxed a three-week search for a successor to Ed Hickey, fired as Marquette coach and athletic director March 26…"

Looking back now, it seems like it was meant to be. For although neither Milwaukee nor Al McGuire knew it at the time, he had arrived. "It's a mortal sin," Al always told me, "to not live up to your capabilities." Now, for the first time in his life, he would finally be given the chance. After 10 years performing off-Broadway, this zany showman had finally found a stage big enough to accommodate his outrageous antics…and let him perform to his full capacity.

How good a basketball coach was Al McGuire? If you want to simply count the numbers, there's no doubt he was one of the best. After coming to Marquette from Belmont Abbey, Al continued his strategy of "repetition, repetition" over the next 13 seasons—during which his teams scored 295 victories against just 80 defeats for a phenomenal .787 winning percentage. Talk about consistency. During his years at Marquette, Al had only one losing season (his first, in 1964-65) and after a 14-12 rebuilding campaign the next year, chalked up 11 straight 20-plus winning seasons. During those 11 years, Al's teams also received 11 straight invitations to postseason tournaments, where they won 27 of 37 games (a .730 winning percentage) and made him one of a handful of coaches whose teams have won both the NIT (1970) and NCAA (1977) championships. (Trivia buffs should also take note: Besides the legendary John Wooden at UCLA, Al was the only coach in history to win a national title in college basketball after announcing his retirement prior to the conclusion of a season.)

Awards? Over the years, Al won a ton. Ironically, his biggest personal "keepers" weren't handed out in recognition of Marquette's two championship seasons, in 1970 and '77, but in 1971 and 1974. In 1971, after his Warriors finished 28-1, Al was named college Coach of the Year by the Associated Press, United Press International, *The Sporting News*, and the United States Basketball Writers Association. In 1974, after a 26-5 season in which Marquette lost to North Carolina State in the NCAA finals, the National Association of Basketball Coaches selected Al for Coach of the Year honors, an award he called "the most important of my career."

Impressive? You bet. But as anyone who knew Al realized, there was a whole lot more to him than numbers and awards. They were simply the outline of the story—signposts that reflected the greatness of his success. What made Al McGuire unique, in the world of college basketball and beyond, was not just what he did, but *how* he did it.

"I'm not an Xs and Os-type guy," Al told me once. "I leave that up to Hank and Rick. What I do is try to create a party on the court and keep it going. You know, Rog, each season is like a life. It's born, it lives to fruition, and then it dies."

That was Al—the master psychologist, who each year took the players he had and created something, for better or for worse, but created it in his own image nonetheless. "We can make a nice sound together," he always told them. "It all gets down to love. If we have love, we'll be good. If we don't, we'll be bad."

Which is not to say that Al's players ever had any doubts about who ran the show. Al was never a "whistle blower"—a coach so regimented that he required his players to all have short haircuts and wear matching sport coats on the road. He allowed them casual dress and outlandish haircuts and even the right to argue with him on court from time to time. But one thing they always knew—once it was "showtime" on game night, Al was always the boss.

"I don't discuss basketball; I dictate basketball," he always said. "I'm not interested in philosophy classes. Hey, the guys know that. Sure, we yell at each other sometimes, there's some give and take, but in the end, I'm the dictator. And one thing you must remember, Rog. The times they scream at me the most is when we're 10 or 15 points ahead. When things get tight, you watch, they listen to me."

What amazed me most about Al McGuire the coach was that he was able to compile the numbers and win the awards he did over the years, given the type of coach he was. For one thing, he had a genuine dislike for recruiting—which deep inside, I think, he felt was nothing more than trying to curry favor with another person, almost like begging, if you will, and which I think offended some inherited part of his Irish pride.

"Recruiting, to me, is very distasteful," Al admitted once. "But it's like part of any job. There are distasteful things you do in life, whether you're a butcher or the president of IBM. There are always certain parts of your day that you find distasteful. But if you're going to succeed, they have to be done.

"Now, I try to keep a certain amount of dignity. I'll kiss the mother once. I'll talk to the high school coach about defense. I'll move the salt and pepper shakers around, and that's about it. The visits, they really drive me nuts. If it rains, I won't get the kid."

One way Al managed to maintain his dignity was that, at some point in the discussion with a player that he sought, he'd always throw out a line that I think he felt kept things in proper perspective. "I'll win even if you don't come," he'd tell him, "but it'd be easier if you came."

The initial "touches"—the phone calls and the first knock on the door—were left to Hank and Rick, or former players like Jackie Burke and Ric Cobb.

"Once Al established himself, he did little recruiting," Burke explained to me. "Rick did a lot of the intros, and me. We'd see a kid two or three times, make him aware Marquette was interested in him, tell him we wanted him to come out and visit [Milwaukee and Marquette], that sort of thing. Once the visit was made, if it was a player they really wanted, Al would make the move."

Hank and Rick were the arbiters, who reported to Al on which particular "blue-chip" player Marquette needed the most that particular year. After which, Al would fly in to the player's hometown, make his one visit to the player's house, meet the player and his family, the whole nine yards, and close the deal.

"I never saw him sit down with the parents," Burke recalled, "that he didn't come away with the kid's name on the bottom line." Another thing that struck Burke was Al's absolute honesty with the player, that he never promised him pie in the sky. "The big thing Al sold was an established basketball program," Burke explained. "And the fact that it was important for the kid to get his degree. If the kid he was talking to brought up that he wanted to be a pro, Al would never guarantee anything. Just that, if he was good, he'd get every opportunity."

Al told me his strategy was to always talk to the player's mother. "If she feels you'll take good care of her son for the next four years, you're in," Al said.

One thing that always baffled me was Al's style of recruiting. Other top coaches of his day—Adolph Rupp, Bobby Knight, Dean Smith, Ray Meyer, and Digger Phelps—always seemed to me to be "loading up" with players, putting together physical powerhouses that were sometimes downright intimidating. That wasn't Al's style. Like old-time Hollywood producers, he believed in the "star system" and there was only one star at a time. So his thrust, each year, was to bring in one more "thoroughbred" to go with the players he had and fill in with complementary players who filled a certain need.

Why, I wondered, didn't Al just go out and make "closing visits" on five thoroughbreds one year, and then blow people out of the water the next three?

"I honestly don't know if Al could have coached five blue-chippers," Burke told me. "Marquette's success was predicated on everybody knowing exactly what their role is, what they had to do to win."

Looking back now, I realize Jackie was right. The key to Al's success was that he, not the players, set the tempo during a game.

Al also had an ironclad rule about when prospective players were to be brought in for a visit on the campus.

"Either you want the kid to make his first visit here or his last," he explained, in the fall of 1974, when future star Bernard Toone (whom Al called "Toom" for the first months he was there) came to visit. "Anything in between is garbage. Now, we asked Toone out here early. I figured the weekend of the Czech [National Team] game was a good one. That game was a lollipop. Everything was fine, no dissension on the team or anything. We were fresh, the cheerleaders and the crowd were fresh. Bernard saw us at our best, everything uptick, with our Sunday go-to-meeting clothes on."

One thing Al didn't want in a prospective player was what he called a "homeboy."

"The priests are always telling me about some 'good boy' in the parish, whose mother is in the altar society and whose father is active in school events," he explained, shaking his head. "I don't want an altar boy. I want someone with a killer instinct."

What Al gravitated to, over the years, were talented, tough, street-smart kids whom he could relate to—kids, frankly, whose roots were similar, spoke his language, and reminded him of himself. Little wonder then, that most of his "thoroughbreds"—George "Brute Force" Thompson, Dean "The Dream" Meminger, Ric Cobb, George Frazier, Earl Tatum (whom Al dubbed "the black Jerry West"), and Butch Lee came from the concrete canyons of New York. Chicago and its environs also provided Al with some great talents, like Bo Ellis (whom Al dubbed "the Secretariat of college forwards"), Lloyd Walton, and center Jerome Whitehead.

"My rule," I heard Al say, "was I wouldn't recruit a kid if he had grass in front of his house. That's not my world. My world has a cracked sidewalk."

The reason Al McGuire—white and in his 40s—could connect with so many talented African-American players during the Civil Rights era of the late 1960s and on into the 1970s was that he knew exactly where they were coming from—in most cases, the streets of the inner city. And he did his best to make sure that after their four years at Marquette were finished, they came away not only with some newspaper clippings and trophies, but a college degree as well.

"We don't run a plantation here," I heard him say more than once. "I want and expect my players to get degrees, even if it takes more than four years."

In the mid-1970s, Al admitted that he had broken NCAA rules by underwriting his players' education costs beyond the five years then allowed by the NCAA.

"What's the purpose of this rule?" he asked then. "Is it to send a man back to the ghetto?"

Rather than punish Al, the NCAA adopted legislation that extend-ed the time allowed athletes to pursue degrees with financial assistance.

That was one thing Al told me often that he was proudest of—that so many of his players (over 92 percent, during the years he coached at Marquette) had gone on to earn their college degrees. And in the later years, long after Al had left Marquette, one thing he never failed to mention when we were talking over a beer and a sandwich was how he had heard from this player or that one recently and how the player was doing. Like a doting father, it really delighted him that his former players—when they had a career decision to make—still called him for his advice.

"You know, Rog, that's what means the most these days. That the guys stay in touch," Al said one day. "They're like an extended family. And you're touched when they come back. You know, I've never had a player I couldn't look in the eye after he finished his career at Marquette. And I've never known a former player of mine not to contact me when I'm in his area. I always tried to teach a type of espirit de corps in which the guys would run through a wall for me. But only because they know it works the other way, too. That I'd run through a wall for them. It's an early American philosophy. But it's genuine."

The phrase that's been quoted most often, of course, is what Al always told his players concerning the sport, their college careers at Marquette, and how basketball could affect their lives.

"Use basketball," he told them. "Don't let basketball use you."

The point that needs to be made is: Al meant it. Even if it caused a setback for him and the Marquette basketball program when they followed his advice.

Case in point: Al lost three "blue-chippers" to the pros in three years—when center Jimmy Chones went hardship in 1972 and forwards Larry McNeill and Maurice Lucas did the same in 1973 and '74. And yet, Al—who had risen from the streets himself—did not fault them doing so. His comment when Chones turned pro spoke volumes: "I looked in his refrigerator. He had to take the money," Al said at the time. "He has a family to support."

Over the years, Al always seemed to have another funny recruiting story ready to tell, even if sometimes it wasn't a case of his landing his man.

"Rick came to me, in 1972 it was, I think," Al recalled, "and told me about this white kid out in Denver. Rick said, 'I know it's a little out of our area, but the kid is six-six and he can shoot. And I think we have a shot at him.' So I asked, 'What kind of grades does he have?' And Rick said, 'He's a great student. He's got 3.8 average.' And I said, 'Forget it. He's too smart. He'll figure us out.'"

Then there was 1974, when Lucasa, a 6'8" center whom many pro scouts called "the best big man in the country," decided to turn pro after his junior year. "Hank was really nervous, cause Luke had just turned hardship," Al explained, "and there was this big forward, six-eight or six-nine, named Landsberger from Minnesota. And Hank really wanted him. So I call up the father and ask if the kid can come down to visit the next weekend. 'Fine,' the father said, 'I'll come down, too.' And so I told him, 'Well, you'll have to drive, then. We'll pay for the gas. We can't pay for the flight, because the NCAA won't allow for that.' And then he tells me, 'But everybody else flies us in.' So I said, 'Hey, you got this all screwed up. We're not recruiting you. We're recruiting your son.'" Al shrugged. "That was the last I heard from him."

And practice? I honestly think Al hated practice. He was once quoted as saying "I've never blown a whistle, looked at a film, worked at a blackboard, or organized a practice in my life." The first time I read that, I thought, oh, sure. But after attending Marquette practices for a season or two, I realized he had been talking gospel.

Most times when I wandered into the gym, Al was sitting on one of the wooden benches against the far wall, huddled in a long black coat over a golf shirt and slacks (the place was always cold; I doubt they ever heated it). Sometimes, Al's face sported five o'clock shadow, and usually there was an almost disinterested look upon his face, like his mind was off somewhere else, contemplating God knows what. It was a luxury he could afford, of course, since he had Hank and Rick—two of the best— always running the practices.

"Hey, Rog," he'd always say, as I approached, getting up and shaking hands. "How's things?"

After a few minutes of small talk, he'd suddenly get down to business. "Is there something you wanted to talk about?" he'd ask matter-of-factly. Or, "Is there someone you needed to see?"

If I needed to talk with Al, we did that first. Then he'd yell out, "Hey, Butch! [Or Earl, or Bo, or whoever.] Take a blow!" Practice would halt momentarily, the player would wander over; Al would tell a reserve on the sidelines to go in for him, then make the perfunctory introduction, "You know Rog. He needs to talk with you a bit."

One thing I noticed. Al always moved down a bench or two before he sat down again. Not once did he ever try to sit close enough to hear my questions, or his player's answers, or do anything that would influence or guide the course of the interview. He'd just sit back down, cross his legs, and stare out across the court, his thoughts again on who knows what.

Like so many other things, I always admired that. Al was never afraid to let his players go one on one with anybody—on or off the court. He never interfered.

As you would expect, Marquette practices provided the grist for a number of great Al McGuire stories over the years. Stories Kevin Byrne and I always stored away in our mental Roladexes for when out-of-town reporters started asking. That was something I noticed immediately, East Coast or West. The guys would always cue up Kevin or me, knowing that—as the team's PR guy and the beat reporter—we were a ready source for the latest Al McGuire lines and funny anecdotes.

Two of the funnier practice stories I ever heard—and which, of course, were passed on down through the years—concerned Hughie McMahon, a six-foot, five-inch forward from Brooklyn, New York, and Dave Delsman, a five-foot, eleven-inch guard from Waukesha, Wisconsin.

In the early years, Al always let the students and nuns come over to the gym and watch practice. One day, McMahon took a pass on a fast break, went up for what should have been an easy layup, tried to convert it into a fancy dunk shot at the last second...and missed the basket entirely. No sooner had his feet hit the floor than McMahon let loose with a string of four-letter expletives that echoed throughout the gym, causing Al (who saw the nuns standing aghast in the far corner of the gym) to quickly rush out onto the floor.

"Hughie, Hughie!" he cried. "Settle down, Hughie! It's all right. Everybody makes a mistake, Hughie. Even I make mistakes. I made one three years ago, when I recruited you!"

Delsman's transgression was decidedly of the physical nature. During one early practice in the 1973-74 season, Delsman and fellow guard Marcus Washington got into an argument, and Delsman slugged Washington in the jaw.

"Hey, Dels!" McGuire yelled as he ran out onto the floor, "If you want to hit somebody, hit me."

Delsman obliged, smacking Al solidly and knocking him down.

"Can you imagine that little squirt putting me on the floor?" McGuire said after. "I should have just hit him on top of the head and been done with it."

On a personal note, my favorite practice story occurred the first fall I was covering Marquette, when I was leaving to go back to the office and write my story, only to see that my car had been towed away. Darkness comes quickly to Milwaukee in October, and I found I had inadvertently parked my car in what an obscure little sign said was a no-parking zone. Cursing my fate, I trudged back into the gym.

Al, whom I had just met for the first time, saw me coming back in and walked over and inquired what was wrong. When I told him, he immediately told me where they had most likely taken my car, then whipped out a $100 bill and said, "Go tell Rick [Majerus] to take you over to the garage. That'll cover the fine."

Feeling blessed (reporters never did make that much money, you know), I mumbled a thank you and started to walk away, only to be halted by Al's voice. "Uh, Roger," he said, "I want the hundred back."

I smiled, and nodded, and rushed off to find Rick before he left the building. I had only met Al McGuire once, but at that moment, his stock had risen 100 percent in my mind. He could have brushed me off ("Geez, that's too bad") or simply given me directions. But he went the extra step to make sure I could solve *my* problem. I was overwhelmed by his generosity—not just the money, but the fact he took the time to care. Man, I thought, and he doesn't even know me.

I was just starting to begin to realize what a great "run" I might have in front of me. Al was, most certainly, an intriguing coach—the colorful quotes I had in my notebook from practice told me that. But he had also shown himself to be quite a special person, more so than most of the big-time celebrities I had covered over the years.

Today, when I think back about that chilly fall night and Al's warm generosity that made it memorable, I always recall a quote of his I read somewhere, when he was talking to someone about the importance of having friends and knowing who they were. "I'll give you the coat off my back, the shoes off my feet, but if I don't know you, I wouldn't give you a straw hat in a blizzard," he said.

And yes, I did pay the hundred back. The very next day, to be sure. I would have been embarrassed to have done otherwise. And I could tell, when I forked up, that I had passed some sort of initial test with Al. Loyalty and trust were important things to him, I could tell. It was black and white. There was no in-between. My only worry? That somewhere down the road, he'd be in need of a quick $100, and I wouldn't be able to come through in return. My fervent hope was that it would be some problem a twenty could handle. Because given what reporters made in those days, that's the about most cash I ever had on me at one time.

During the years I covered Marquette, so many people asked me, "What's the secret? Why is Al McGuire so successful?"

If they'd been listening to Al, of course, they would have known the answer. As he said so many times, "I don't know if I coach. I think I'm like a master of ceremonies. I create a party on the court and keep it going."

People might chuckle, but Al wasn't kidding. Al McGuire was the best bench coach I have ever seen. Bar none. A psychological genius. On game night, when it was "showtime" and everything was on the line, his strategy was always the same: Create, orchestrate, and control the tempo of a game. No one was ever able to do it better. Why? Because Al's teams were so strong defensively and because he had an innate ability not just to react, but to correctly anticipate changes in momentum, the ebb and flow of a game, from the bench.

Defense was the trademark of Al's Marquette teams. His Warriors were never a run-and-gun bunch, and winning scores were often in the 50s. Control, remember, that was the key. Control your opponent (and the tempo of the game) with strong defense, use up the clock, and force *them* to make mistakes at the end. But always, always, be in control. That was McGuire's formula, and with some notable exceptions, it served him well over the years.

The defensive mindset was, of course, a carryover from his scrappy, hard-nosed playing days. "I'm a defensive coach," McGuire said many times. "I couldn't shoot when I played, so now I teach defense." It was control, remember, control. Hard work and heart could produce good defense. Offense was less predictable, like a fickle woman you couldn't control. "You can't count on offense," Al explained. "One night the basket is a washtub, the next night it's a teacup."

Not that Al didn't try to control his offense, as well. At Marquette, plays were designed to get the ball to one man, in a certain spot, for a certain shot, and that was that. There were no options. The only time Al allowed his troops to improvise was if they had grabbed an unexpected steal on defense. "Our offense is Simple Simon," he said. "Our All-Americans know they should have the ball and the other guys know they should get it to the All-Americans."

All of which, I realized, went a long way in explaining Al's recruiting philosophy of surrounding blue-chippers with what he called "complementary players"—players who knew their roles and were happy to fill them.

The best example of this I saw was Bill Neary—the rangy Marquette forward who was a member of the starting lineup on Marquette's 1977 NCAA championship team and who never got as much credit as he should have for their success. Many Marquette fans thought that Toone, who was a much better shooter, should have got that starting spot instead.

Problem was, Al had two other great shooters on the team—Bo Ellis and Butch Lee—and there was only one basketball to go around. What he needed was a guy, well, kind of like himself when he was a player—who was willing to go out there and play a physically tough, aggressive defense, throw the picks and the elbows and battle underneath, all the time setting up the shots for the All-Americans.

Which was just what Neary did. Al usually put him on the other team's leading scorer—which many times meant that by the end of the first half, Neary had exchanged enough elbows and hips that the other guy was on the bench in foul trouble. That defense breached, Al would then send in Bernard to shoot away during the second half, knowing the other team's "big gun" had to play tentatively and couldn't guard him nearly as closely.

Longtime Warriors fans shouldn't have been surprised. It was a tactic Al had been employing for years. Always trying, especially in his early years when his teams were often overmatched, to swing the odds just a little bit more his way and perhaps get one more number in that winner's column.

Bob Wolf, one of the top scorers in Marquette history, who played for Al in the mid-1960s, recalled how Al made a desperate attempt one season to even things up with his "Scrambled Eggs Defense"—reserves Dane Matthews, Craig Leonard, Billy Joe Smith, Joel Plinska, and Joe Mimlitz—whom he sent in with the sole purpose of disrupting the other team.

"It was early on, when we weren't winning," Wolf remembered, "and Al was trying to develop interest in the program. So he came up with the 'Scrambled Eggs'—guys with limited, if not questionable, ability. But he'd send 'em out to run around and try to steal the ball, foul if they had to, anything to break up the tempo of a team who was making a run at us."

Al's tactic of putting a scrapper on the other team's star resulted in one of the most famous stories of his coaching career. The scrapper this time was Pat Smith—a 6'3" forward nicknamed "Evil Dr. Blackheart" who wore Coke-bottle glasses and was averaging all of 0.5 points per game. Against archrival DePaul University at Alumni Hall in Chicago, McGuire sent Smith out to rough it up with Bob Zoretich, DePaul's high scorer. Shortly after the opening tipoff, the two exchanged shoves, Smith threw a punch, and both players were ejected.

DePaul coach Ray Meyer was outraged. "I lose my star," he fumed, "and Al loses a guy who can't throw the ball into the ocean if he were standing on the beach."

The opportunity was too good to pass up. The next day, back in Milwaukee, Al and the team's publicist, Max McGowan, took Smith, a basketball and a *Milwaukee Journal* photographer to the shores of icy Lake Michigan, where Smith lofted a shot…and hit his target. The picture of his feat ran on the national wire services, along with Al's gleeful quote that Lake Michigan was actually a much harder shot because it was smaller than the ocean.

Timeouts and technical fouls were Al's secret weapons, and I never saw a coach who used them more effectively. Unlike most coaches, if Al had, say, a 10-point lead, and he sensed momentum was shifting, he'd take a timeout to slow things down and break the spell immediately, rather than waiting until the other team had closed the gap and was back in the game. Control, that was the key. Never let things get out of hand. And never did I see a coach who was able to use the technical foul so effectively as a defensive weapon as Al. With one well-timed and accurately placed outburst, he could not only stop the clock, slow or diffuse the other team's concentration, but get the crowd (and his players) fired up as well. How many times did I hear Al, once he'd returned to the huddle, look at his players indignantly and yell, "Hey! They're trying to take this game away from us! What the hell! Call a foul like that! You gonna let 'em take this game away?" Sometimes, if you were sitting close enough to the bench, you could just feel the anger and the resolution flow from McGuire to his players, and when they went back out on the floor, most times he had them galvanized, ready to strike again. That's when Al was at his best, with his back against the wall.

What most people remembered, of course, were McGuire's flamboyant acts of indignation, the mincing words, charging the official to guarantee the slap of a T. What most forgot were the circumstances when it occurred—usually at a time when the other team was starting to make a serious run at Marquette and Al saw he needed to buy his troops a breather and put their psychological compasses back on track. Another point: Yes, Al did get some technicals called on him simply because he was upset with a particular official or call. But when he *wanted* to get a technical, he had a standard operating procedure: "When I commit a technical on purpose," he said, "I do it when the opponent has the ball, not when I have the ball." That way Al made sure he cut his losses. His outburst might cost him two points, but not two points plus possession (and two more points his team might have made). Calculating? You bet. Al did not earn his nickname "The Fox" for nothing.

Defense and control. They were the heart of Al McGuire's coaching philosophy.

As he once put it: "Basketball is a simple game. Most of the time it's like kindergarten. When you have the ball, you're king. But when I have it, I am king. And when you dribble, you are king. But when you stop, I am king."

*"Only God could be a good official.
He's the only one who could please
the other 50 percent."*

Chapter 4
"Technical-ly" Incorrect

The fall of 1974, my first season on the Marquette beat, was a pivotal time for Al McGuire. It was then, I think, when he first began to seriously entertain the thought that no matter how good a basketball team he put together, he was never going to win the NCAA championship. His fiery persona, especially towards the officials, had become legendary over the last decade, and now that very reputation, he felt, was starting to turn on him, especially in "big games" where a lot was on the line.

From time to time, Al voiced a growing suspicion that the officials who worked Marquette's games were being "prepped" (as he called it) by the NCAA and came onto the floor determined—if not downright predisposed—to keep a tight rein on Al McGuire, the flamboyant showman, handing out technical fouls (even at the slightest provocation) to prove they could not be intimidated. Was it, he wondered, his ironic fate to become his own worst enemy on game night?

Al's thoughts, I felt, were a result of a summer of simmering following Marquette's 76-64 loss to North Carolina State in the 1974 NCAA championship game the previous March, in Greensboro, North Carolina. In that game, Al had drawn two costly technical fouls in the second half that allowed NC State to score nine straight points and put the game away for good. "I lost the championship with those two technicals," Al admitted. He shrugged. "It's something I'm not proud of, but it's something I did. We were up five points, then down by four. And there were 42 million people watching."

Little wonder, then, when Al got slapped with four technical fouls in Marquette's first five games of the new season that December, he out-of-the-blue told me one day at practice—just prior to the annual Christmas Classic tournament—that he had finally "got the message" and that he planned to keep quiet and stay seated from then on.

"I'm not going to get off the bench," he said. "I'm going to stay seated and keep my mouth shut for the whole Classic. I'll probably need some kind of seatbelt to keep me strapped in there, but I fully intend to stay in my chair. Call it an early New Year's resolution. I may stand up for the huddle when we call time out, or kneel in front of the bench, but that's it. I'm not going to say one word to the officials."

I rolled my eyes in disbelief and told Al flat out there was no way he could do it. Who did he think he was kidding? He just laughed. "I know it's a hard statement for me to make," he admitted, "but I am going to try."

Naturally, I asked him to elaborate on what "the message" was— and who he thought was sending it to him.

"The message is a carry-over from last year," Al insisted, "when I got the technical fouls in the NCAA championship against North Carolina State. The message is that Al McGuire should sit down and shut up. Well, all right. I understand. And I'm going to sit down and be quiet." Asked again about who was sending it—the NCAA or the officials—Al turned evasive, knowing full well that my notebook was open and he was on the record. "Let's just say some people are trying to get the message to me," he replied. "They have succeeded."

The amazing thing was, Al did it. He kept quiet throughout the Christmas Classic as promised and picked up only one technical foul in the final 19 games of the Warriors' season, during a highly charged 71-68 victory over Notre Dame at the Arena. And that happened midway through the first half, after a flurry of fouls by Marquette that put Notre Dame into a bonus situation, causing Al to erupt off the bench, go into his familiar "Act" and shake things up a bit.

"What the hell's going on here?" he screamed in the official's face. "We don't even have a foul shot yet! What are you guys trying to prove?"

Outside of that one outburst, Al remained "technically correct" the rest of the year.

Al McGuire's relationship with college basketball officials, you must understand, was always uneasy—and sometimes volatile—*at the best*. It was that control and tempo thing, remember. From tipoff to final horn, both Al and the "zebras" (as he called officials, because of their black and white striped shirts) had the same thing in mind: Keep control of the tempo of the game. It was just that Al's idea of control and tempo often was a whole lot different than that of the officials. Morever, it always irritated and worried him that they could so easily disrupt a winning rhythm he had so carefully set up with a single blow of the whistle, if they (for whatever reason) changed the style or frequency of their calls.

Don't get this wrong. Al was smart enough to know that he had to adjust to the personality and mood of the officials who were working his game on a particular night. The key to the whole thing was knowing the officials well enough, and how each was different, so that he (i.e., his players) could adjust as soon as possible.

"I really don't think there's any such thing as a dishonest official," Al told me once. "But you must learn to change to his style of game, that is, the style of game he's calling, in the first five minutes. Some officials are what I call 'high school officials,' with the quick whistle. Others let you play football underneath. You have to let your players know what's happening, and quickly."

What Al looked for in officials was consistency. Given that, he told me, it was just a matter of adjusting and conducting your game plan accordingly. "Most officials," he explained, "got to the top doing things one way, and they aren't going to change. You must learn what they do and change to accommodate. They call things the same if it's Palm Sunday or Yom Kippur. It's you who [must] adjust."

Officials, Al went on to say, were just like the players. Each had his own particular style, and normally that didn't change throughout the game.

"Earl Tatum doesn't change his style from one half to the next, and officials don't either," Al said. "Now, on the close calls, some call charging, others call blocking. Some favor the big man, others the small guy. But it's ingrained. It's constant."

The other thing Al said a successful coach has to learn about officials is their little "quirks"—things they call that most other officials don't. Learn an official's style, he said, and his "quirks," and you always have the odds on your side.

"One guy may be really aware of three seconds in the lane," Al explained. "Another guy is more lax, gives you four seconds. Some allow Chinese steps, that half a step extra before they call traveling. But you see, you have to get to know these things, learn their habits."

It was that rare time when an official suddenly changed his style during the middle (or late minutes) of a game that got Al up and shouting. That's when you heard the cries: "Hey, how can you make that call? What's going on here? You haven't made that call all night!" Consistency. That was what Al looked for in officials, so that he could adjust his psychological template to theirs and increase his chances of winning. It was as simple as that.

"So why do you always yell at officials?" I asked him once. I figured, hey, once you got the pattern down, why bother?

"Sometimes because you disagree with them," Al said, "but most times, you're really yelling to keep face for your ballplayer. To keep him up. To make sure he knows you're in his corner, no matter what."

Writing this now, it brought to mind that night, during Al's championship season, when Bo was really getting picked on by the officials in a game against DePaul at Alumni Hall in Chicago. Once, twice, then a third time, Bo—who on the other side was really getting hammered defensively by the Blue Demons—was called for charging. The third charging call had Al up and screaming, voicing his displeasure as the official who made the call passed by the Marquette bench. "Hey, what the hell are you doing out there?" Al yelled at him. "You're calling high school fouls on us, pro fouls on them." Then he angrily chided the official, asking: "What do you want us to do with the guy? Send him home?"

Al told me more than once that, over the years, he had never asked for a particular official (one he thought might be more partial to his style of play), blackballed an official (refused to let him work any of his games), or rated an official (sent a ratings form back into the conference office). And I believe that. Marquette, an independent, always used Big Ten officials, and Al had the option to rate their performance, just like a conference member. But he never did, and he didn't think other coaches should follow that practice, either.

"I don't believe in that," he said simply. "I don't believe a coach has the ability to rate an official. He sees things through tinted glass, after all, depending on whether he won or lost."

The only restriction Al placed on who would call his games at the Arena was that he didn't want an official from Wisconsin. The perception—right or wrong—of the other coach feeling he was being "homered" was just too great. "I've always felt that when a team comes in here [to Milwaukee] from 2,000 miles away, to have an official from the state just isn't right," Al explained.

Which is not to say that there weren't some officials Al just didn't like. I can think of two (who shall remain nameless, but diehard MU fans will know) right off the bat. Whenever I took my seat on press row and saw that one of them (worse yet, both!) was officiating that night's game, I knew for certain that one of them (if not both) would be nose to nose with Al before the game was over. Why? Because the two guys I mention here were not particularly consistent. One game, they'd call things tight as a drum, the next you wanted to hand out shoulder pads. And the bad thing was, if the game was close near the end, they were totally unpredictable. Out of nowhere might come a call they hadn't made all night long…at a moment when it hurt the Warriors most.

That was why, I knew, Al didn't like them doing his games: because of their lack of consistency and competence. But never once during my years on the beat did he publicly complain after the game about either one of them to the media or, to my knowledge, try to get them off his games. That just was not Al's style.

Not that he didn't try, during the game, to get things back into what he felt was the proper perspective, when the officials' calls weren't going his way. Tom Collins, the radio announcer who did Marquette's play-by-play, tells one of the better stories about Al's relationship with officials.

"The Warriors were 18-4 and they already accepted a bid to the 1969 NCAA [tournament]," Collins recalled. "Marquette was playing at Denver, a team that had only won two games. It was early in the second half, and Marquette was getting beat. Al called time, walked out to the officials, and in a voice that could be heard all over the Rockies said, 'Hey, what are you guys trying to do to me? We're going to the NCAA, and these clowns aren't going anywhere!' When play resumed, Denver was charged with traveling, charging, basket interference, you name it, and the Warriors went on a scoring rampage to win, 65-61."

Al didn't get his first technical foul until the third game of the 1975-76 season. Which is not to say that he didn't have a lot on his mind. All through his career at Marquette, Al was drawn to controversy like a flagpole in an electrical storm—and as opening night of that season drew near, it struck once again...big-time.

The problem was, as the beat reporter, that this time I got drawn into the melee...a circumstance that tested my friendship with Al for the first of only two times during all the years I knew him.

When I think back about it now, I always remember something Al told his players. "You have to know what's important," he said. "Don't come to me with a haircut problem. Come to me with a hit-and-run problem. Go after a parrot with a slingshot, not a cannon. If you need the howitzer, roll it out. But don't roll it out to stop a cold."

The problem was that, this time around, the "haircut" turned into a "hit and run." It came about, as many big problems do, because of little ones that were left unresolved.

This time, the problem was called parking tickets.

Because Marquette played all their home games at the Milwaukee Arena, they practiced there quite a bit as well. And during November of 1975, two of Al's starting players—senior guard Lloyd Walton and junior guard Bo Ellis—ran up an inordinate number of parking tickets. Problem was, they'd get out of class, then rush to get across town to the Arena (not wanting to be late for practice), only to find nothing open next to the building. Their solution to that crisis was to simply park wherever they found a spot—handicapped, restricted, whatever—hurry on in, and worry about it later.

This, of course, the Milwaukee police frowned on. Thus, after two or three weeks, Lloyd and Bo found themselves in possession of all these pink slips that had been tucked under their windshield wipers. Tickets that, for whatever reason (lack of funds or excessive ego), they simply ignored and refused to pay.

So it wasn't long before the police were calling the University, and Al, who was both men's basketball coach and athletic director, suddenly found himself bombarded by calls from school officials. And when in spite of his ordering the two players to pay their tickets, the calls kept coming, Al took them to task in the locker room prior to Marquette's preseason exhibition game against the Russian National Team on November 2.

"Jesus Christ, Lloyd!" he yelled at his diminutive guard. "Will you pay your f—ing parking tickets? Who do you think you are, Mayor Maier?"

"Hey, you know how things are," Walton retorted with a shrug. "I don't have any money."

"Bullshit," Al insisted. "Just pay the tickets, will ya?"

At that moment, to me, the outsider, it was actually a humorous sort of thing—the down-and-dirty, nitty-gritty coach-and-player exchange that Al always allowed his players to have. In fact, I thought, the relationship was kind of neat.

A month later, however, any thought of humor was gone—when the situation produced some sobering consequences.

At 4:05 a.m. on December 1, the morning of the day before Marquette's season opener against St. Joseph's of Indiana, Bo Ellis was stopped by police on the 1500 block of Milwaukee's W. Kilbourn Ave. and arrested on a warrant citing him for 11 unpaid parking violations.

Had that been the extent of things, I would not have been surprised. For one thing, I knew Bo, like Lloyd, was not paying his parking tickets. And second, the Milwaukee Police Department, back then, had a reputation of being a racially prejudiced force, and I had no doubt that when the officers involved saw a young *black* man driving alone at that hour—in spite of the fact he was not speeding or driving erratically—they immediately called in for a license plate check and then simply pulled him over to see what they could find.

What they found, when they searched the vehicle, was 22.9 grams (less than an ounce) of marijuana in a hat in the back seat. Suddenly, the stakes went up tremendously.

In addition to the unpaid tickets, Ellis was also officially arrested for possession of marijuana. And that's where I came in, when I arrived at work the morning of December 1 and was immediately briefed by our police reporter on what had transpired thus far. Because of his age (and status, I'm sure) and the fact he had no previous record, Bo was referred to Milwaukee County's Special Evaluation Unit. What that meant was that he had to agree to six months of informal supervision, and if he maintained a clean record during that period, no charges would be filed and the whole matter would be dropped.

Bo, thank God, agreed to the program and signed on the dotted line immediately.

Still, the whole degrading situation saddened me, because I honestly liked Bo an awful lot. Not only was he a talented athlete, but he also had a unique vision of life on this planet and the people who inhabited it and a good sense of humor that his shyness often hid. Still, as a reporter, I knew what I had to do. My job was to write the story about all that had come down in those early-morning hours—a story that would appear in the *Journal* the afternoon of Marquette's opening game of the season.

Armed with the facts (and a ton of apprehension), I went across the street to the Arena, where the Warriors were conducting an afternoon practice, and confronted Al with the situation.

When I told him I was going to write a story and that I needed to ask him some questions, first I was told there was no story to write, and when I persisted and insisted there was, I got a broadside similar to what I'd seen Al give an official, when the guy made a call he didn't agree with.

"Raaah-ger!" he screamed, as we squared off, toe to toe at courtside. "How can you write a story? The kid hasn't been charged with anything! He hasn't done anything wrong!"

"Al," I retorted, "he's on the record book! He was arrested for tickets and possession! It's there. I could show it to you right now!"

"But he hasn't been charged!" Al shot back. "How can you write something if he hasn't been charged? Listen. If they charge him with something, okay. Then I got no problem with this. But right now, he still hasn't been charged. It's not fair to write anything until he's been charged. Until he's been charged, he's not guilty of anything!"

"Al, my job is to write what happened. Don't yell at me! I didn't refuse to pay my parking tickets! I didn't have marijuana in my car! Bo did! And you have to understand, I have to report all that. It's on the record. You know it, and I know it. My boss knows it. By now, all of Milwaukee knows it! So I have to write the story. OK?"

Al shrugged. "OK, Rog. You do what you got to do," he said coldly. And then he walked away.

A bit later, when all the TV stations arrived, Al saw it was no use, and so a press conference was held right then and there, where both he and Bo tried to put the best spin they could on the whole affair.

"They just told me I was under informal supervision for six months," Bo told the reporters. "But I wasn't charged with anything. I was not guilty of any wrong."

Al, after affirming that Bo would start against St. Joseph's that night, insisted, "As far as I'm concerned, there's no guilt. So I can't react to a situation that right now isn't there. Unless more things are brought to light.

"All I know about Bo is that he's just a wonderful young guy. He's been our leader for the last two years and set an outstanding example on and off the court."

The key question asked of Ellis was: Had he had any marijuana in his possession at the time of the arrest?

"No," he said.

What Bo was claiming, of course, was that the marijuana wasn't his and he had no idea how it got into his car. And in fact, perhaps it wasn't and he didn't. For example, it could have accidentally been left there by a friend. I knew right then that unless some surprise witness popped up somewhere, the real truth would never be known for sure. And that's why I think the police decided it was far better to opt for the Special Evaluation, rather than pursue the case any further. Instead, Bo pleaded guilty that day to 11 unpaid parking citations, at $10 each ($110).

Al, speaking to the TV cameras, said he thought too much was being made of the situation. "There were no implications of guilt," Al insisted. "No findings of guilt. He was not charged.

"But we're dealing in a situation where the celebrity is not expected to be treated like the nine-to-five guy. It's part of being a celebrity. For every pat on the back, there's a kick in the pants."

Pat or kick, it didn't matter. I had one obligation: to write my story, which I did, no holds barred, giving every detail of Bo's arrest and the deal that was struck with the district attorney's office.

Tuesday night at the Arena, no sooner had the National Anthem been played than Ellis grabbed the microphone at the scorer's table and made a surprise apology to the capacity crowd—and then went on to play one of the best games of his life.

"I just want to say that I'm sorry for everything that's happened," Bo told them. The response was a rousing wave of applause. After which, the six-foot, nine-inch forward scored 16 points, grabbed 11 rebounds, blocked a number of shots, and stole the ball twice—leading Marquette to an 87-60 route of St. Joseph's.

Al, as expected, was beaming afterwards. "Bo had a great game. But then, he's a great player," Al told reporters. "I've said all along, the way he goes, or Lloyd Walton goes, so we go."

"I just wanted to put all that has happened in the past," Bo said, after the game. "It [the apology] was something I just felt I should say. I talked it over with Coach before I said it. It didn't do anything to change my game, though. I was just being Bo Ellis out there, trying to give my 150 percent."

The next afternoon, I showed up at the gym as usual to cover practice and walked over to where Al was sitting on a bench against the wall, draped in his old black coat. Given all that had happened, I was a bit nervous about how he'd receive me. As I drew near, he glanced up in my direction, but said nothing.

I decided, the hell with it, let's get right to the quick of things, so I know where I stand.

"Well," I asked, with a sigh, "are you still mad at me?"

Al looked up, a puzzled look in his eyes. And then said to me the words I have never forgotten to this day.

"No," he said, a bit wearily. "You know, Rog, I was just doing what I had to do—trying to protect my player. I hope you understand that. And I know, you were doing what you had to do—just trying to do your job." He looked me squarely in the eye. "But Roger, you have to understand one thing. If you hadn't written that story, I would have had no respect for you. It's as simple as that."

At that moment, I felt like a million dollars. As far as I was concerned, Al had paid me the ultimate compliment.

What Al was telling me—even though we were on opposite sides this time around—was that he recognized that I (like him) was a professional in my given field and that we could still be friends. That while he might disagree, he didn't doubt my sincerity. That meant an awful lot to me back then...and it still does today.

Not to say that others in the Marquette entourage didn't carry a temporary grudge. Hank was upset with me, I knew. And for a while, Doc Eichenberger, the team physician, looked the other way when he saw me coming and refused to speak. Of the players, Lloyd Walton was the angriest. He didn't speak to me for three weeks after Bo's arrest. He felt, sincerely I'm sure, that I had betrayed his friend when I wrote the article detailing everything that happened. That, of course, was the downside of my profession. I knew that as long as the articles were positive, I would be considered an OK guy. But when something negative (like Bo's situation) happened and I had to write about it, I suddenly became the person everyone—school officials, players, alumni, fans, and sometimes the coaches—loved to hate.

I think Al understood that. And that's why he said privately what he did to me that day.

Publicly, of course, it was another story. A few weeks later, in his remarks prior to a Milwaukee Classic dinner at the Lime House Restaurant, Al took time (in the middle of his usual running litany of funny stories) to turn serious and criticize the press for our coverage of Bo's scrape with the law and for what he called a negative outlook in sports reporting.

"I've never said this before in 20 years, but I will today," he remarked. "The first time I ever argued with a reporter was over the Ellis thing. I just don't want to see everybody get so negative. Hey, if you want to find something wrong with anybody, and if you probe long enough, you'll find it. With Marquette, Wisconsin, even the Lime House Restaurant. But the thing is, we're not pros. This is college amateur sports. I know I'm saying too much, but it's time." Al laughed, then added, "I've got my safe-deposit box. I wouldn't have dared say this years ago."

When the laughs subsided, he continued. "I know things go on," he admitted. "I have skeletons in my closet. Everybody does. But suddenly there is this tendency by the press for investigations. What I'm saying is, 'Don't get spoiled.' Enjoy the success you've got. It's going to end someday.

"I've seen [Green Bay Packers coach Vince] Lombardi, the old [New York] Yankees, the New York police department. Everything comes to an end. While you have it, enjoy it, milk it. Because it'll end, and then you'll sit dormant for 15 years."

Did Al's criticisms bother me? Not one bit. Because I understood, too, that he was doing once again what he had to do—just as he had when he confronted me, three weeks before at the Arena. That was his job: to talk the talk, and walk the walk. To circle the wagons, in times of crisis, and defend his "family" from whatever enemies seemed to be threatening at that moment or on the horizon. In spite of our own personal friendship, I never lost sight of the fact that to the Marquette faithful, the media—like the "zebras"—were always considered a necessary evil, somebody they put up with, at best, when things were going good. But let something—or somebody—go astray, and immediately we became the villains for calling that particular call or writing that particular story. If you're a fan, that's the way things are, always have been, always will be.

Al knew that, too. And when the occasion demanded, he had to play to his audience.

No sooner had the Bo Ellis controversy died down than Al's penchant for drawing technical fouls returned with a passion. In December alone, he was slapped with three technicals in six games (all during lopsided Marquette victories), and in January he picked up four more—giving him seven technicals in 23 games, or about one in every three. Diehard Marquette fans thought it was great, of course, and more than one was overheard to say after a game at Major Goolsby's (a favorite watering hole across the street from the Arena) that it was great to see "the old Al back." Critics, however, merely noted that he—like a person with a chronic drinking problem—had "fallen off the wagon."

To me, Al seemed more of a "driven" man during his next to last season at Marquette than I had ever seen him. Hank Raymonds said once he believed Al coached "out of fear," and if that was the case, well, Al was carrying around a lot of demons in his psyche right about then—because of intense pressures, self-imposed or otherwise. Even before the regular season began, Marquette watchers were already proclaiming "this was the year" the Warriors would win it all, and even Al admitted to me privately that, in terms of sheer talent, he thought his current squad was "my best team ever."

Right from the start, the national rankings supported such speculation, and while the Warriors rolled to an astounding 25-1 regular-season record, the wire services continued to rank them No. 2 and 3, right behind Bobby Knight's No. 1-ranked Indiana powerhouse. By Christmas, there was already talk of a possible MU-Indiana matchup in the NCAA final—a "dream game" for the championship that had Marquette fans buzzing.

One other factor came into play, as well. Al had said for a number of years that "coaching is just a passing fancy for me," and I knew he was already employed by Medalist Industries—a company that manufactured sports equipment—in some sort of public relations capacity. Had he decided, I wondered, that the time for a career change was at hand? Did he see this season as his last, best chance to grab the brass ring and bring an NCAA title home to Marquette?

Given all those factors, I think Al was under more strain than he ever admitted, feeling a heavy obligation to do everything possible to get the most and best out of his team that year, before Walton and Tatum both graduated. It would certainly explain why, in a number of games where Marquette was playing well and winning big, he was still up on his feet and yelling at his players, to the extent that even I felt he was overdoing things at times. And why, in spite of his claiming to have received "the message" from the NCAA and the officials the year before, he had reverted to his earlier combative stance with the officials once again.

"I'm just trying to teach these guys the killer instinct," Al told me, when I asked if he wasn't getting on the players a bit too much after an 82-66 route of Wisconsin in the Christmas Classic, a game in which Al drew his third T of the month. "To go for the throat when you got 'em on the ropes. To go in and get 'em out of there as quick as possible." He paused, then added, "There's a time, you know, when every team is ready to be beaten."

Perhaps, but I still wasn't convinced.

Two weeks later, on the road against Oklahoma City University, Marquette was winning by 24 points when the Warriors turned the ball over twice and the lead was cut to 20. Instantly, Al was on his feet, angrily calling a timeout, during which he really chewed the players out. There were all of seven seconds remaining. "I was angry because we break our back to get to a certain point and then we start that one-on-one stuff," he explained later. "That doesn't impress me."

Tempo and control, I knew, were Al's watchwords. But with a 24-point lead and seven seconds left? I had a feeling the screws were being turned a little too tight here.

On February 16, things finally came to a head. Marquette was hosting Tulane at the Arena, and with 12 minutes 50 seconds left in the game, the nation's No. 2-ranked team had just played seven of the prettiest minutes of basketball imaginable (much to the delight of the Marquette fans) to outscore Tulane 20-8 and take a 22-point lead. In that remarkable span, Al's troops made 10 of 13 shots from the field, out-rebounded Tulane 8-2, and stole the ball four times.

And yet, while the fans were roaring their approval, there stood Al before the Marquette bench, continuing to harangue his players as if they were losing to a cupcake. Finally, it was just too much for Walton, who, when Al yelled something at him as he ran past, turned and yelled right back, "You want everything, right!"

It broke the ice. Even Al had to laugh. And after the game, he admitted that maybe he was pushing his players too much.

"Sometimes, I do yell too much," he explained. "But that's the only way I know how to coach. Hey, the guys ran a smooth run there, it was good. But I coach under winning. You understand? Create static while you win. Never show contentment. Berate. Anger. Don't accept faults after you win. If you accept them now, you have to accept them when you lose, too. I can't do that."

I understood Al's logic, of course. It was something I had heard him say many times. Never accept anything in victory you would not accept in defeat. My fear, of course, was that if he kept pushing the envelope, sooner or later at least one of the players might decide there was no way he could please his flamboyant coach...and simply give up trying.

Lurking in the back of my mind, too, was the continuously mounting number of technical fouls Al was chalking up. How long, I wondered, until another message would be sent?

Four games later, on March 5—the day before my 30th birthday—Al got "the message" again, this time in Cincinnati, where Marquette drubbed Xavier University, 74-49, in one of the most bizarre college basketball games I have ever seen.

First off, the game was a horrible mismatch, or as Al would put it, "like an 18-year-old kid taking on the bouncer" in a New York bar. The No.2-ranked Warriors had far superior talent. (Al, by the way, was the only coach on the Marquette bench; Hank and Rick were off scouting.) Second, the two officials working the game, Jerry Menz and Bob Schockley, were by far the worst I ever saw at the college level. There was no consistency to their officiating. They called things tight one minute, loose the next, and some things they didn't call at all.

The result was a game that got out of hand early on and never got any better. Five technical fouls were called, there were two near fights and a lot of angry words, and at one point the game was halted so that a canful of beer hurled onto the court by an angry fan could be wiped up off the floor.

At halftime, Marquette led by only six points, 33-27, thanks to great shooting by Whitehead and Toone. The scoring burden fell on them, believe it or not, because Tatum, Ellis and Walton all were on the bench with three fouls before the crowd's popcorn had begun to cool. When Walton drew his third, Al stood up and yelled: "Twenty-two?!" (which was Walton's number) and then walked off the court and behind the bleachers. While Al took a few minutes to cool down outside, the coachless Warriors (unless you count Bob Weingart, the trainer) played on as best they could, until he returned to call a timeout and regroup.

It was midway through the second half, when Marquette had already put the game away, that Al's fiery reputation caught up with him again. When Tatum was whistled with his fourth foul, Al stood up and yelled something to him. Menz, standing close by, whirled and slapped Al with a technical foul. And when Al began to protest, he slapped him with a second T.

After the game, Al was nothing short of dumbfounded. "What happened was a misunderstanding," he said, shaking his head. "A sad misunderstanding."

Xavier coach Tay Baker, who also drew a technical during the game, not only lambasted the officiating of Menz and Shockley after it was all over, but he also defended Al's actions. "Al didn't deserve those technicals," Baker said. "He wasn't trying to incite, and he didn't show disgust at the call. I've seen guys do a lot worse and not get slapped with a technical, much less two."

Those "guys," Baker might have added, weren't Al McGuire. His fiery reputation, put somewhat to rest the year before, had been resurrected in the officials' minds, I felt, by a season of repeated technical fouls. And now, it seemed, it had come back to haunt him once again.

In this case, like many others over the last three months, it didn't matter. Against a "bunny" like Xavier University, Marquette's sheer talent had been enough to save the day. Two weeks later, however, against No. 1-ranked Indiana in the final of the NCAA's Mideast Regional, that would not be the case.

What Al wanted was to meet Indiana right away. Never in his 12 years at Marquette had he had a chance to upset a No. 1-ranked team, and now, there the opportunity was—hanging in front of him like forbidden fruit, if only the cards fell right. It was just another bit of pressure—in what had already been a pressure-packed season—factored in.

"If we're going to get to Philadelphia [the Final Four], we're going to have to meet Indiana sooner or later," he told a businessmen's luncheon in Milwaukee, two days before the bids were announced. "Now the way the bids are drawn out of a hat, we could meet Indiana in the first round, March 13 at Notre Dame. I'd prefer this. Indiana's been close to getting beat a few times lately, and so I think they could be tightening some.

"On the other hand, I think we're at the top of our game right now. It's just a question if we can stay on top of it for the next few weeks. But I'd like to get at Indiana as soon as possible. The sooner the better. Too many things can happen in a tournament, when you're looking ahead."

As things turned out, Al was right.

The No. 2-ranked Warriors were anything but sharp against Western Kentucky in the first round in Dayton, Ohio, a game in which Al was continually on his feet, alternately exhorting and berating his troops, especially Ellis and Tatum. "Hey!" he screamed, again and again. "Come on! Cut the crap out there! Play ball! Come on, Bo, play! Hey, Earl! Wake up! Get the boards! You want to come out?"

Round two—a 62-57 squeaker over Western Michigan, in Baton Rouge, Louisiana—was even worse. In one of its sloppier games of the year, Marquette actually trailed by a point with six minutes left, then finally charged back to take command. Al's postgame comments showed where the players' minds (and his) had really been. "If Indiana isn't sleeping now, they'll never sleep," Al told the press. "We couldn't shake 'em. Hey, Western Michigan gave us all we could eat. Made us look bad. I was trying to be patient with the game, not panic, but they had us in the panic stage at the end."

When I asked Bo about the Indiana factor, he didn't blink an eye. "We might have been looking ahead to Indiana," he told me. "I hope we were. If this is all the better we can play, then we might as well take a plane home tonight, instead of taking a beating Saturday."

Saturday. The regional final. That, I sensed, was what had really been on the minds of Al and his players all along. And how could it not be, with so much at stake? There it was, the chance to topple powerful Indiana, take away its No. 1 ranking, and advance to the Final Four—all in one game. There was biggest prize on the block waiting for them, just around the corner, and Al, from the time the bids were announced, was not altogether certain if he and his team would even get the chance.

"I personally don't think we'll meet [Indiana], because in history I've never had a chance to get at number one," he told the press a few days earlier. "It's never happened to me in 12 years at Marquette that the thing everybody has been thinking about has become a reality."

Looking ahead? I think no matter how hard they tried, Al and his players were wearing telescopes those first two games. Given the situation, if they hadn't, they wouldn't have been human. And they could take consolation in the fact that maybe Coach Bobby Knight and his Hoosiers were fighting the same problem, since they struggled to a five-point, 74-69 win over Alabama to earn their spot in the long-awaited "dream game" on which so much was riding.

Al's sense of humor, however, endured through it all.

When Knight showed up in a green sport coat for practice on St. Patrick's Day, the day before Marquette's game against Western Michigan, Al (who was wearing a yellow sports shirt, red slacks, and tennis shoes) scoffed. "Wait until the banquet tonight," he told the press. "I'll have a green sport coat on, too. Hey, Bobby's like all the others, he likes to pretend he's Irish. Like my black ballplayers do. Everybody's Irish on St. Patrick's Day."

Then he asked a writer if he could borrow his pen. Was he going to chart plays? the reporter asked him, as he reached into his pocket for a folded sheet of paper. Al laughed and shook his head. "Nope, just checking on tickets," he explained wryly. "That's the job of a head coach. To see who has the comps."

Once we'd arrived in Baton Rouge, it quickly became obvious that the differences between Al's band of footloose Warriors and Bobby Knight's National Guard drill team ran a whole lot deeper than their No. 1 and No. 2 rankings. This square-off for the Mideast Regional title was not going to be merely a matter of strength vs. quickness, offenses vs. defenses, or one-on-one matchups, once the ball was in the air. The difference between Marquette and Indiana, that spring of 1976, was a total difference in lifestyles. These were two teams that were light years apart in every way but one—winning.

On one hand, you had Bobby Knight—the domineering General Patton of college coaches (who years later would finally lose his job at Indiana, just as Patton had lost Third Army, because his superiors were fed up with his excesses). On the other, there was Al, whose alternately off-the-wall and down-to-earth comments made him seem more akin to Willie and Joe, the two ordinary buck privates of World War II whom cartoonist Bill Mauldin made famous.

On Friday, the day before the game, the differences between Al and Knight were drastically evident during their pregame press conference. Knight talked basketball and made a point of saying his team's practices would be closed. Al told stories and said his team's practices would be open. The closest Knight could come to humor was when a writer asked him if he'd ever ridden a motorbike (like Al). "Yes, but not very well," Knight answered curtly. "I couldn't get it started, so I slammed the damn thing down in a ditch and kicked it."

The laughter was faint, and strained, to say the least.

Al, on the other hand, went off on one of his usual tangents, complaining about how he had been asked to speak at a clinic in Baton Rouge later that summer, but refused when he was told they didn't pay. (Having heard this lead-in many times, I knew what was coming next!) Out came the old "Do you ask Frank Sinatra to sing for nothing?" lament, and how could you "ask a carpenter to fix the front stoop and then say, 'See you later?'" No matter. Al knew his audience. While I sat smiling, the other writers laughed aloud and scribbled furiously.

After that, Al left us all (including myself, who had never heard this one before) shaking our heads when—24 hours before one of the biggest games of his career—he suddenly decided to put in a plug for tourism in Milwaukee that had even Mayor Maier smiling when he read it in *The Milwaukee Journal* the next day. "We need more conventions in Milwaukee," Al insisted. "So when all you guys go home to your areas, plug for conventions for Milwaukee. I mean it. It's a nice town, but we need more conventions."

And up and away he went.

At that point, I knew one thing for sure. No matter which team won the "dream game" the following day, Al had just trounced Bobby Knight when it came to personality and wit. With a turn of the hand and a few good phrases, Al the Showman had captured the Fourth Estate, and so would get the headlines the next day. (Not that Knight cared, I'm sure. Laid back was just not his style.)

Even more telling had been watching the two teams when they ate breakfast earlier that morning in the hotel cafeteria. Knight's players were as neatly dressed as freshmen from an Eastern boarding school, wearing leisure suits or sport coats and dress shirts. Al's minions, on the other hand, who were sitting close by, were the epitome of casual, clad in cut-off blue jeans, tennis shoes, and T-shirts with witty sayings across the fronts.

As I ate my scrambled eggs and bacon, I enjoyed watching the two squads surreptitiously eyeing each other while they partook from the buffet. At the table on my left were Indiana's three star players—Quinn Buckner, Scott May, and Kent Benson, looking for all the world like three young corporate types discussing the stock market over breakfast. Had one of them been reading *The Wall Street Journal*, I would not have been surprised.

By contrast, on my right, sat Bo Ellis, wearing a leather eyeshade, like a croupier at Caesar's Palace, and Bernard Toone, in a Civil War-era planter's hat. And when Toone got up and walked by Benson—en route to seconds at the buffet table—the big Indiana center gave him a look reserved for visitors from another planet.

Benson just couldn't believe it, and neither could Buckner, who leaned over to Marquette's Lloyd Walton, who was seated at the next table, and asked, "Man, you all go around like that?"

Walton gave Buckner his friendliest riverboat gambler grin. "Yeah," he replied smoothly, with a shrug. "We're free. We can do what we want. All that counts is that we produce on-court. As long as we don't hurt the school's name."

Buckner's jaw fell just about a foot. He nodded and turned away.

Later, when I asked Lloyd what he really thought about Indiana's regimentation, he told me it was something "out of the 1940s."

"But you can't say it's bad," he added. "If you're undefeated, it can't be bad. I'm just glad I had the opportunity to pick. I went through that [jacket and tie] stuff in high school. I knew I had to go somewhere I could grow a mustache."

The next day, Al's premonitions came true, for the second time in three years.

Talk about déjà vu.

The first Marquette basketball story I wrote for the *Journal* had actually been two years before, when Marquette played North Carolina State for the 1974 NCAA championship. Mike Kupper was the beat reporter then, covering the game, and I was watching on TV back in the office so that I could write a short "topper" for his "A matter," filed at halftime so we would have a story for the early edition. I saw, of course, Al commit those two technical fouls that cost him and the Warriors the national title.

Now, on March 20, 1976, in the Mideast Regional final, I saw it all happen again, like a sad sort of Passion Play that had been acted out many times before.

Against No. 1-ranked Indiana, Al's fiery reputation cost him dearly—as I had feared for some time that it would—when he protested two calls by the officials in key situations during the game and was slapped with a technical foul in each instance. The result was a shocking (to me) 65-56 Indiana victory that ended Marquette's season prematurely.

To this day, I still think Marquette could—and should—have won that game. But coupled with the Warriors' inability to take full advantage of 19 Indiana turnovers (including five straight late in the second half), what I had begun to think of as "the Al factor" came back to haunt the volatile showman once again.

Make no mistake. Al did not deserve the first technical, which was called with 12:54 left in the game—after Bo Ellis had been brutally stripped of the ball by Benson and Tom Abernethy and no foul was called. Yes, Al was upset. And yes, he did get up and kick the scorer's table. But he didn't say a word, initially, to referee Jack Ditty, who called the foul. Yes, an angry comment was made, but it came from another person (non-player, non-coach) on the Marquette bench.

The point is that Ditty was looking. Just as the officials had been looking at Xavier, two weeks before. Just as they had been looking at the start of the season, the year before. Al wasn't lying, after the game, when he said that first technical was "not intentional" and insisted, "I didn't say a word"—and though he knew, he never betrayed the person whose angry remark had caught Ditty's waiting ear.

How costly was that first technical? Very. It put Marquette behind the eight ball for the rest of the game. First off, it added an additional point to Indiana's lead *and* gave Indiana possession of the ball, which allowed them to stall away two minutes off the clock. That, in turn, forced Al to pull his team out of the 3-2 zone they favored into a man-to-man, which the more talented Hoosiers used to increase their lead to 55-46 with 3:31 left to play.

The second technical was the killer.

It came about because when no foul was called when Ellis missed a jump shot with 44 seconds left, and Indiana got the ball, Al was up and steaming. Twenty seconds later, Marquette was forced to foul just to try to get possession, and when no one else heeded Al's call, Earl Tatum (the team's leading scorer) deliberately picked up his fifth—which put him out of the game. Little wonder Al went berserk. Try as he might, he had lost control. It was all coming down around him now, and his emotions just spilled forth as he stalked from one end of the scorer's table to the other, arguing until Ditty finally threw a second T.

In a heartbeat, Al's second technical changed things dramatically.

Instead of going to the line with a one-and-one situation and only a slender, three-point lead, Abernethy now had both the one-and-one *and* another shot off the technical *and* guaranteed possession of the ball. After a couple deep breaths at the line, he sank all three shots, and Indiana had the ball with a commanding 61-54 lead.

The game, for all practical purposes, was over.

In my mind today, I can still see Al as he stalked off the court that afternoon. Glaring angrily over his shoulder, knowing exactly what had happened, but more importantly *why* it had happened. His worst fears had come to pass. His stormy reputation as a "ref baiter" had again come round full-circle, and once again, his team had paid the price.

Once he'd reached the Marquette locker room, Al threw the press a bombshell when he announced that he had just coached his last college tournament game. Leaning against the wall, he seemed not just subdued, but genuinely depressed.

"I will not come to another tournament," he told us. "If we are fortunate enough to make it again, I'll let my staff, Hank Raymonds and Rick Majerus, handle the team. I'll stay away. I think, because of my reputation, that I put too much pressure on the officials in the big games. I think it affects them, my team. I don't know, maybe I push too much. But there's something there."

Al shook his head and looked up, and our eyes suddenly met. For a heartbeat, he locked me in, then added a weary admission, "I've created a monster. A monster that's eating me. That I can't control."

When asked, both Ellis and Tatum defended their coach.

"Bo turned around for the jumper and didn't make it," Tatum said. "He was hit, but there was no call. The technicals hurt us, but they were legit."

Ellis agreed. "I thought I got hit. You can't fault Coach for saying what he thought was right. It didn't shake me up, because after you're around Marquette and Al McGuire for a while, you're used to it."

That, of course, was Al's whole point.

"I think because of my reputation, I put too much pressure on a game," he explained to the reporters gathered around him. "I think I'm tightening up the officials too much. Hey, they're good officials, but they're under so much pressure from committees and such, too much emphasis on how well they do. Hey, I've always said, an official never determined a game."

Silently, I felt differently. To my mind, Ditty's unfair call stamped his mark on this particular game, just as Menz's two calls had two weeks before at Xavier. Were either of the technicals intentional? Al was asked again. He shook his head. "[After the fall of 1974], I swore I'd never do that again in my life," he answered.

Al was pressed regarding his statement that—in future years—Hank and Rick would handle the team if Marquette got a bid. Did that mean, he was asked, that he would simply sit on the bench, or in the stands?

"No," Al replied. "I mean stay home."

A year later, of course, it would all seem so ironic. But at that moment, none of us could have predicted what a surprising and marvelous season lay ahead.

"Help one kid at a time. He'll maybe go back and help a few more. In a generation, you'll have something."

Chapter 5
The Game of Life

During his lifetime, Al McGuire coached two very separate—but at the same time, very intertwined—games throughout the years. One, of course, was the very public (and controversial) game of national college basketball, in which he battled not just opposing teams, but often officials, media, and even the alumni and faculty in his role as Marquette's flamboyant head coach. The members of his profession, he liked to say, were truly "the last cowboys"—who were required to step out in the street and put their talent on the line, night after night, with no guarantees or job security. "The ideal coach," he quipped more than once, "has a mother with money and a wife fully employed in a civil service job." Because, Al knew, once the ball went up, there were no excuses, no instant replay.

There was another game Al McGuire knew quite a lot about as well. One he learned growing up in the streets of New York City and behind the bar at McGuire's in Rockaway Beach. Only in this case, he was coaching not just his players, but his associates, friends, and anyone who was smart enough to listen. It was called The Game of Life, and to Al, it was always more important than what happened after the opening tipoff in some noisy, smoke-filled arena.

Why? Because Al was so much more than just a coach. Once you were around him, it didn't take long to realize that he was not only a straight talker, but a real teacher, motivator, and one of the greatest "people persons" God ever put on this planet. That, I always felt, was the secret of Al's success as both a coach and human being—his ability to communicate, to genuinely touch the people he met. Anyone who met him, I found over the years, never forgot him. He was just that down to earth.

The rock of his strength, of course, was his straight-in-the-eye, dead flat-out honesty when it came to dealing with his players. During the turbulent 1960s and early '70s, Al took some heat because he let his players wear their hair long, dress casually on the road, cultivate their own lifestyle, and even argue with him on court during the games. What he was trying to do, of course, was give them the freedom of their own identities and at the same time instill in them the real importance of pride, fulfilling their potential, and playing together well as part of a team.

Do those things, he felt, and you've earned your right and respect as an individual. Ignore them, and you're nothing. "A poor man," I heard him say more than once, "isn't a man without a cent. It's a man without a dream."

Like any parent, he could also go ballistic when he felt one of his players had made a serious mistake off the court, as well as during a game. When Hughie McMahon told Al that he was engaged, Al retorted, "Engaged! Do you know the price of butter?"

At the time, Al was a pioneer in race relations—what he called "that checkerboard thing," the ability of his players, black and white, as well as society in general, to get along. The way to solve the problem, Al felt, was simple. Treat everybody the same, black, white or whatever. And that was what he did.

What Al offered all his players—black and white—was a fair exchange. You help me win games, he told them, and I'll help you get your college degree and the chance for a good career and life for you and your family later on. He did not promise them the pie in the sky of professional contracts and millions in the bank, because he knew quite honestly that it just didn't happen that way all that often. If it did, fine. Then he told his players who had the chance to go hardship—like Jimmy Chones or Maurice Lucas—to walk away, take the money and secure their future. They owed him nothing. What he gave them, especially the poor black players from the big cities, was the chance—through their God-given talents—to overcome their poverty, overcome prejudice, and *earn their chance* in life like everyone else, and by doing so, to be able to hold their heads high and command the respect that they deserved as individuals.

The only reason, I believe, Al was able to do this so successfully was because he was truly color blind. (Can you say that? Can I?) Never, in all our years together, did I ever hear Al McGuire utter a racial epithet, tell an off-color racial story, or see him treat anyone in a racially derogatory manner. As Rick Majerus, his assistant coach, so aptly put it, "Al never saw color; he saw character." It was something, I always felt, that his players saw back in him, as well. Which explains why he was able to go into some of the toughest neighborhoods in New York City, Chicago, and other cities and bring top-notch players to Marquette and the Midwest.

"Both Hank [Raymonds] and Al came to my little ol' ratty house that I lived in with my eight brothers and sisters," said Joe Thomas, who played for Al in the late 1960s. "I was embarrassed about the whole experience, but they came in very humble, just treated me like everyone else. What really sold me was that they talked about academics."

George "Brute Force" Thompson, one of Al's early "thoroughbred" recruits, who went on to become Marquette's all-time scorer, put it best.

"Al was from New York," Thompson said. "Everybody understands that race is an issue. But in New York, people live in closer proximity than a lot of places. Often times, it boiled down to it wasn't how you look. If you're a decent guy, you're a decent guy. If you are a jerk, you are a jerk."

Bo Ellis, a thoroughbred Al dubbed "the Secretariat of college forwards" and who led Marquette to the NCAA title in 1977, agreed. "He treated us all the same, white and black," Bo said of his former coach. "He was just straightforward and down to earth. He understood where we lived, where we were from and our background. It was never about your color or where you were from. It was all about where he wants you to go."

What Al understood was that if he wanted a really successful team, his players had to know each other. To achieve that, he made sure Marquette players roomed with players of a different race. It was mandatory. "Consequently, you'd have a guy like myself from Bed-Stuy rooming with a guy like Jim Langenkamp from Merrill, Wisconsin," Thompson said. "And that had to change you."

Be they black or white, Al was brutally honest with his players. When George Frazier (black) and Allie McGuire (white) were battling for playing time at guard in their sophomore season, Frazier confronted McGuire about the situation. McGuire told him, "George, I love my son. For you to play, you have to be twice as good as him."

In practice, Al wanted his players to play as a wholly integrated team and nothing less. If he thought he saw favoritism on either side of the color line, he applied his sharp-edged tongue towards any offenders, no matter what their skin color. "Hey!" he yelled at Bob Lackey once during practice. "You haven't passed to a white man in four days." And likewise to Gary (Goose) Brell, "Goose, don't you see any brothers open?"

That was Al. He never hesitated to lay it on the line.

"Why not be frank?" he said to a reporter who asked him about his remarks during practice. "We talk about differences, and we don't stop when practice ends. I don't want my guys going back to 1870 as soon as five o'clock comes."

For me, a white man born and raised in an Iowa farm community with mainstream Midwestern values, covering Marquette was an eye-opener to say the least. It made me stop and realize that not every young person in our country had the God-given opportunity to be raised by a good, Christian family, grow up in a safe, friendly, protected neighborhood, partake of three good meals a day, and after high school be financially assured of going off to college and earning a degree. I mean, where I grew up, in the tiny farm town of Williams (population 517), nobody locked their doors at night. So the more I got to know about guys like Bo, and Lloyd, and Butch, the more I realized just how fortunate I was to have been raised the way I was, and where I was. Not that I didn't work hard—but they worked just as hard to get where they were, and without most of the aforementioned advantages.

Bo was *the* player who always fascinated me. He told me more than once that he was certain the world was not far from coming to an end. "Everything just keeps speeding up, going faster and faster," Bo would say, shaking his head slowly, "and someday, I think everything's just going to happen so fast that the world's going to just spin out of control and come apart. Just like that."

A shy, soft-spoken guy, Bo was the product of a Chicago ghetto area, 71st & Normal, on the South Side. Luckily, he grew up loving basketball, and the only thing that kept him away from the basket was gunshots.

"I lived right between two railroad tracks, and there was this big park right next to our house," Bo told me once. "And sometimes, when we were playing on the court, the gangs would start shooting at each other across the tracks. We'd hear the shots and run. Once, I was sitting by this house, just watching, you know, and the bullets started hitting in the house right behind me. First I thought the shots were firecrackers. But then I heard the bullets smacking into the wood above my head. Fa-whooomp! Fa-whooomp! Fa-whooomp! Heck, basketball was all I had. It was either that or the gangs."

Bo admitted to me that he had been a member of a gang. "They were my friends, you know," he explained, almost sheepishly. "The African Sniper Gangsters." He paused and smiled. "But when the fighting started, I was gone." I asked Bo what he did when he wasn't playing basketball. The shy grin reappeared. "There wasn't much else to do, except steal," he replied. "You didn't just walk around the neighborhood, you know. 'Cause you might get jumped or killed yourself, if you did."

I remember asking him once, too, if he was a Black Muslim. Bo just laughed. "No, no, man, I ain't got nothing to do with all that. I'm no Muslim. I'm just Bo Ellis, out there trying to make it."

Trying to make it. That, Al realized, was what most of his players were attempting to do. Basketball was their way out. A chance, if they succeeded, to significantly better not only themselves, but their families as well. I'll never forget Lloyd Walton's answer, when I once asked him why he wanted so badly to succeed in the world of basketball. "The thing I want in life is to be able to support my mother and grandmother," Lloyd said fiercely. "I want them to have it all. Because when I was growing up, I was never in need of anything. If one didn't have it, the other did. I want to do things for them."

Al, thank God, understood and did his best to give his players that chance.

Rick Majerus, who did a fare amount of the scouting for Al during the late 1960s and early '70s, always came back with stories that raised my eyebrows—stories about what that other side of life was like, the one we, who were so lucky, did not often see.

"It was just an experience to go to some of those places I'd go," Rick said. "Like Harlem, for instance. Down there, a white guy in a business suit and tie is one of two things—a basketball scout or a cop. Otherwise, he'd never go down there. So when I'm walking down the street, these kids are yelling at me, 'You a scout or a cop?'

"The gyms are something else. The lights are about as good as what's in the Milwaukee sewer system. Armed police stand around the courts. They play in the afternoons a lot, in these old buildings that are dark on one end and bright sunlight on the other, where the sun streams through big open windows. It's so bright you need sunglasses to see.

"It's just a segment of society not everybody gets to see. The crowds are small, but they scream like banshees. When you visit the schools, there are police in the corridors, and fights are breaking out all the time. It's a little bit scary. And there's no clocks or timers. Score is kept on paper. At one game, they took five points away from one team after the game was over because somebody hadn't added right."

Al understood all that. He knew that except for their marvelous on-court talent, those kids had little or nothing going for them at that point in their lives. His job, he knew, was to get the most out of each player, which in return would do *the most* for them career-wise and for the Marquette team as a whole. To do that, he knew he not only had to assess a player's on-court strengths and weaknesses, but be aware of his personal insecurities and needs as well. Like it or not, he *was* the "Father Figure de'jour" at that time in their lives. And to create a winning "family" each year, he had to not only apply discipline, but also be receptive to his children's individual needs.

"Dealing with problems, with differences—that's what coaching is," Al always said. "Running patterns is not coaching."

"It was really a good way to end up. But I have no idea why it happened. It certainly wasn't preconceived... but it might as well have been preordained."

Chapter 6
Charmed

Twenty-six years after it happened, the same word comes back to me today when I think about Al McGuire and his incredible final season of coaching basketball at Marquette University. A word, fittingly, that evokes all that's grand about "the luck of the Irish" and the storied centuries of leprechauns and shamrocks that go with it.

Charmed.

There's just no other word that says it better. No better way to try to put into perspective why all the cards finally fell into place on Al's last ride on the merry-go-round. I mean, how else can you explain a coach winning the NCAA national championship three months *after* he has announced his retirement? How else can you explain how, after being counted out by the pollsters and almost not receiving an NCAA tournament bid at all, Al and his gutsy players were able to bounce back in fairy-tale fashion and make their magical "Run for the Roses" to the Final Four at the Omni in Atlanta, Georgia? And once there, they survived two "white-knucklers" to grab the NCAA's brass ring—and bring it back to their loyal, long-suffering fans in Milwaukee.

And for you of little faith—who don't drink green beer or celebrate *Erin* each year on March 17—I'll say just one thing: Those were just the highlights. From start to finish, when it mattered, Al was charmed that final season. Charmed beyond belief. How he managed to capture as many of the "little people" as he did over the years and hold them in reserve for this critical pass is anybody's guess. All I know is, every time he needed one, he had a "little guy" on his sleeve that season to grant him one more wish and bring him a step closer to the pot of gold he'd sought for so long.

And which, of course, was finally his.

Where do we start? Why, at the beginning, of course. As the Irish would say, is there any better way?

Al's troops reeled off four straight victories to start the 1976-77 season, but he got his first good news a month before the season even started, when he learned that his senior forward (and food freak) Bo Ellis—whom he had dubbed "the Secretariat of college forwards" and who was this year's designated star—was actually eating meat again.

Ellis, who had performed superbly as a freshman and sophomore, had fallen off markedly as a junior, when he started substituting things like sunflower seeds for U.S. No. 1 sirloin. What that meant was that his six-foot, nine-inch frame shrank to a wafer-thin 190 pounds, and he showed a marked fading in the second of half of games, so much so that, along with his meat intake, his points, rebound production, and his shooting percentage had all fallen off as well. Little wonder that by the holidays that previous year, Al was already on his case.

"Jesus, Bo!" he stormed, as the team was getting dressed in the locker room, prior to a pre-holidays game. "Will you eat some meat for a change? Christ, look at you! You're nothing but skin and bones. No wonder you got no stamina for the second half! How do you expect to have any lead in your pencil if you eat nothing but seeds?"

Al's ravings had done no good at the time. But for some reason, Ellis suddenly was back on the meat wagon his senior year. For Al, that had to make it a whole lot easier to say, "As Bo goes, we go!" when he talked about the year's designated star and the upcoming season. What I wanted to know was: Why had Bo quit eating meat in the first place? And why had he now returned to the red meat he had previously boycotted?

I never got a convincing answer. Because when asked, Bo addressed only the first half of my question and not the second. "I quit because of the food in the dorms," he told me at the time. "I ate the meat there and got sick a couple of times. That's why I quit." So what had changed this year? Bo was elusive. "I try to eat what's being served once or twice a week," he demurred. "Or else I go out and get a good meal."

Why couldn't Bo have done that before? My guess is that Al finally solved the problem, at some point, by making sure (through a deal with some local restaurant owner?) that Bo could get a decent weekly intake of whatever type beef he chose—hamburger, ground round, or New York strip—and thus build up his strength and stamina again. I can't prove it, but I can't think of any other answer, either. The point is, no matter how it was accomplished, Al had to be happy knowing his "Secretariat" had all the oats he needed.

Al had two major decisions to make before his team opened the season at the Arena against tiny St. Leo's of Florida—the designated "opening cupcake" that year. With Walton and Tatum gone, he had two starting spots to fill, and as everyone knew, once Al named his starting lineup, he never changed (barring illness or injury) for the rest of the season. At guard, he had Gary Rosenberger and Jim Boylan, both juniors, battling for Walton's old spot, and Bernard Toone and Bill Neary for Tatum's vacated forward position.

Privately, I had no doubt that Boylan and Neary were going to get the nod. True, there was no doubt that Rosenberger and Toone were the better shooters. But Al already had three cannons on the team—Bo, Butch Lee and center Jerome Whitehead—and only one basketball between them. What he was looking for were two "complementary" players to get the ball to that trio, and both Boylan (who was a great ball handler, with the cool saavy of a riverboat gambler) and Neary (a good passer, consummate hatchet man, and totally unafraid), filled those roles to a T. And that still left him with Rosenberger and Toone for additional offense, if it was needed in the second half.

The day before Thanksgiving, Al announced that Boylan would be his other starting guard, and six days later, two days before the season opener against St. Leo's, he gave Neary the starting nod at forward as well. What I remember most was how, on the day he announced both decisions, he softened things in his usual humorous way by insisting he had other, equally important things on his mind.

On the 23rd, when he officially named Boylan, Al said what he was pondering most was which restaurant his mother, Winifred, would enjoy most when he visited her in the Big Apple on Thanksgiving weekend. "I plan to take a day or two off, Monday or Tuesday, [and] fake a recruiting trip to visit my mother in New York," Al quipped. "I think there's a great player two houses down from where she lives. Then I'll take her out for dinner and offer her a scholarship. She's pretty good with a knife and fork."

On the 29th, after confirming that Neary was his choice, Al poohpoohed the idea that starting really meant all that much, anyhow, and then said he had two bigger problems to confront. "The biggest thing about starting is the National Anthem," he said. "And I'm going to change that a few times this year to *America the Beautiful*. We'll try both of 'em and see which the fans prefer. But that's my biggest decision, more than the starting team.

"And, of course, I don't know whether to change the names on the cheerleaders' uniforms to numbers. That's a big topic of conversation right now. If we give 'em names, we have to give 'em the jersey when they retire. Or do we just button the name tag on?"

Al also admitted that the *last* thing he had on his mind was worrying about St. Leo's (which had an 8-18 record the year before) in the season opener. "If I have to go to the sweat box at the opener, I'd better take my sabbatical soon," he remarked. "But remember, the score is still nothing-nothing at the start. It's easy to give something away when you don't have it.

"Like the story with the dog. The guy says, 'Hey, come on in, this dog won't bite.' Well, he knows it, and I know it, but does the dog know it?

"Or like the lady who wanted to buy some pork chops. She went into one store and asked the guy, 'How much are your pork chops?' He says, '60 cents a pound.' She says, 'I'll take three pounds.' He says, 'Sorry, I don't have any.'

"So she goes across the street to another store and says, 'I'd like three pounds of pork chops. How much are they?' The guy says, '80 cents a pound.' '80 cents!' she says. 'They were only 60 cents across the street.'

"So the guy asks, 'Why didn't you buy them?' And the lady says, 'He didn't have any.' And so the guy says, 'Well, hell, lady. If I didn't have any, I'd sell 'em for 40 cents a pound.'"

Al was right. He didn't have to worry. Marquette trounced St. Leo's, 80-39. Which led me to ask Al afterwards if he really was able to learn anything from a game like that. "I found out my guards are out of shape," he replied. "They're hitting the bars too much. Not Rosey [Rosenberger]; he was sick. But Boylan looked out of condition. The first sign is when the guy starts putting his hands on his hips. The second is when he turns blue."

But was it really worth anything, playing a game like this? I pressed.

Al gave me an impatient, sideways look, like I was asking a stupid question.

"Sure," he insisted. "It gets you off the snide. You know, like when you're playing poker and you can't win a hand. Can't get off the snide. It becomes something that eats at you, can cause dissension. But now we've won one, and we can get on with the season.

"Hey, this is not uncommon, playing a bunny right off. It's just that other coaches won't admit it."

Three victories and 16 days later, on December 17, 1976, Al dropped a bombshell that changed forever the fabric of his professional life and which, for different reasons, would alter our personal relationship soon after that as well. In a hastily called press conference in a barren, poorly lit little anteroom at the aging Wisconsin Club, Al stepped up before the klieg lights and announced his resignation as Marquette University's athletic director and basketball coach, effective at the end of the season.

Dressed in a stylish dark three-piece suit, Al told us he was quitting the world of college basketball to become vice chairman of the board of Medalist Industries, the Milwaukee-based sports equipment firm he had been associated with since 1965. As he spoke, I could see that Al was clearly uncomfortable. The few stories he told seemed forced, and he was pretty much somber and stoic throughout the 20-minute ordeal.

"This is no General MacArthur speech, no 'Old soldiers never die' routine," Al began. "I have a tremendous season ahead of me. This is not a farewell, no last hurrah thing. But there's always a time in everyone's life. And it's my time to move on to the next strata. I guess I'm at the crest of a wave. And now I want to build another crest with Medalist."

Sitting there, scribbling down Al's words, I felt numb. For an instant, my mind flashed back eight years, to the spring of 1968, when—as a sportswriter for the *Miami Herald*—I had covered Mickey Mantle's retirement from baseball at the Yankee Clipper Hotel in Fort Lauderdale. For only the second time in my sports writing career, I felt a tremendous void and a true sadness. Another era in sports history was clearly ending.

Al had almost left Marquette once before, in the spring of 1968, when he was being wooed by the Milwaukee Bucks of the NBA, but the school refused to let him out of his contract. This time, even though Al had one year left on his current contract, that was not the case. "I met with Father Raynor [president of Marquette] last night, and he gave me his blessing," Al explained. "In my letter to Father Raynor, I said that all carnivals and merry-go-rounds come to a stop sometime. That this was the time for me to go my own way."

The most puzzling aspect of Al's announcement was: Why now? Why not wait until the end of the season? I got no straight answers to that one that afternoon. First, Norm Fischer, Medalist's president, insisted the announcement had to be made immediately for what he called "business reasons."

"Medalist is a publicly owned company," Fisher said, "so we have to announce publicly any decision as important as this immediately, because of its effects upon the company. It would have been better if we could have forestalled it. But we also felt it would be better for the Marquette basketball program if we made the announcement now, effective next May, so there could be an orderly transition."

Orderly transition? I thought. Who is this guy kidding? Doesn't he think this will affect the players? Or the outcome of the season? Al had always told me that each season was like a life—that it was born, it lived, and it died. If so, then this life, I felt, had suddenly and prematurely been dealt a serious blow, if not cut short altogether. And what about Hank Raymonds, the obvious heir apparent? Was he now to be left hanging as the season wore on, with no guarantees? Nothing, I felt, could have been more unfair for all of those concerned.

When Fischer finished speaking, Al said that the idea of quitting had "been in my mind for a number of years. But I had been concentrating on it for the last eight or nine months." But why now? He was asked. Why not next month, or next year? Al, to my surprise, started laughing.

"I was gonna say Bernard Toone," he replied, referring to his ongoing struggles with his sophomore forward. "The guy's unbelievable. No, I truly love Bernard Toone. Anyone I whip verbally or physically, I love to be around. No, it's a natural thing, a natural flow. I believe that a man was meant for more than one career.

"I may miss the ego end. It's nice to have smoke rings blown at you, I don't know what it is not to be a celebrity. A lot of people think I need the ego end, the applause…and maybe they're right. I'm not sure."

As expected, Al ended the press conference with a joke, when asked what the duties of a vice chairmen were. "The vice chairman, I believe," he quipped, "puts the gas in the chairman's car."

Four days later, watching practice with Al at the Arena, I brought up the subject again—and this time got yet another insight as to why, in the prime of his career, Al had traded in his colorful ringmaster's coat for a gray flannel suit. We were sitting in the 25th row, looking down on the players below, when I reminded him that he had said a lot of things at the press conference and yet really said nothing. The real question remained unanswered. Why now, all of a sudden? And in the middle of a season?

Al paused, looked thoughtfully out across the Arena, and then told me it was because he had suddenly realized one day that he wasn't being true to himself. That his priorities had changed. Somewhere along the line, he said, he found that producing for the bottom line for Medalist gave him as much of a thrill as beating, say, Notre Dame at South Bend. And so, psychologically, he put basketball on the back burner, and as long as the Warriors kept winning, he found it easy to rationalize that he was still giving 100 percent.

Until that day, not too long ago, he said, when he found he couldn't fool himself any longer. "I've always said, Rog, there's no way a man can serve two heads," Al told me. "I just felt that I had been cheating on the kids and on basketball for too long."

Al continued, choosing his words carefully, staring fixedly at his white sneakers on the chair back before him as he spoke.

"It's like the guy who takes his first dime out of the till and says, 'I'll give it back'…and a year later he's taking a dollar a day out and still hasn't paid it back," he explained. "Well, about seven years ago, I starting cheating on the kids." Al looked up and shrugged, with a sheepish sort of smile on his face. "And so now I'm a $10 a day guy."

That same day, Hank gave me another insight when I asked him what his take was on the whole situation after practice. Al, he felt, had suddenly realized that because society was changing, his time was past. "I think Al realized it was the end of the era for the type of player he was able to coach," Hank said. "You have to realize, Al was *the* coach for his era [the late 1960s and early '70s]. In a time of unrest, campus revolt, a time when all sorts of authority was ridiculed, he was someone of the establishment who could relate to that type of youngster. The poor blacks, the ghetto kids. Now we're getting into a more stabilized society. More like the 1950s. And blacks have made their mark now. Al's type of player is on the way out."

True, perhaps. And yet, as I drove home that day, I thought of another reason why Al suddenly made the decision he did—perhaps the most intriguing possibility of all. What kept coming back to me were the clowns—those sad, vacant-eyed clowns I saw in his office that day—and how they reflected Al's own doubts and insecurities as to where he really fit into the grand scheme of things. At some point, he must have felt that no matter how great his success at Marquette, he would still be considered the eccentric, the showman, and at times, the clown. What Medalist offered was something Marquette could not—respectability. Bottom-line success at Medalist, surely, would finally prove he was more than a mere attraction—a court jester or a clown—because gray flannel must always be taken more seriously than checkered satin.

Was that the nub of it all? For some intuitive reason, I felt it was. And so I broached the subject with Al the very next day.

He frowned at my suggestions.

"I don't know. I'm deep, but I don't know if I'm that deep..." he said, pausing. "There's one misunderstanding here. You all think that I'm going to change and become a long mahogany table or something. But the formula I used as a lifeguard, a bartender, a wild lather...it'll be the same on top-floor business." He grinned. "The only difference is that now I'll have a key to the washroom." Once again, he had completed the tangent.

"Now, obviously, I'm not going to wear sneakers to the annual stockholders' meetings. But I won't lose that earthiness and open face that got me here in the first place. It's like the girl who marries the guy who drinks and thinks she'll change him. And so he becomes a member of AA and she ends up an alcoholic."

My thought, right then, was that I was right on target on this whole thing and that Al was protesting a bit too much. But before I could ask him that, the philosopher vanished and the showman reappeared.

"Hey, this is good stuff, isn't it?" Al asked, beaming.

Yeah, pretty good, I admitted.

"What do you mean, 'pretty good?'" Al retorted. "This is a $10,000 interview you're getting here."

I couldn't help but laugh. He was one of a kind, this poet, con man, actor. My only disturbing thought was: How do I really know when he's acting?

What was my final read upon all this?

My mind kept going back to what Al had said at the press conference: "I guess I'm at the crest of a wave. And now I want to build another crest with Medalist." There, I felt certain, was the key. Al had come close to winning the NCAA championship twice in the last three years, but each time his hopes (and those of his players) had been agonizingly crushed by the "monster" he had created—his reputation as a ref baiter that now was causing him to draw costly (albeit sometimes unfair) technical fouls at the very worst of times in the very biggest of games. When Marquette was playing a cupcake, it didn't matter. Sheer talent on the floor prevailed. But in the NCAA tournament, where almost every game was a mano a mano with another team that sported equal (or perhaps better) credentials, Al had seen repeatedly that just one premeditated call by a "programmed" official in a close game could irretrievably tip the scales the other way.

I really think Al felt the Indiana debacle the year before had destroyed his last real chance at an NCAA championship. And I think that's why he announced his retirement decision when he did: to give his last team the best shot it could have for a successful season. If the NCAA had sent him a message over the last three years, he was now sending the people "in smoke-filled rooms" one back: "Hey, guys! Enough, okay? I'm on my way out here. Peace. Let's just play out the string. But let's do it fairly. Don't take it out on the kids."

To this day, I truly believe Al could have made his retirement announcement at any time he chose. It had nothing to do with "business" or "legal" reasons. The timing was solely his to decide. The truth was, the job description for Al's position hadn't even been drawn up when he went before the lights that December afternoon. Hence his humorous line, when asked about his duties, that he was responsible for "filling the chairman's car with gas." As was often the case, humor was Al's best camouflage. Yes, he had decided he was ready for a career change. But genius that he was, he had figured out a ploy he hoped would help him control the tempo one final time. The showman in Al would not allow him to walk off-stage before he had given himself—and his players—the best chance he/they could have to go out a winner. And that meant letting the NCAA know ASAP that the "monster" was soon to be off their backs—that after this one last fling, he was stepping aside.

As I had feared might happen, Al's retirement announcement, unfortunately, had an immediate negative effect upon the players—although he wouldn't admit it. The No. 2-ranked Warriors were upset twice in the next four days in their friendly home-court surroundings at the Arena—by Louisville, 78-75, in overtime on national television the day after Al's press conference at the Wisconsin Club, and then, three days later, by Minnesota of the Big Ten, 66-59.

After both games, Al insisted his retirement announcement had not had any impact upon the players or the outcome. After the loss to Louisville, however, he broke his long-standing habit of an open locker room and refused to let the press talk to the players. That alone told me Al knew his announcement had caused some damage. How serious? That was more difficult to assess. Yes, the Warriors had not played well, suffering their first loss in 23 games at home. But Louisville was always a tough opponent, and the defeat was by just three points, in overtime.

Three nights later, however, there was no masking anything. From the start, it was obvious that something was very, very wrong. Marquette shot just 16 percent (making only six of 37 shots) the first half. At one point, they went almost 11 minutes without scoring, missing 21 straight shots. So bad was their performance that, for the first time, I heard the home crowd boo them as they walked into the locker room at the half.

Al let them have it during intermission, telling them their pride was at stake, that they had to regroup and go out and play again. The players responded, charging back to outscore Minnesota, 41-29 in the second half, but the 19-point lead they had given the Gophers at half-time was just too much to overcome.

Afterward, the obvious question was asked again. And again, Al insisted his retirement had nothing to do with his team's poor play. This time, however, the locker room was again open, and Butch Lee, when asked, admitted he wasn't so sure.

"The players have talked about it," Butch said. "Nobody is going to come out and say it, nobody is going to say whether it is or it isn't. But something is wrong."

Al's sudden announcement, I felt, was nothing short of a cultural shock for his players. Most of them were at Marquette for one reason— they wanted to play basketball for Al McGuire. He was the type of coach they could identify with, and the team's style (right down to how they dressed on the road) was a direct reflection of Al's lifestyle and beliefs. To them, not just basketball, but life itself, was just as Al had described it— a cool, hip, flashy trip uptown. Seashells and balloons, ribbons and flowers. And the brass ring waiting at the end.

Little wonder then, when the "original flower child" turned corporate and bought a gray flannel suit, it was a psychological shellburst for his young troops. For their generation, it was something akin to Timothy Leary suddenly running for Congress, or Abbie Hoffman taking up teaching high school civics. Initially, it seemed to them, the guy they believed in had moved to the other side of the street. Al had thrown their beliefs akimbo, and subconsciously they were scrambling. And so, in the midst of a basketball season, they were suddenly forced to think about other things. The point being, it *was* a distraction, and something (as Butch had indicated) that each player was going to have to deal with in his own way.

Al was a great motivator, I knew. If anyone could heal the hurt his move to Corporate America had caused his team, it was he. But privately, I also wondered, how long would it take for those same players to recover? By the time they did, would there be anything left of the season worth saving?

Looking back now, I realize I shouldn't have worried.

The leprechauns, as I said, were on the job. Al was charmed. Somehow, in the week prior to the Milwaukee Christmas Classic, he was able to mend the fences and connect with his players once again—and they responded by reeling off 10 straight victories in the next six weeks, with winning margins of 10 points or more in all but three. To this day, I don't know how he did it, but it was a remarkable turnaround—the first of two in that incredible championship season.

During that 10-game run, Al had to deal with just two problems. One was his love-hate (and worsening) relationship with Bernard Toone, the Warriors' talented 6'9" sophomore from Yonkers, New York. The other was with me.

The Bernard problem, of course, was much more serious in the whole scheme of things. Because, as the weeks and months went along, you could see it develop almost like a cancer, growing to the point that— sooner or later—it *had* to be cured if the team was to make any kind of a run at season's end.

The problem was, Bernard was a shooter—a fantastic shooter, to be honest. But all he wanted to do was shoot. Day in and day out, he showed little interest in playing good defense. Bernard could consistently thread the needle from 20 feet, but he also was a nice, good-looking kid who had little desire to get in underneath, fight for rebounds, or play tough D. In short, he wasn't a scrapper. Little wonder that Al bristled. Strong defense, after all, was his forte. He already had three older "shooters" in the lineup in Bo, Butch, and Jerome. Al's star system had worked for years, and he was not about to compromise it for Bernard. His day, Al felt, would come. But not this year, not as a sophomore. Bo had earned the spotlight this year, as the "Secretariat of college forwards." "Name That Toone" time could wait.

Before the season started, Al was on Bernard's case, basically because he didn't feel Bernard took the game seriously enough and for his inability to play heads-up defensive basketball. "His attention span is, umm, about seven seconds," Al told me once at practice. "Now with the help of God, we're going to expand it. And hey, it's better than last year. Last year, it was three and a half seconds."

When it started to look like the rough-and-tumble Neary (whom nobody wanted to play against in practice), rather than the sharpshooting Toone, was going to get Earl Tatum's vacated starter's spot, I asked Al what Bernard would have to do to retake the favorite's role.

Al minced no words. "Be more aware," he said. "Play defense. Rebound. But I don't think it'll happen because at this point in time, it's not in Bernard's world...Bernard has to realize that being a beautiful person isn't enough. We're in a profession where you have to get your hair messed, be unruly, once in a while." Al threw up his hands and shrugged with frustration. "I've tried everything. Bernard has to be more streetish. But he won't. He just likes to play.

"Like the other day, he drops the ball, and I yelled at him, 'Bernard! For shoot's sake! You dropped the ball. What's the matter with you?' And he said, 'But Coach, I didn't drop it on purpose.' Hey, don't get me wrong. Bernard is a fantastic player. There's no doubt he's a star. He has a magnificent body. The one or two times he jumps in a game, it's frightening. There's no doubt he can get you 20 points a game, but will it cost you 24 to get it?"

As the weeks wore on, Bernard became more resentful. His goal, of course, was to make the pros someday, and like a lot of youngsters, he was in a hurry. What he could do well was shoot. So what he wanted *now* was more playing time and more shots. What he couldn't understand was that it just wasn't going to happen under Al, who was looking for Bernard to pay his dues before he was allowed to step into the spotlight.

"We need a complementary-type player," Al said, when I asked him about the Neary-Toone rivalry. "By the time you get past Bo, Butch and Jerome, it means that the other two starters have to be complementary shooters. Not looking for 16-18 points out there, just a garbage shot here or there."

What Bernard never could understand was that Neary—the tough, in-your-face brawler—was so much like Al 20 years before. He knew his role and played it to the hilt. "I do what I'm supposed to do," he told me once. "I play defense, rebound. You're not going to get anything spectacular out of me. I just play defense."

I would disagree. There were quite a few games, and not just that season, that Al did get spectacular play out of Neary—even though it didn't show up as points in the box score afterwards. Again and again, I saw him tear into the opponent's leading scorer (many times at a decided weight or height disadvantage), and by sheer force of will, the ability to take a hit and give one back, make the guy a non-factor for six or seven minutes at a time. Or, best-case scenario, he would get the guy so angry at his bump-and-shove, elbowing presence that the guy lost his cool and was on the bench in foul trouble early on.

Little wonder Al defended the mustachioed senior forward to the limit. "Bill Neary has ability," Al would say. "He knows the system, and he never contradicts me. And it's not easy to take people writing that Bernard Toone is two times better than you are. But I'm happy for Bill. It's nice to see someone who has the same type of ability I did go out and make it."

By the time the Christmas Classic came around, Bernard had become Al's public whipping boy. He was losing patience with his talented but lackadaisical 6'9" sophomore, and his remarks became more pointed. At the Classic press party, Al got his monologue going by admitting he was worried about his team's back-to-back losses at home to Louisville and Minnesota. "I'm not saying I'm desperate," he told the crowd, "but I even went so far as to have Bernard Toone to dinner at my house the other night. I don't know if it'll help or not." The problem, Al reiterated again, was Bernard's refusal to put as much effort into his defense as he did into his shooting. What he needed were solid, all-round ballplayers, and Bernard—for whatever reasons—just wasn't interested in being one.

"Hey, Bernard is an unbelievable guy," Al lamented. "But he doesn't take basketball serious. He never plays basketball in the off season. Never. The other guys, they want to scrimmage with the pros in the summer, but Bernard, he's always got hemorrhoids or migraine headaches or something."

Al's remarks drew laughter, as expected. But behind the laughs, a serious problem remained. By his repeated public chastising of Bernard, Al was—whether he knew it or not—beginning to publicly paint Bernard as the main cause of Marquette's problems. And that was just not the case. Certainly, Bernard was the main cause of Al's frustrations, but the timing of Al's resignation had more to do with the losses to Louisville and Minnesota than anything Bernard did or didn't do.

Unfortunately, things were about to get ugly.

In the first game of the Classic, against Clemson, Al's mental teapot finally boiled over, when he yanked Toone from the game late in the first half after Bernard let a Clemson player get around him to score. In previous games, Bernard had endured Al's verbal wrath all the way to the bench, and in one instance, it left him so upset that he kicked the back of his chair before he sat down. But this time, Al kept after him once he had taken his seat, bending down and screaming at him as he sat with his head in his hands.

After a minute or so, Toone could take no more. Looking up, he pleaded, "Go away! Get away from me. Just leave me alone." When Al did go away, Bernard began to cry.

This time, Al's treatment of Toone had gone too far. During intermission, as I typed my A matter for the early edition, I could actually hear people talking angrily about it behind me. Most, I knew, were season ticket holders, who were used to Al's outbursts and harangues. This time, however, it was clear they were upset. When Bernard finally returned to the game in the second half, the home crowd stood and gave him a standing ovation, and later on, when he sank two baskets, he got a huge cheer each time.

After the game, Al downplayed his tirade, saying "I yelled at him, and he yelled back. I wouldn't call it a Sister Mary Applesauce thing. It was just an exchange."

Incredibly, Bernard refused to really criticize Al, although it was clear that he was anything but happy. "I thought it was unnecessary," he told reporters. "I guess he's doing it for a reason, but not starting has had an effect on me. I felt I deserved the spot on past performance. He thought differently, and he knows what he's doing.

"Ulice Payne said to me at halftime, 'You're playing for yourself, so you can't be down on yourself all the time.' Then, when the crowd went with me like that, I felt like everything would be all right."

In the days following, many people wrote angry letters about Al's actions, not only to the Marquette athletic office, but to the sports department at the *Milwaukee Journal*. Example: In an "Open Letter to Al McGuire" sent to Bill Dwyre, the sports editor, Thomas F. Schmit of Brown Deer (a Milwaukee suburb) wrote:

> Your conduct at the Classic Monday night toward Bernard Toone was disgraceful. Observing an illustrious coach indulge in such immature antics saddened all of us who have so highly respected you. Surely your actions were detrimental to Bernard's athletic career; but more important, to his sense of worth and personal well-being. A public apology is called for.

On January 10, Al replied.

Dear Tom,

Thanks for your letter of December 28. I genuinely appreciate your including your name and address so that I could reply.

Bernard Toone is an outstanding young man with an unlimited amount of God-given athletic talent. I would not be doing my profession justice if I allowed him to throw this out the window because of his age. He's being treated exactly the same as 30 other great players in the last 24 years who don't realize that the merry-go-round stops and that the Bowery is full of Einsteins.

God-given ability, environment, heredity—does not mean automatic success. It's usually misery and despair.

Hope you have a pleasant '77.

Sincerely,

Al McGuire
Director of Athletics
Head Basketball Coach

How did I feel about Al's tirade at Bernard? Personally, I thought he went overboard, although I know he did it out of sheer frustration. During the previous year, I knew he had tried to motivate the kid in many ways, but it was like the irresistible object meeting the immovable force. "Christ, Rog!" Al blurted out to me one day. "You know what's going on here? Four years from now this kid will have a pro contract, and I'll be in an insane asylum."

That was the problem. No matter how much Al alternately cajoled or screamed, Bernard was going to be Bernard. And Al was most certainly going to be Al. That's where I felt Bernard was stupid. Did he really think Al was going to change for him? Change for him a winning system that had been successful for over a decade? If I had been Bernard, I'd have taken a few elbows, even a bloody nose, and really tried to play better defense. That done, I think Bernard would have seen his playing time increase and his relationship with Al improve. Unfortunately, it never happened.

Earlier, I mentioned how I felt early on that the "Bernard problem" was a cancer that—unless checked—could cause even worse problems down the road. Well, it did. On January 18, during that 10-game winning streak, Marquette traveled to Iowa and just was able to edge Drake University, 62-60. The outcome was a controversial one for a number of reasons, but the thing that bothered me was an argument that ensued during a timeout, when Al proceeded to chew out Jimmy Boylan, Jerome Whitehead, Bernard and Bo, and Bo, totally out of character, jumped right back at Al to take the side of his teammates.

It was clear that since Al's outburst at the Classic, the "cancer" had been spreading—a growing resentment among the players that he was being too rough on not just Bernard, but all of the rest of them as well. Al knew he had to do something, and so, two days later, he sat his troops down to see "the film."

Profile of a Coach was a 20-minute documentary that had been shot of McGuire during the Warriors' 1971-72 season, when his team included Jimmy Chones, Bob Lackey, and his son, Allie McGuire, among others. And while it certainly was no *Gone With the Wind*, it was, in its own way, a classic.

The film showed Al at perhaps the wildest stage of his career—at various games and practices—screaming at players and officials, kicking chairs, knocking over cups of Coke. Glaring as only he could do. Except for a few bleeps here and there (which didn't matter because you could read his lips easily), it was G-rated material, but the point Al wanted to make was clear: You guys got it easy, compared to the way it used to be.

"I just want them to see that they're not being treated any different than the top money makers," Al told me, when I asked about the showing. "That the stripes are still the same. And that they will be until March." He laughed, then added, "The only thing is, my vocabulary is a little better now."

Thanks to Kevin Byrne, of course, I had been given a private showing of the film, so I knew what it included. And believe me, I wish I had a VHS tape of it today, just so I could listen once again to Al, the wild man, in his prime.

The highlights included:

Halftime of the DePaul game, Al screaming at guard Marcus Washington: "What the hell's going on? Nobody pays any [bleeping] attention! For Christ's sake, Marcus. I put you on the bench and you're making goo-goo eyes at some girl in the first row!"

Second half, DePaul game, when Lackey took one shot too many, and Al was up and screaming, "What the hell are you looking for, Lackey, a contract?"

DePaul cuts Marquette's lead from 17 points to five, Al calls time out and is on Lackey again. "Oh, stop the [bleep-bleep], Bob. I'm tired of it. You want go back and live in the jungle, then live in the jungle!"

Stalling with a slender lead, Kurt Spychalla not once, but twice goes for the layup. Makes one, misses one. At the horn, Al grabs him, shakes him, and yells at him: "Kurt! What'd I tell you? Don't take the layup! And you take the layup!"

Next the scene switched to practice, where Al screams over and over for someone to take a long jump shot, and nobody does. He runs out onto the floor, stops, jumps up and down in one spot. "I want the jump shot! I want the jump shot from here! Right from here! Hey, can we be this bad? You're awful! You're numb to abuse. We can't abuse you! Only one guy is jumping; that's Larry McNeill. His wife isn't telling him yet that he's a star and doesn't have to, or he won't be either."

And of course, there was a scene with an official, at the Loyola game, where Al and a ref are eyeball to eyeball. "Now, ref," Al snarls, "I don't want no trouble. But do me one favor. Just stop and think what you're doing. Okay?"

Naturally, I wanted to know what the players felt after they saw the movie. Most seemed to think that, compared to back then, they had it a lot better off today. "I can't imagine what it must have been like," Bo told me. He grinned, then added, "I don't know if I'd have wanted to play for him back then. I don't know if I could have stood it."

The one exception was Bernard. "It looks like it was the same then as it is now," he said simply, shrugging his shoulders. "Same old stuff."

Toone's remarks bothered me. It was clear, from the look in his steely hazel eyes, that the chasm between him and Al was still there—and still wide as a canyon. Theirs was a relationship, I felt, that would never be close. Why? Because while Al understood Bernard perfectly, Bernard never understood Al. Al's philosophy was simple. It didn't matter if Marquette was winning by 10 or losing by two, the rules still applied—you played Al's game and nothing else. No freelancing, no "Hail Mary" shots. And always, aggressive, in-your-face defense. Until the final horn, he expected one thing: that you run the "patterns" so you could govern the tempo of the game. Anything else was heresy.

Al had said publicly many times: "I will never accept anything in victory that I won't accept in defeat." If Bernard had just taken time to understand that one statement, I think their relationship might have improved. But as I said before, Bernard was Bernard and Al was Al. Given that, I felt certain more trouble lay ahead.

Looking back, I'd like to think that my problem with Al, compared to his frustrations with Bernard that January of 1977, was pretty miniscule. But given his reaction to it at the time (and what transpired over the following 23 years), I guess it must have been more important to him than I thought. One thing I do know—it commanded his immediate attention...and action.

The problem that arose between us was a book. To be more specific, a book on Al. In late November and early December, I had started researching it, gathering as much immediate background as some initial interviews and the *Journal* library clip files could supply. Al, I felt, was not just a winning coach, but a unique human being, with a fascinating philosophy on life that superseded the basketball court, and for all its struggle, angst and humor, needed to be told.

Besides, I was reporter, remember, and there was nothing I loved better than a good story. And Al's, I knew, was a *great* story. An *extraordinary* story. So, as fall gave way to winter, the first snows fell and Lake Michigan began to freeze, I was busy calling people like Frank McGuire, Al's brother Johnny, his former players and associates, compiling their best Al McGuire stories and piecing together the colorful fabric of this remarkable man's life, trying to show not just who he was, but why he was who he was, as well. When Al announced his "retirement" on December 17, I speeded up the process, devoting every minute of my free time to calling, interviewing and gathering, feeling the time was ripe (which to this day I felt it was) for what I had tentatively titled *Seashells and Balloons: The Best of Al McGuire.*

The only problem was that when the "remarkable man" heard about it, he went ballistic.

"Raa-ger!" he screamed at me, a few days before the Northwestern game in Evanston, Illinois, on New Year's Eve. "Holy shit! I didn't know you were doing a book. You can't do a book! You think I'd have told you all that stuff if I knew you were doing a book? I don't want you to do a book! This is not the right time for a book! Christ, if I wanted a book, I'd do one myself! I mean it, Roger! I don't want you to do a book."

I was stunned. I tried to explain to Al that this wasn't a negative thing, but a celebration of who he was and why. No matter. Al remained firm. He didn't want a celebration, he didn't want any kind of book done about him, and he told me up front he would fight it in any way he could.

Today, of course, I realize why Al reacted the way he did. Al was thinking about the bottom line. He didn't want any book done on him unless he was included in the profits. Furthermore, any book now, he felt, would take away from "the book" he planned to write later on and perhaps affect the size of another "safe-deposit box" he was counting on down the road. Shrewd businessman that he was, Al wasn't about to let anyone interfere on that.

The day after my talk with Al, my boss, Bill Dwyre, called me into his office. Al, he said, had called him earlier and brought up the subject of my projected book.

"Al doesn't want you to write a book," Dwyre told me. "He says if you continue with it, he'll refuse to talk to you."

"So let him," I countered. "He's public domain. There is no way he can legally stop me from writing a book on him."

"The point is," Dwyre replied, "if he stops talking to you, you're no good to us on the Marquette beat. And I want you on that beat. Your job is working for the *Milwaukee Journal* sports department, and a big part of that job is covering Marquette basketball and Al McGuire. I don't want anything interfering with that."

The threat was veiled, but barely. It was clear to me that if I continued with my project and Al refused to talk with me, my job at the *Milwaukee Journal* could be in jeopardy. And at 31, divorced, with alimony, child support and who knows what to pay for each month, I needed a job. I knew a book on Al would be a bestseller for the short term—but what about after that? When it came to the support of my kids, I wasn't ready to take the risk.

As I should have known, Al knew what buttons to push. Legally, there was nothing he could do, but still, he had me in a corner. So the next day, I put the files away and called Al and told him I'd go along with his request and forget the book for now. It was one of the lowest points in my life. I was disappointed that Al, whom I considered a friend, had treated me so shabbily. And I was disgusted that Dwyre, who in later years would back Dave Begal, another *Journal* sportswriter, to the hilt in his feud with Green Bay Packers coach Bart Starr, had failed to stand behind me.

The next time I saw Al privately was the first week of January, when we huddled on the sidelines during practice, and I give him credit, the first thing he brought up was the book. "I hope you understand, Rog," he said. "This is just not the right time. A book now, well, it's too final. And if I'm going to have a book done, I want to have control of it. I don't want anything in there that I think might hurt Pat."

The control theme, I understood. Something that would hurt Pat? That boggled my mind. To this day, I don't know of one thing I ever knew about Al McGuire that could have hurt his wife, other than his saying, after he had made it big time, "She still buys her dresses at Treasure Island." Yes, once in a while, Al liked to stay out late, playing gin rummy with the guys. But to my knowledge, he was always a faithful and loyal husband, and all I ever saw between Pat and Al in the 26 years I knew them was love and genuine respect.

Maybe it was the scene in the rowboat, with the beer and sandwiches and the Coast Guard. I don't know. Did Pat not know what a scrapping wildman Al had been in his early years? Again, I don't know. I never will. But to this day, I do respect the fact that he cared enough about Pat that he never wanted—for whatever reason—to cause her any embarrassment on his behalf. It was the family man side of Al that few people ever got a chance to see.

What I remember most about our talk that day was what Al told me next. And I knew it was in response to the sacrifice (financially) he knew I'd made out of my loyalty to him. Al and I had talked a lot. He knew my domestic situation, where I was sitting. "Rog, I promise you, if I ever do a book someday, it'll be with you."

It was a promise I abided by, and believed in, for the next 23 years. I only wish, at some point along the way, Al had decided the time *was* right. God, what a book we could have done together. (Hey! I'm not that way. When it came to the numbers, I'd have even let him decide the split.)

At a late-morning press conference on the MU campus on January 28, Hank Raymonds was officially named to succeed Al as Marquette University's basketball coach and athletic director. As I sat there, taking notes, I felt a great relief for Hank, that his wait was finally over. Nobody, I felt, was more deserving. Publicly, Al had always said that Hank "was the reason for my success." And he was right. For it was Hank—the "Xs and Os guy"—who had created the disciplined offense and multiple defenses that were such a big part of Marquette's success. Thanks to Hank, Al's teams were always solidly trained in the basics—which allowed him the psychological freedom to coach from the head in his own unique way.

Honest as always, Hank said he knew it wouldn't be easy to follow Al, who in 13 seasons had guided the Warriors to 10 postseason tournament bids in that flamboyant style that was all his own. "You don't replace Al McGuire; you succeed him," Hank told us. "Hey, I know it's not going to be easy. People will want to make comparisons, but that doesn't bother me. Let 'em say anything they want; I don't care, as long as we win.

"Listen, there's no greater person than Al, but I've got to be myself. I'm a different person. He's a legend. John Wooden was a legend at UCLA. Vince Lombardi was a legend at Green Bay. Hey, I know what I'm getting into. I wasn't born yesterday.

"I admit that I'm no Al McGuire. There's no way I'd want to be. It's not my lifestyle. I don't intend to change at all. I'll just be me."

As far as I was concerned, that was more than enough. Under Hank, I felt confident the program would continue in good hands.

Near the end of the press conference, Hank got in a good line of his own, when one reporter asked him if he was worried about having to match some of Al's colorful statements. Hank laughed. "No, you're going to have to learn some basketball now," he told the guy. "I won't give you all that baloney."

By mid-February, Al and the team seemed to be back on course. The shock of his resignation, his controversial feud with Bernard, all that appeared to be behind them as they put together an impressive 12-1 streak (the only loss being to Cincinnati by one point on the road) that left the Warriors with a 16-3 record and a No. 7 and No. 9 ranking in the national polls.

At which point, disaster struck.

"The Slump" is how it's usually remembered these days, by anyone who was watching Al's final run back then. "The Slump." A dismal six-day period in which the bottom fell out, when Marquette lost three straight games *at home* and appeared to have thrown away any chance for an NCAA tournament bid in Al's final season.

To this day, I can't believe it happened—that such a stark turnaround occurred so quickly. Bo had finally hit his stride, as Al had hoped, proving with timely points and rebounds that he was indeed "the Secretariat" of college forwards that Al had proclaimed. Plus Jerome was maturing by leaps and bounds—providing points along with his rebounding and tough defense inside. And Butch? He was sensational, throwing in jump shots from the outside and then, if a defender played him a bit too close, suddenly faking him out, going around, and driving inside for the bucket (and often a bonus foul shot) instead.

So what happened? For three straight games, the Warriors just simply fell apart, that's what.

Believe it or not, DePaul—a team Marquette had beaten by 21 points *on their home court* just 17 days before—took the Warriors to *two* overtimes before finally defeating them, 77-72, in the friendly confines of the Arena. After which, Detroit came to town two nights later and nicked Marquette by a point at the final horn, 64-63. And then, to add insult to injury, Wichita State ruined the final home game of Al's career, 75-64, although that defeat was as much a result of some of the poorest officiating I have ever seen as anything else in the game.

Although I didn't write it publicly back then, I always described those three games to anyone who asked as "two white-knucklers and a rape." Depressing? You bet. I was used to seeing ups and downs, routs and upsets, after 10 years in the business. But it absolutely boggled my mind that Al's team could take such a sudden dive when everything seemed to be going so right. Plus, from a personal standpoint, I admit I suffered with Al—in this, his last hurrah—when all the fates had suddenly seemed to turn against him. (And don't let any sportswriter tell you they don't experience those kinds of feelings. A *truly* honest writer will admit, given your choice, you always would much rather cover a winner than a loser. Throwing bouquets is a whole lot easier—and a lot more fun—than proffering excuses or attempting to assess the blame correctly.)

The losses to DePaul and Detroit were the result of nothing more than an amazing failure by Al's players to execute one of the basic tenants of his "game" philosophy—to hold a lead in the final minutes. Against DePaul, with 4:43 left and a four-point lead, Al sent his team into its usual delay game, designed to allow them to run down the clock and keep things in control.

Which is exactly what didn't happen.

Instead Butch, for whatever reasons, tried twice to dribble *between* two defenders and lost the ball both times. And Rosenberger missed a layup with 29 seconds remaining. That allowed DePaul to tie the game at 60 with nine seconds left—all of which had Al frantically walking the sidelines, tearing at his hair like a madman, and rubbing his face in sheer disbelief. Luckily for Marquette, DePaul's star, Ron Norwood, missed a jumper with nine seconds left, and his teammate, Dave Corzine, missed a follow-up hook at the horn, allowing Marquette to stay in the game.

Al's troops played no better in the first overtime, when they threw the ball away twice, Rosenberger missing a layup and Jerome doing the same on his follow-up dunk shot with 1:01 left on the clock. The only reason the game went to a second overtime was because of DePaul's continued poor shooting, when DePaul's Gary Garland missed a jump shot as the horn sounded.

Al's luck finally ran out four seconds into the second OT period. Garland made a jump shot, and Bo fouled another player after the shot. That gave DePaul a three-point lead, and when Butch threw up another air ball, that was it for all practical purposes. With seven seconds left, Al got up and walked over to shake hands with his longtime adversary *and friend*, DePaul coach Ray Meyer, and was, as I expected, generous in his comments after the game.

"I was sad for my team, but happy for Ray," Al told us. "It meant a lot to him. He ate a lot of humble pie the last few years."

Al was so depressed that he admitted to the press for the first time that he didn't think his team would be going to the NCAA tournament this time around. "I personally think it's very doubtful that we'd get a tourney bid," he told us. "One more defeat and we're out. Because there's never been any love affair between us and the NCAA."

Detroit's 64-63 thriller at the horn two nights later was an exact turnabout of the game between the two teams in Detroit the year before, when Marquette had triumphed by a point on guard Lloyd Walton's jump shot as the clock ran out. This time, it was Detroit, not Marquette, that trailed the whole night, and yet salvaged the game on one last desperate shot.

Lightning struck in the form of Detroit's center, Terry Tyler, who with 35 seconds left stripped Bo of the ball to gain possession, after which Detroit coach Dick Vitale (who was under the assumption he had no timeouts left, when in fact he had one) did the only thing he could— scream for his team to move the ball out front and stall for a final shot. As the final seconds ran down, Detroit guard Dennis Boyd had the ball, and when neither Neary or Boylan guarded him close enough, he lofted a long, towering "Hail Mary" jump shot that swished the net as the horn sounded.

As the hushed crowd filed out of the Arena, I will never forget the contrast between Al, who stood before the Marquette bench with a stunned expression on his face, and Vitale, who was doing a victory dance with his team out on the floor. Both realized that Boyd's shot had probably decided a whole lot more than that game. Vitale's troops had now won 21 straight for a 22-1 record, while Marquette had slipped to 16-5 with three defeats in its last five games. Since both schools were Midwest independents, the Titans had clearly gained a big heave over the fence in a race for an NCAA postseason bid by defeating Marquette at home.

Vitale, as expected, was ecstatic. "Wow! I feel like crying," he declared, when I ventured out on the court, where the dancing and back-slapping continued. "I haven't been this choked up since I lost my eye when I was a kid."

Al, on the other hand, was like the pilot who sees the mountain before him. He was stoically calm and resigned to his fate when the press gathered round in the locker room a few minutes later. "I guess turn-about is fair play," he started off, as if not knowing exactly what he want-ed to say. "We beat 'em that way last year." When asked about his team's chances for an NCAA bid, Al indicated he felt they were not just slim, but none. "It's over," he said, tight-lipped, shaking his head. "It's been a nice year, but it's over. Maybe now we can become spoilers or something. But there's no way we could get an NCAA bid now. No way."

Al pointed out to us that after his home finale against Wichita State, the Warriors' last five games were on the road, another reason he felt a postseason tournament bid was no longer in the picture. "No way, no way," insisted. "We can't win at home, so how can you expect to win on the road?"

Then Al added an interesting comment, which (whether he meant it to or not) had everyone—fans and media alike—buzzing the follow-ing day. "I don't think we could qualify for the NIT or the NCAA," he told us.

The NIT. Until that moment, when Al mentioned it, I doubt any-one had seriously considered that option. I know I certainly hadn't. And yet, by the following day—thanks to Al's remark—the idea had spread like wildfire among students, fans, and the media. Suddenly, it seemed, everybody was talking NIT—a brand new scenario Al had offered up about how his final season might actually end.

No matter how you looked at it, the idea of Al McGuire and Marquette returning to the National Invitation Tournament—the annu-al 12-team affair played each year in Madison Square Garden in New York—on his final go-round was nothing short of tantalizing.

First of all, of course, because Al had already won it—and the story behind that was a classic.

Back in 1970, the NIT had been a viable competitor to the then 25-team National Collegiate Athletic Association tourney, luring many top teams to the Big Apple on a regular basis. This was before the NCAA began its drive to force all teams into conferences, the reward being that *any* NCAA conference champion was guaranteed a bid to postseason play. (In short, the NCAA, being the Microsoft of college basketball, was doing everything it could to eliminate the competition.)

In 1970, however, General Motors ran head-on into a guy named Al McGuire.

That year, the NCAA decided to send Marquette (then 19-3), out of its region to the Midwest Regional at Fort Worth, Texas, giving the two at-large bids in the Mideast to Notre Dame (20-5) and a real outsider, Jacksonville of Florida (20-1). Al was incensed, ripping the NCAA for what he called "power politics," and made national headlines when he spurned the NCAA and accepted a bid from the NIT instead.

"It's crazy," he told reporters. "With a 19-3 record, we're only third in our region? The way I look at it, Notre Dame must have got the word around that they wouldn't play if they had to go down there [to the Midwest]. I guess I should have done my homework. I should have been on the phone last week.

"The thing is, I couldn't get anyone to give me any reason. You can't get any information from anybody. One time they talk [caliber of] schedule, the next they talk record. If you talk schedule, we played a tougher schedule than Jacksonville. If you talk record, we're better than Notre Dame. It was just power politics.

"It's a shame, because probably more than anyone, I wanted to go to the NCAA. If I could have got any explanation, if anyone in the NCAA would have stood up and given me a reason—right or wrong—we probably would have gone to the Midwest. But you say something, and they say, 'We're dealing with a nut up there.'"

Clearly, the NCAA's decision was a slap in the face to Al, and given his Irish pride, it's no surprise he refused to accept it. He did what he had done all his life when a bully ruffled his hair. He didn't hesitate. He went for the throat. And told the NCAA to stuff it.

Not that Al didn't get some pressure from school officials to reconsider his decision. "I got this call from the [MU] president's office," Al told me once, "and this priest, his assistant, told me the president thought we should go to the NCAA. That it really was what was best for the school. I told him, 'Father, I don't hear confession and you don't coach this team.' A few minutes later, he called me back and said, 'You're right.' And that was that."

The thing was, Al won. He took his team, with their outlandish suits and a lot of moxie, to the Big Apple, where they ran off four straight victories to bring the NIT title home, and Dean Meminger was named MVP. Included was a 101-79 thrashing of Louisiana State University, in which Jackie Burke handcuffed LSU's star shooting sensation, "Pistol" Pete Maravich, who would later sign a $1.8 million pro contract. Press Maravich, Pete's dad and LSU's coach, had ridiculed Marquette's defense-oriented style, saying it was "as exciting as watching grass grow." To which Gary Brell responded, "We're gonna mow his lawn." Added Burke, after the game, "If they let me play Maravich every night, I'll play pro ball for cab fare and a hamburger after each game." Ironically, Marquette beat Al's old school, St. John's of New York, 65-53 in the final.

Now, seven years later, I felt the odds of Marquette winning the NIT again were heavily in Al's favor, should he choose that option. The NIT in 1977, after all, was a mere shadow of its former self, whose field normally included what few decent teams were not already chosen by the ever-expanding NCAA. If Al and his No. 7-ranked Warriors went to New York, I had no doubts they could triumph over the "crumbs" the NCAA had left behind. And the thing was, what a story it would be! Al McGuire, the hometown boy, born and bred in Rockaway Beach, graduate of St. John's, returning to Madison Square Garden to close out his colorful career. If that wasn't a promoter's dream, I figured, what was?

To gauge the sentiment in the Big Apple, I called Rob Franklin, an old friend from my days covering the New York Yankees' spring camps in Fort Lauderdale, who was then assistant vice president of production for the Garden. Rob agreed with me wholeheartedly. "Al McGuire and Marquette would be a *very* marketable commodity," Rob assured me. "They would be any year. But this year, with Al closing out his career, they most certainly would be."

Officially, the NIT field wasn't chosen by The Garden, but the Metropolitan Intercollegiate Basketball Association, a group of five athletic directors from East Coast schools. But, as Rob confided to me, The Garden had a lot to say about who made up the field. "It's strictly up to them," he said, "but they do check with us on which teams are financially attractive. Now being it's Al's swan song, I think it would be an honor and very appropriate for him to coach his last college game back in New York, in Madison Square Garden, and possibly in the championship game of the NIT."

Rob and I both knew what he could and couldn't say. But the message was clear and simple. You want it, Al, you got it. We'll welcome you with open arms. Franklin, and the others at the Garden, knew the kind of national press attention that would generate—and it was something that, frankly, the sagging NIT really needed.

What was my read right then? I still thought Al had a shot for an NCAA bid, despite his remarks to the contrary. But given this new wild card that had been thrown out on the table, I felt that if the NCAA did pass him by, he wouldn't hesitate for a shot at one last blaze of glory amidst the cracked sidewalks and concrete canyons where he had been raised.

Twenty-four hours later, however, my thoughts had changed dramatically, after watching Al's humiliating 75-64 defeat by Wichita State in his home finale at the Arena. After that, I felt, Marquette's only shot for a postseason tournament bid would come from his home turf, the boroughs of New York.

The key to the Wichita State debacle—or "Dunkirk" as Al would call it—was actually something that had occurred a month earlier. That was when, on February 18, Marquette had beaten Drake University of the Missouri Valley Conference by just two points, 62-60, on the road at Vets Auditorium in Des Moines.

A bit of background is needed here.

Al had a philosophy on officiating in which he tried to make things as fair as possible for both teams involved. Marquette was an independent, but used Big Ten officials. Al's philosophy was "yours at home, ours at home"—that is, if you hosted Marquette, Big Ten officials were used, and if you were visiting at the Arena, your   conference officials were used. That way, the officials would hopefully offset some of the home-court advantage either way.

Unfortunately, after the game—which was decided on a Butch Lee jump shot with six seconds remaining—Drake coach Bob Ortegal ripped the Big Ten officials as "idiots," insisting they had stolen the game by not giving Al a technical when he walked onto the court at one point and not calling Bo Ellis with a foul when he stole the ball away and set up Lee's final basket.

"It was the most gutless example of officiating I've ever seen," Ortegal stormed. "Al McGuire deserved a technical. He took over the officiating with 18 minutes left in the game. Ellis's cheap shot was a flagrant foul. He should have been kicked out. The ballgame was decided by the officials. It's unfortunate Al McGuire can get away with these things. If Bob Ortegal did them, there would be technicals all over the place. It's ridiculous."

The only ridiculous thing was Ortegal's charges. Why was he so upset? Because his team had played well, yet suffered its third straight loss, leaving Drake with a dismal 4-10 record and a nothing season. Remember, too, an upset of nationally ranked Marquette would have allowed Ortegal to salvage something out of an otherwise horrible season. From what I heard at the time, Ortegal's job was on the line, and he just self-destructed.

Unfortunately, his remarks triggered a wave of anti-McGuire sentiment all over the Hawkeye state. (I know, because my hometown is an hour north of Des Moines, and I got all the newspaper clips and comments from my folks in the mail and on the phone.) The consensus was that Big Ten officials stole the game from Drake. But just wait, the callers on the talk shows ranted. Wait until Wichita State (another Valley team) comes to Milwaukee...with *our* officials. We'll see what happens then.

That threat wasn't rooted only in irrational talk show callers. The week prior to the Wichita State game, I heard through the grapevine that Valley officials Ron Spitler and Jack Savidge—who were officiating the MU-Wichita State game—had a little "going away present" for Al in his appearance at the Arena. Naturally, I hoped the rumors were false. Unfortunately, from what I saw that night, I have always thought since that they were true.

For Al, the night turned into a nightmare. To start with, his team did not play well the first half, although still only trailing by five, 33-28, at intermission. Al, as I recall, was on his feet much of the time, verbally skirmishing with Spitler and Savidge, who made more than a few questionable calls. Then Al and his family were called to center court for what turned out to be an emotional farewell ceremony—one of the few times I ever saw Al at a loss for words. I can still see him to this day, standing there next to Pat and his family, as the tributes and presents flowed from the University alumni and friends alike. There was a black rocking chair, a gold plaque, a beautiful oil portrait of Al, a silver basketball presented to him by George "Brute Force" Thompson, and finally, a magnificent grandfather clock. After this, Father Raynor, Marquette's president, had the crowd up and cheering when he thanked Al for all he had done for the university and told him, wherever he might go in the future, "You give 'em hell, Al!"

What a moment. Toilet paper sailed down from the rafters. Cheers rocked the building. Pat was crying, and Al was trying not to, repeatedly wiping the tears from his eyes. "I'd like to thank the players, the student body, and most of all, thank God," he told them, struggling with the words. "It's been great, but as I said in December, the merry-go-round has ended…Thank you!"

That's when it really hit me, right then. *Damn, I thought. He's really going. He's going to be gone soon. No more Al.* I couldn't help it. As I stood there, courtside, I was overcome by a heavy sadness. As the cheers came down, my lips trembled, and tears formed in my eyes. Because I knew in my heart that I didn't want Al McGuire to leave. He was one of the most enjoyable and charismatic people I had ever met, and no matter what the situation, I always looked forward to his next witticism or tirade with equal pleasure. As I sat down and got ready for the second half, I knew one thing for sure—there were 10, 938 people around me who would most certainly agree.

Just over a minute into the second half, after Marquette had closed to within two points, Spitler made a questionable call (on guard Jimmy Boylan) that finally sent Al over the edge. Angry that no call had been made on Wichita State's Robert Elmore in a similar situation seconds earlier, Al charged out onto the court, at which point Spitler slapped him with a T that caused the crowd to go wild, hurling another barrage of toilet paper onto the court. Up went the familiar chant, not heard all season: "Give 'em hell, Al! Give 'em hell, Al! Give 'em hell, Al!…"

Al didn't disappoint them. Enraged, he lashed into Spitler with yet another barrage of his finest buzzsaw vernacular…at which point, Spitler gave him a second technical for his efforts, and things really got out of control. After screaming for a timeout, Al turned on his heel and waded back into the fray, most certainly questioning Spitler's parentage (although I admit I was lip-reading at the time, because the noise was so great). Now the crowd began to turn ugly, hurling not just streams of toilet paper, but programs and soda cups onto the floor, followed by wave after wave of threatening boos—and not just from the safety of the cheap seats up top, but from behind press row as well.

For another five minutes, the tumult went on. And then, once things had finally quieted down, Al and his Warriors paid dearly for the uproar.

First Wichita State guard John Kobar made one of two foul shots off Boylan's foul. Then his teammate, Bob Trogele, sank three of four awarded (two for each of Al's technical fouls). That gave the Shockers a six-point lead…and possession of the ball. To make matters worse,

Elmore made a jump shot seconds later and a free throw off Whitehead's foul…leaving Marquette trailing by nine.

The rest of the game was predictable. Marquette would close to five or six points, there would be a questionable call, and Wichita State would regain momentum and surge ahead by 10, 12 or 15 points again. I could see that Al was frantic. This was his "last hurrah" at the Arena, before the home fans, and it was rapidly dawning on him that—thanks to the deadly duo of Spitler and Savidge—the tempo of the game had been taken out of his hands.

With 22 seconds remaining, Marquette trailing by 11, and the crowd getting uglier by the second, Al suddenly called a timeout and huddled with Spitler, Savidge and some security guards. What I learned later was that in spite of what those two apes had done to him, he was still enough of a gentleman to be worried about their safety, and so he let them know that there would be a cordon of security guards ready to escort them to the locker room after the final horn.

And that's just what happened, as the refs exited under a snow-storm of toilet paper to the locker rooms. Al, I could see, was brimming with frustration and disappointment. And so, in spite of his humanitarian efforts moments before, he couldn't resist firing one last broadside of bitter words at Spitler, to let him know how he really felt as they left the court nearly side by side.

"You pigeon!" Al yelled at the zebra. "How did you get assigned to this game?" That night, after I had filed my story and downed more than a couple beers, I sat contemplating the whole sorry mess. For Spitler and Savidge, I had nothing but contempt. What they had done was easy, taking their revenge (and probably becoming heroes back in Iowa and throughout the Missouri Valley Conference) by making calls that couldn't be questioned later on, no matter what. And what they—and Al—both knew was that once it was done, the game *was* in the books. It was over. Finis. They had stolen something crystal clear and fine away from him, something he could never gain back. His home finale. For the rest of his life, he could never recall that night fondly. And for all you holier-than-thou officials out there, who are going to insist that nothing like this ever happened in college basketball, just stuff it. Al was human, you're human, I'm human. End of discussion. Don't get on your pedestal and tell me jealousy, hubris, reputation, revenge, public opinion, or your personal feelings don't enter in when you are officiating a game. Bullshit. It all depends on whose ox is getting gored. And you know it. We are all children of the same garden, the one the snake lived in. I know you try your best, but don't tell me you're perfect. Because then I'll bring up the

Above: "Hey! What the hell's going on here?" A familiar sight to Marquette fans—Al throwing down the gauntlet in the heat of battle. *Courtesy Marquette University Archives*

Below: Al makes a point as only he can during an argument with referee Jim Bain at the Arena during his final season at Marquette. © *2004, Journal Sentinel, Inc., reproduced with permission*

Above: Business as usual: If the score was close, heated exchanges were the norm when the Warriors huddled during a timeout. *Courtesy Marquette University Archives*

Below: Two technicals and out: Al angrily stormed off the court after losing to Indiana, 65-56, in the 1976 Mideast Regional Final. *Ernest Anheuser, © 2004, Journal Sentinel, Inc., reproduced with permission*

Above: Pat McGuire—the lovely and gracious queen of Al's Camelot career. *Richard Brodzeller, © 2004, Journal Sentinel, Inc., reproduced with permission*

Below: All-America guard Butch Lee was the spark plug of Marquette's 1977 NCAA championship team. *Courtesy Marquette University Archives*

Above: The Moment: With an NCAA championship 14 seconds away, Al fights back tears as assistant coaches Hank Raymonds (center) and Rick Majerus begin to celebrate. © 2004, *Journal Sentinel, Inc., reproduced with permission*

Below: Basking in the glow of a national championship: Al and his family join the cheers of happy Marquette fans on the court at the Omni in Atlanta. © 2004, *Journal Sentinel, Inc., reproduced with permission*

Above: The fruits of victory: Al shares a laugh with problem child Bernard Toone, while center Jerome Whitehead (54) looks on. © 2004, *Journal Sentinel, Inc., reproduced with permission*

Below: A treasured gift: The photo Al sent me (I'm the guy with the dark moustache) a few weeks after Marquette won the NCAA championship at the Omni. The inscription reads: " '77 NCAA, Roger, Send money. Happiness. Al." *Courtesy of Roger Jaynes*

Above: The team that made Marquette history: (L-R) Jim Boylan, Bill Neary, Ulice Payne, Butch Lee, Jim Dudley, (seated) Gary Rosenberger, Bernard Toone, Jerome Whitehead, Jim Butrym, Robert Byrd, and Bo Ellis. *Courtesy Marquette University Archives*

Below: The only time Al claimed to be at a loss for words—when he met President Jimmy Carter at the White House. He was one of 14 people chosen for Carter's Commission on Physical Fitness. *© 2004, Journal Sentinel, Inc., reproduced with permission*

Above: The NBC Trio: Al, Dick Enberg and Billy Packer delivering pregame commentary. © *NBC Sports*

Below: Al shares a laugh with the crowd as he limbers up prior to the start of the 1981 Milwaukee Journal/Al's Run on 15th and Wisconsin. The event raised more than $2 million for Children's Hospital in the nine years Al participated. © *2004, Journal Sentinel, Inc., reproduced with permission*

Above: Life is good! Al strikes a Chairman Mao-like pose as he takes a private swim off a friend's dock in a lake west of Milwaukee just weeks before his 60th birthday. © 2004, *Journal Sentinel, Inc., reproduced with permission*

Below: The free spirit: Thanks to NBC's generous contract, Al had loads of time to explore the countryside on his motorcycle in his post-Marquette years. *Courtesy Marquette University Archives*

Xavier game of Al's last season, or his last home game we have just recounted.

The only reason I bring this up at all is that Al deserved better than what he got in his final home game at the Arena. I don't say he deserved any favoritism because of the circumstances, and I know Al wouldn't have wanted any. But holy crow! At least he deserved an honest shake.

With five games left to go in the regular season, Al and his team now faced a tremendous challenge if they were going to get any kind of a postseason tournament bid in his final go-round. The three straight losses *at home* had left them with a mediocre 16-6 record and serious doubts in the NCAA hierarchy as to their ability. After the Wichita State disaster, I firmly believed they could not afford to lose another game if they hoped to snare an NCAA bid. NIT? I knew the East Coast folks would be more forgiving because of Al's New York background, but in my heart I really didn't want to see him have to close his career as the top banana in a second-rate act. Al McGuire deserved to go out in style on center stage—win or lose, first game of the NCAA tourney or last—but on center stage, where the real stakes were resting. And yet, given the gauntlet he and his team faced on the road—starting with archrival Wisconsin at Madison, followed by Virginia Tech, Tulane, Creighton, and finally Michigan, another Big Ten foe, I seriously doubted that Al could pull it off.

Hello, New Yawk! I kept telling myself, when I thought about postseason. Get ready for the Garden. The lines from the song "New York, New York!" kept drumming in my head, because that's where I really thought it was all going to end.

What I didn't realize, of course, was that Al had come nowhere close to using up the stash of leprechauns he held in his personal reserve. And that, combined with the phenomenal talents of a player like Butch Lee, his spark-plug junior guard, and Bo Ellis, his "Secretariat of college forwards," would be more than enough to see them to the pot of gold at the end of the rainbow that they were seeking—an NCAA bid.

Butch and Bo. They led the way on that final regular-season run. Marquette, in an amazing 17-day stretch, charged back like the thoroughbreds they were to win an amazing four straight games on the road and then battled to lead Big Ten foe Michigan by five at halftime *in Ann Arbor,* at which time the NCAA bids were announced and Al found he had been given one final shot at the brass ring.

Butch and Bo. All season long, they had been Al's equivalent to what Maris and Mantle had been for the New York Yankees a decade before. Like the "M&M boys," B&B were the two players, Al knew, who had to perform if Marquette was to "go Uptown." They were the two guys who really made things click.

In the first game of that stretch, Marquette's 73-58 victory over Wisconsin at Madison was no surprise. The surprise would have been if the Badgers had ever been a factor in the game. For outside of Coach Bill Cofield's Sonny Liston-like glare, they had no real weapons, and once Al turned Butch loose in the second half, he put on a "run and gun" show for seven straight points that gave Marquette a 10-point lead and all but put the game away.

What I remember most about the Wisconsin game was that it was the first in which Al donned what later would come to be known as his "lucky suit"—a black three-piece he told his players he was going to wear until Marquette got an NCAA bid. (While I can't prove it, I also believe it was the same suit Al had worn on back on December 17, the day he announced his retirement at the Wisconsin Club. Same tie, too.) At any rate, when the Warriors continued to win, the suit continued to ripen.

"It became a superstition thing," Al told me, years later. "I used to stand in the corner and jump in and out of it, because if anyone realizes what a coach goes through, there's no way you'd keep it on after the game. We didn't clean it or anything." He chuckled. "In fact, it became the job of the 12th guy to carry it on and off the bus."

Butch's finest moment of the season, I felt, came just five days later, when Marquette was playing Virginia Tech in a noisy, overcrowded, snake pit of a gym in Blacksburg, Virginia. That's when Al told him, after calling timeout with the 7:50 remaining and the game up for grabs, "Time to go, Butch. Score's close." Looking back, I think it was *the* moment Marquette could have faltered. When they could have succumbed to the pressure, lost the game, and with it, quite likely, their last chance for an NCAA bid.

But they didn't, because Butch Lee didn't falter. In that dark, noisy little snake pit, he rose to the occasion that night. For the next two minutes he put on a one-man "shake and bake" clinic on offensive basketball that iced the game. First faking out his defender, then driving in close and scoring on a short jump shot. Then faking out not just one, but two defenders and driving in for another basket. And finally, faking, driving, faking and driving again, taking the foul...and then sinking both free throws. Suddenly, Marquette had a 10-point lead and was able to go into its delay pattern, forcing the Hokies to foul them and settle the contest.

Butch did more than spark a victory that night—he lit the spark that would grow into the Warriors' chances for an NCAA bid. In the locker room afterwards, the team was actually cheering. Cheering! Including the more normally reserved Hank Raymonds, who declared to anyone and everyone who would listen, "We're not dead yet!"

Al was more subdued, both in the press conference and after. "There is a bit of light at the end of the tunnel," he admitted when he faced the press. What I remember most is what he told his players, before he spoke to the media that night, and which he repeated to them after the next two games as well.

"Hey, guys," he told them, "just one game at a time, OK? Just one game at a time."

I knew where Al was coming from. It was starting to hit him. Yes, this is not my best team here. But maybe we do have a shot to go Uptown. And what kept haunting him was that he might, in spite of himself, self-destruct and ruin it for his kids. The staggering losses to North Carolina State and Indiana in previous years, I believe, were still clouds he lived under in his mind. And so, while I have no evidence of it, I believe that Al, after the resurrection in Blacksburg, didn't necessarily pray just for another victory after that. Instead, I think he also asked that "the monster" he had created wouldn't reappear—as had happened in those crucial games before—causing him to lose control so that he would have to watch not just a victory, but his final season slip away.

The only two things memorable about Marquette's 63-44 win over Tulane in the Superdome happened at practice, the day before the game. That's when Al fell in a hole, and Bernard somehow managed to find a basketball so the team could hold a practice at all. (I was more amused than surprised; when you traveled with Al, these things always seemed to happen.)

When we walked inside the shadowy, cavernous arena, no one from Tulane was there to greet us, and there were no basketballs, towels, or any other equipment anywhere in sight. So there the players stood, in practice clothes, until Al, after stewing for about five minutes, angrily stalked off into the darkness behind the huge portable bleachers to find someone—anyone—who could set things right.

Minutes later, he returned, limping...and while I sympathized with him, it was all I could do not to laugh.

"There was a hole back there, where the hydraulics are that move the bleachers," he explained, grimacing. "And I fell in it. It was about two feet deep, I guess." But not even the pain could suppress his Irish sense of humor. "Maybe I should say I got whiplash," he remarked. "I'll need a good lawsuit if we lose here."

Not that Al wasn't impressed with the huge Superdome, which had been built especially for the National Football League Saints and the Jazz of the National Basketball Association. "It's so big," he said, gazing off into the darkness above us, "that you could spend a year here—if you had some way to get food—and never pay to see an event. You wouldn't have to, because nobody could find you."

Which didn't solve the problem of no basketballs. During the next few minutes, some stadium officials wandered by, but no amount of arguing by Al, Hank or Rick did any good. So what did Al do? He hollered for Bernard.

"All right, Bernard," he told him, pointing off into the darkness at the end of the court. "I want you to go off that way and don't come back until you find me a basketball. One lousy basketball!"

And so off Bernard went.

Five minutes later, he returned, grinning like a Cheshire cat, with one basketball in his hands.

Al turned to me, shaking his head, but quickly told me he was not surprised. "Roger, I'm telling you. When Bernard smiles, he can get anything out of anybody. He could sell the Eskimos deep freezers. The man just has the touch."

How did Bernard do it? He hunted down Don Sparks, the trainer for the New Orleans Jazz, who had earlier that afternoon played a game against the San Antonio Spurs. Sparks, after a bit of convincing by Bernard, had grudgingly given up a basketball. It was half flat, and it bounced funny, but it was all the Warriors needed to get a practice going.

Not that they really needed it. The game was a slopfest right from the start, in which Marquette managed to win easily in spite of giving up the ball 30 times. That's because Tulane had 28 turnovers, made only three baskets the first half, and shot .276 for the entire game. "I think we set college basketball back 10 years tonight," Al remarked afterwards. "But 19 wins are beautiful."

At that point, Al knew how precarious his team's position still was. He realized that, while not yet in the tournament, Marquette was already playing one-game seasons, each time his players took the court as they struggled to secure a bid. "Russian roulette, that's what we're fooling with right now," was how he put it, as our bus headed back to the hotel.

In my own mind, I still couldn't get over what a horribly played game I had just witnessed. Given all that slop, would the final score really matter? "Well, I hope all the NCAA sees of this one is the final score," I replied. Al smiled faintly and nodded, but said nothing, staring off into the night.

Two days later, just before the Creighton game, the Bernard-Al situation flared up again, when Bernard publicly made a pitch for more playing time...once Marquette had secured an NCAA bid. "I'm willing to forget about all the stuff that's happened this year," he said, referring to his run-ins with Al, which had caused him to spend a lot more time than he wanted on the Marquette bench. "I say, let's just get the bid and start over...the way it's supposed to be."

Translated, of course, "the way it's supposed to be" meant Bernard starting ahead of Bill Neary, which had not been the case all season.

"There's no question in my mind that the starting job should have been mine," Bernard insisted. "Evidently, he [Al] saw things differently. Maybe I wasn't the type player he thought could fill the role. He wanted a strong, brutal man around the boards. I don't have to play like that to get the job done.

"The thing is, he's never left me in there long enough to have a good look at my defense or rebounding. I've never had enough time to be relaxed. Always I'm coming in cold off the bench, and no wonder I make some mistakes."

To back up his words, Toone pointed out that against Wichita State, a game in which he'd played 25 minutes (much more than usual), he had not only made seven of 14 shots for 14 points, but grabbed three rebounds and blocked a shot.

Al, as I expected, was not impressed when I informed him of Bernard's plea.

"It's up to the situation," Al said, with a shrug. "If the situation arises, fine. But I would not create more playing time for him. We don't operate that way. We're not a better team with him in there than Neary. Hey, we've won 19 games with Neary. That's a lot of games."

Al's message was clear. Unless there was a foul crisis, or an unexpected injury to a starter, things were not going to change. It was the same message he had been telling Bernard all year—either fill the role I've given you, or fill no role at all. For whatever reasons, Bernard just wasn't listening. Perhaps, because he had so much pure talent, he felt he could buck the system. No way, not with Al.

How many times had Al said it over the years? "I'm the boss and the players know it. There's give and take, but in the end, I'm a dictator."

A guy who did understand was Jim Dudley, a six-foot, six-inch sophomore from Milwaukee, who had transferred to Marquette from Michigan State the year before and was willing to bide his time. Al's role for Dudley (who was a fantastic leaper) was clear-cut—when Bo was getting beat up in the second half and needed a breather, or Jerome went into a sudden drought, Al sent the tall blonde in to create more action underneath. Which Dudley did. Against Detroit, he scored four points and grabbed six rebounds in just 11 minutes, and he had four and four against Wisconsin in the same amount of time.

The thing was, Dudley was smart enough to understand his role, or as Al put it, "wait his turn." His biggest supporter was Butch. "Jim Dudley is the highest-jumping white guy in the world," Butch said one day. "He's unreal. I looked at him in the Wisconsin game and I thought, 'Man! And he's only a sophomore.'…I'm proud for him. Real proud."

So impressed was Al with Dudley's talent (and potential) that two days before the Virginia Tech game, he gave him not only a high compliment, but his own unique place in Marquette basketball history.

Al had handed out a lot of nicknames in his 13 years as head coach—like "Dean the Dream" for Dean Meminger, "The Black Swan" for Bob Lackey, "Trickster" for Jackie Burke, and "The Enforcer" for George Thompson, just to name a few. That day, while we were watching practice, he suddenly came up with what he told me would be "my last nickname." He had been saving it for a couple years, he said, waiting for the right guy to come around.

The right guy was Dudley.

"He's the 'Cloud Piercer,'" Al said. "In a few years, when he comes into his own, it'll catch on. It's what the natives on the South Island of New Zealand call Mt. Cook. The mountain was so high that most days you couldn't see the peak."

Al's analogy triggered an immediate, if off-the-wall, comparison in my mind. One, I felt, that summed up Bernard's problem precisely. He, like Dudley, was a sophomore, and Bernard most certainly was far more talented. But psychologically, Bernard was not—and never would be—a "Cloud Piercer." Unlike Dudley, his vision was not high enough that he could see the forest for the trees.

Five days after the sloppy win over Tulane, Al's troops did a 180-degree turn and played a fine game to whip Creighton, 72-60, in Omaha, Nebraska, to clinch Al's 11th straight 20-game winning season and the 399th victory of his coaching career. As expected, Butch and Bo led the show, with 18 and 15 points respectively, and Whitehead gave an indication that his dog days were over, scoring 14 points and 10 rebounds. Even more encouraging was guard Gary Rosenberger, who showed Al he had yet another potent scoring weapon off the bench when he threw up 14 from intercontinental ballistic range.

Afterwards, Al was clearly pleased. "I think there's no doubt that we're an NCAA cut of cloth," he insisted, referring to the tournament bids that were to be handed out the following day. And then he pulled out his PR ace in the hole, referring to the Midwest's other top independent, Notre Dame, which had been a thorn in his side seven years before. "Notre Dame beat San Francisco, so we're both 20-6," Al said pointedly. "And we beat them [earlier in the season]. Now, in 1970, the year I turned down the NCAA for the NIT, the argument was that Notre Dame deserved a bid instead of us because they beat us. So now, I think turnabout is fair play."

Al knew exactly what he was doing when he made those remarks. His players had done their part by charging back and winning the games. Now he was doing his—by effectively putting the NCAA selection committee on the spot.

Talk about tension. The following day—Sunday, March 6, 1977—was my 31st birthday. It promised to be anything but dull. At 1:30 p.m., Al and his players faced a daunting task—taking on No. 3-ranked Michigan in Ann Arbor in the regular-season finale. At 3 p.m. (approximately halftime), the NCAA would officially announce its tournament bids. At which time, we would all find out if Al's last ride was indeed over, or if the merry-go-round would go on.

In my heart, I felt Al and his players had already done what needed to be done. They had come back. They had won the tough ones on the road. They had earned that NCAA bid. But I also knew that Al was anything *but* the NCAA's poster child and how fickle the fates could be.

What hit me most, on the flight from Omaha to Ann Arbor, was the sudden, looming inevitability of it all, and that while I might personally want Al to get the bid, there was nothing I could do to change whatever was going to happen. At one point, I felt I wanted to talk to him, on the plane, but then decided to keep my distance. He had his own demons to wrestle with, I realized, without me tossing my psychological baggage in his direction. So I kept my distance and stayed in my seat. I even made sure I didn't sit next to him on the bus.

C'est la vie! I finally thought that night, after I'd had dinner and a few much needed drinks, and my head hit the pillow. That's life. What will be will be. And then, in my mind, I recalled Al saying how life was never fair, and so I tossed and turned a few more hours before finally drifting off to sleep.

Al's new suit was the signal, the first sign any of us had that Marquette had indeed been awarded a National Collegiate Athletic Association bid. After wearing his black three-piece "Lucky Suit" the first half (during which Marquette took a 40-35 lead over Michigan), Al emerged while his players were warming up for the second, clothed in a light green check.

Al had gotten the news from Kevin Byrne, the Marquette SID, as he was going into the locker room. This time, there was no anger about being sent out of region. Frankly, as he told me later, Al was just damn glad he was being sent somewhere...anywhere. With tears in his eyes, he told the players.

"It was a very emotional moment," Al told us after the game. "I guess I didn't know I wanted it that bad. Or didn't let myself know that I didn't want to go to the NIT in New York. If we hadn't got a bid, I'd have gone if the kids and the school wanted, but personally, I would have been in the minus pool.

"It was an emotional moment for the kids, too. Something we all wanted so bad, but couldn't talk about. We knew if we tripped up on that last road swing, there was no possible way. It was an awful lot of tension."

As things turned out, while Al got the bid, he didn't get that 400th victory. With just under four minutes left to play, Bo (who had 16 points and nine rebounds at that point) fouled out. After which, the Warriors collapsed, throwing away a six-point lead and losing to Michigan by a point, 69-68. "Bo Ellis is like our Mickey Mantle, our star," Al said, after the game. "We need him in there. Need the name in here, even if he isn't hitting. He's our leader. When Bo wasn't in there, we lost our composure."

By any count, Marquette simply fell apart in those last four, frantic minutes—turning over the ball four times and committing five fouls. But I think why it happened was that the players—like Al—realized at that point it really didn't matter. "The fish dies from the head," he'd always said. And they, like him, knew that in the whole scheme of things, the outcome of the game no longer mattered. That's why he threw off the shrouds at halftime. They all had what they wanted—the bid. That chance for a shot at the title. And that, they all knew, was what it was all about.

"The won-loss record didn't mean that much, once we knew we had the bid," Al said after the game. "I still wanted to win the game, but the bid made the season a success, no matter how it came out."

That night, the phrase "c'est la vie" was back in my thoughts again—only this time from an Emmylou Harris song (written by Chuck Berry) about a Cajun wedding, and the relatives' remarks about how unpredictable life can be. In my mind, I could hear Emmy Lou's twangy voice: "C'est la vie, said the old folks. It goes to show you never can tell."

Damn straight, I thought, before I drifted happily off to sleep.

On Monday, the day after the Sabbath, Al and his troops finally rested.

And on Tuesday, when I showed up for practice, I knew exactly what I wanted to ask him. And I could tell, by the resigned look on his face, that Al knew what was coming when he saw me walk in with my usual notebook and pen in hand.

What I had on my mind, of course, was that statement he had made after the loss to Indiana in the Mideast Regional the year before. "I will not come to another tournament," he had said then. "If we are fortunate enough to make it again, I'll let my staff handle the game. I'll stay away."

The thing was, back in December, when Al had announced his retirement, he was already hedging. "If we get the bid, I'd really like, by popular demand, to do it this last time around," he admitted then. "If you give me an out, I'll jump in—if we get a bid."

From what I could see, there had been no obvious groundswell (primarily, I suspected, because nobody had really believed what Al had said in the first place, a year ago). The question, however, begged to be asked, and so I asked it. And got one of the greatest off-the-cuff replies from Al I ever heard in return.

"Well, you got the bid," I said to him. "What I want to know is: Given what you said last March, are you going to the tournament or not?"

Al frowned.

"Roger," he muttered, shaking his head. "I knew this was coming. I just knew it. I told Pat this morning at breakfast that you were going to ask me about this."

Al stretched mightily and then wiped his tired face with his hands. He was wearing his old black coat, jeans and scuffed white tennis shoes, as usual. "Give me a minute, will ya?" he asked, after which he wiped his face again, squared his shoulders and composed himself, and then proceeded to create his own "groundswell" right then and there.

"By popular demand, by a petition signed by 800 people in Rockaway Beach, New York, passed around by my mother in the Irish bars, led by Monsignor God Bless You, I have been asked to return," Al declared. "Hank Raymonds and Rick Majerus tried to rip it up, but I said I'd do it. I will put back on the 'Lucky Suit'—the one I wore until we got the bid—and we'll have at it."

As I scribbled furiously, I couldn't help but chuckle. Would he never run out of those $75 lines?

But don't you feel bad, I asked him, about saying one thing and then doing another?

"Seeing that this is my last hurrah, and that we're in the area of St. Patrick's Day, I feel certain the Lord will hold me in the hollow of his hand, that the wind will be at my back and we'll be okay," Al replied confidently.

He paused, then lowered his voice for effect.

"Bernard Toone is searching for that petition right now," he told me, in mock confidential tones. "He wants to burn it. But I've got it hid." Al paused a second, and laughed. "I can see all the letters to the editor right now if we blow the game big," he added.

"But Al," I asked, pointedly. "Why did you make such a statement, and then renege?"

"Because I am emotionally unstable," he said simply.

I couldn't help but start laughing now. That was a $100 line! I continued chuckling as Al continued to elaborate. "Some of my other famous quotes have been: Television is only a fad. Mickey Rooney will be a bachelor. And Kareem Abul-Jabbar will be a jockey. I noticed it when he was in grade school, by looking at the size of his feet."

Was he angry at all that the NCAA had sent him out of his "home" Mideast Region? I reminded him that, in 1970, that was enough of an affront that he chose to go to the NIT instead. After which, Al reminded me that this was not 1970. "This year, I would have played in East Taiwan with reject sandals on," he said.

"I'm just happy for my family. And I'd like to thank God."

Chapter 7

The Slap, the Shot...and the Golden Ring

What I didn't realize at the time was that at some time during the six-day interval between Marquette's clinching an NCAA bid and the Warriors' first tournament game against Cincinnati in Omaha, Nebraska, the ongoing (and always simmering) Al-Bernard relationship had boiled over once again. This time it resulted in Bernard (for a few days at least) being kicked off the team...and almost sent home.

The problem, as I was told, was that Bernard didn't think he had to go to class. And after he missed a mid-semester test, Al warned him that he'd better start showing up or else. Given his status, Al explained to him, professors were usually more than lenient when it came to grades—as long as the athlete made an honest effort to attend the class and learn.

For a while, it seemed as though Bernard had gotten the word. And then Al found out he had started skipping once again.

This time, he laid down the law. "You miss one more class," he told Bernard, "and I'll get another player just like you. You'll be gone."

Again, no problems...for a while. And then, when Al heard Bernard had missed another test...well, it was just too much.

The next day, when Bernard walked into practice, Al was all over him immediately. "You're done!" he screamed. "You're outta here!"

"My grandmother died!" Bernard shouted back.

"And that's the last time she'll die!" Al retorted, after which he hauled Bernard off the court for a private conversation.

What I was told later was that, after that incident, Al actually called Bernard's mother and told her, "Mrs. Toone, I am sending your son home. He has the attention span of a three-year-old, and I cannot handle him. He is driving me insane!"

Hank and Rick, of course, felt if Marquette was going to go anywhere in the tournament, they had to have Bernard. From what I was told, Bernard was kept under wraps and out of sight for a couple of days, until they had convinced Al to keep him on. It was only then that he magically reappeared at practice.

Whether this is true or not, I can't say for sure. It's been 24 years, remember. I would like to think that I couldn't have missed Bernard in practice for two days running, and not asked about it. But then, maybe I did and got some answer from Hank, or Rick, or Kevin, like "He's studying for an exam" or something. To this day, I really can't remember. But I do know I was told later by *someone* about Al's call to Bernard's mother and his being "hid out" while Hank and Rick worked to change Al's mind. And I do know the shouting match related above did occur. For whatever reason, the fact is the bad feelings between Al and Bernard escalated a lot during that in-between week…and then exploded during the Warriors' first postseason tournament game against Cincinnati on March 12.

Al's near-fight with Bernard at halftime of the Cincinnati game in Omaha, Nebraska, is one of those sports incidents—like Babe Ruth calling his shot during the World Series at Wrigley Field—that has become the stuff of legend over the years. Why it happened, how it happened, is today still the subject of controversy. Everyone who was there seems to have a different version of the story. But one thing is certain. When Al slapped Bernard, he not only shook his team out of the lethargy of the poor game they had been playing, but instilled a spark in all of them—including Bernard—that caused them to rise to levels they (and Al) previously hadn't imagined and become a championship team.

"Sometimes I wonder, 'How did it happen?'" Al recalled, 10 years later, when we did a story for the *Journal* commemorating Marquette's run to the title. "I had seven or eight better teams than that. One reason, I think, was the fight at halftime with Bernard during the Cincinnati game, the first game of the tourney. I hit him, and the whole room ignited to break us apart, and for some reason, right there, was a championship wristwatch. We came out the second half…We had the Big Mo, and the next thing I knew I was crying [in Atlanta] where Sherman burned the city down."

What really happened?

Well, first off, Cincinnati looked to be a very, *very* tough opponent. Gale Catlett's troops had beaten Marquette the last three times they had played, including a 63-62 defeat at Cincinnati earlier in the season. "Look at it any way you want," Al told me, "and there's not a dime's worth of difference between us."

Personally, I was not so sure. Yes, the Bearcats' 25-4 record was better than Marquette's 20-7 mark. But Marquette had played well on the road all through the season, whereas *all* of Cincinnati's losses were away from home. Outside the friendly confines of Riverfront Coliseum (where they were undefeated), they definitely were not the same team.

Al, of course, was in his "Russian Roulette" mode with reporters, when they asked about how he felt going into the game, which could either be his last bow or the start of his last run at an NCAA title. He likened it to a high-stakes poker game, where you played like there was no tomorrow.

"It's where you shoot the works," Al told me, the day before the game. "It's the last hand of the night. You've been playing until one in the morning, and now you're going for the pot. You don't save anything, and you don't look back."

You don't save anything, and you don't look back.

Given Al's frame of mind, what happened the following afternoon against Cincinnati should not have been surprising.

Al got help from two more leprechauns in that game. The first came after Marquette had out-shot and out-rebounded Cincinnati the first half, but because of nine turnovers, went into the locker room at intermission trailing by three, 31-28. Al was particularly angry with Bernard, who missed a crucial one-and-one opportunity late in the first half that could have given Marquette the lead, and then, as time was winding down, threw up a wild baseline shot that actually went over the basket.

Furious, Al pulled Toone from the game, and as Toone passed him, screamed, "Another f—-ing shot like that, and I'll cut off your hand!" After which, as Bernard flopped down in his chair, he minced no words telling (Bo, as I recall) that he'd had enough of that "motherf—-er." Which Al heard.

The horn sounded, and into the locker room we went. No sooner had I got through the door than Al stormed in and grabbed Bernard, who was standing not two feet away. Furious, he shoved him against the wall and stuck a finger in his face. "Don't ever call me that again!" Al screamed. "You ever call me that again, and I'll kill you!" He then slapped Bernard hard across the face, and the two squared off.

At that point, Butch Lee, Bob Weingart, Hank, Rick, and some of the other players all stepped in between, and Rick physically pulled Bernard out into the hall, where he tried to calm him down. Like many of the others in the room, I was stunned.

Looking back now, I realize that incident could well have been the end of Al McGuire's final run. His angry slap at Bernard could have ripped the heart out of his struggling team, triggering a wave of resentment and disappointment so strong that they simply folded up their tents the second half. But for some miraculous reason, it didn't happen. In fact, just the opposite occurred. What could have been a season-ending negative turned out to be an inspiring positive. Instead of being emotionally ripe for the picking, Al's players came out in the second half almost galvanized and outscored Cincinnati by 18 points to win in a runaway.

Why? Because once again, Al was charmed. Yes, he had to do what he did to maintain his self-respect and, I'm sure he felt, to maintain the respect of the other players as well. When push came to shove, when the street-smart kid had his back pushed to the wall, he did what his whole life had taught him to do: Push back. Don't save anything, and don't look back. (Plus which, I had no doubt, those leprechauns on his shoulder were on the job as well.)

In the second half, Al got one more bit of luck when he needed it, when with 8:47 remaining and Cincy leading by one, Whitehead was fouled underneath by Cincinnati's Bob Miller as he made a dunk shot. Initially, the officials signaled the basket did not count and that Whitehead would get two free throws. But since the play had occurred on Marquette's end of the floor, Al was able to intercept them and do some fast talking, arguing that the basket should count on that type of play and Whitehead should get one foul shot.

Like I said, the leprechauns were in Al's corner once again. Before Catlett, who had the misfortune to be at the other end of the court, could get to the scene and get his two cents' worth in, Al had convinced the officials to reverse their call. Whitehead's basket counted, and he made the free throw, giving Marquette a two-point lead.

"That was a big call," Bo told me after the game. "That particular play got us going. I think Coach pressed the refs into making that call. And that got us rolling. He pressured them into it, and that turned the game around."

At that point, Cincinnati folded. Ignited by two baskets by Bo, Marquette ran off 10 straight points to put things out of reach with 3:37 left, while MU fans in the audience, anticipating the NCAA's next round in Oklahoma City, began chanting, "Oklahoma, here we come!"

After the game, Al was in prime form as he held court with the press, giving credit for the win to his "Lucky Suit"—that black three-piece he had worn on the Warriors' final road swing until they secured an NCAA bid. "There is no way they could defense my lucky suit," he gloated. "They tried to steal it, but we got it back. It's not lucky at home, but it is on the road. It's made of traveling threads."

What Al was referring to was the loss of his suit bag during the Minneapolis stop of our flight to Omaha two days before.

"The first thing I asked was if Catlett had been on that plane," McGuire recounted. "But then I asked the airlines guy to trace the suit. I told him I needed it before game time today. He said he'd be willing to buy me a tie and a shirt if I'd settle. I said, 'That suit is worth $140,000 to Marquette University, and if you don't want to get sued, find it.'

"So they traced it and got it here this morning. And I knew everything would be okay. You know, I wore that suit through four victories on the road, and the first half of the Michigan game, until we found out we had a bid. And then today. So now the suit has a record of 5 1/2 to 1/2. Like I said, once it showed up, nobody could stop us."

More significant, I felt, was Bernard's play the second half. While he only scored one basket, he did play solid defense, grabbing four rebounds and stealing the ball three times. Most important, not once did he commit a turnover or take an unauthorized "Hail Mary" shot, or even a bad-percentage shot. It made me wonder what might have been, if Al, rather than issuing verbal slaps in the face all through the season, had given Bernard the real thing early on.

The "monster" Al dreaded most came back to haunt him (of all days) on St. Patrick's Day, March 17, when Marquette squared off against Jack Hartman's sharpshooting, strong-rebounding Kansas State club in the Midwest Region semifinals in Oklahoma City. That was the day Al came within a hair of being his own worst enemy at tournament time for the third time in four seasons, and Marquette won the game with a truly incredible finish. After which, in one of the angriest diatribes I have ever heard, Al let loose the reins on his Irish temper and gave the NCAA a no-holds-barred piece of his mind.

The first half gave no hint of the "white-knuckler" the game eventually would become. The Wildcats controlled the tempo of the game from start to finish, shooting an astonishing 59 percent from the field and out-rebounding Marquette 23-17. Not once were the Warriors able to take the lead, and had Kansas State not committed 10 turnovers, the Wildcats would have taken far more than an eight-point, 36-28 lead into the locker room at intermission.

Al, as expected, was up and screaming before the bench, obviously upset at how things were going. But his frustration was directed mostly at his players, who shot a dismal 34 percent and committed eight turnovers of their own. For the most part, I felt, he was actually doing his best to keep out of trouble with the officials. Only once, late in the half, did he throw out the bait, after three straight fouls had been called against him.

"Hey!" he screamed, as Kansas State brought the ball back down the floor. "Did somebody talk to you before the game?"

I winced. Those were the kinds of words that usually got an official into what I liked to call "the T frame of mind" real quick. Luckily for Al, nothing happened. That time.

It was with 11:56 remaining in the game, with Marquette still trailing by eight, 52-44, that disaster struck when Al's fiery reputation did him in again. Yes, the Warriors were in trouble, but Kansas State had just turned over the ball twice, and Al—sensing that the Wildcats were faltering—jumped up off the bench and yelled to Bo and Butch as they ran past that it was time to go for the jugular.

"They're choking!" Al screamed, repeatedly placing his hand to his throat. "They're choking!"

Unfortunately, referee Frank Buckiewicz was right behind Butch—and no sooner did Al utter those words than he slapped him with a technical foul. The ironic part was that Buckiewiscz wasn't even looking at Al when he shouted the words to Bo and Butch. But he did *hear* them. And given Al's reputation as a ref baiter, there's no doubt his first thought was that Al was referring to him.

Flabbergasted, Al walked over to Buckiewiscz and tried to explain, at which point the referee walked away. Next, he turned towards Hartman, who listened as he angrily pleaded his case, and then (from one coach to another, I guess) he gave Al a sympathetic pat on the shoulder. As Al returned to the huddle, I sat in shocked disbelief. "Why!" I scribbled in my play-by-play notebook. "Tech on Al...MU had the ball!" I was incredulous. Could anyone really believe Al would provoke an official in that situation—trailing by eight with 12 to go, the Wildcats suddenly panicking, and with *his* team in a position to cut the lead to six and really apply the pressure? It just didn't make sense.

When Kansas State's Curtis Redding made the two foul shots off Al's technical, it looked like a "Dunkirk" was in the making. For not only did the Wildcats now have a 10-point lead, they also had possession of the ball and were in a position to take control for good.

Instead, however, Al's troops showed their mettle once again. Led by Bo, who pumped in five points, Marquette used the unfair foul on Al as a launching pad, charging back to outscore Kansas State 14-4 and tie the game at 58 with 4:16 remaining. After that, it was a "white-knuckler" to the finish, with the teams exchanging baskets, and the lead, until Butch's jump shot with 18 seconds left gave Marquette a three-point lead that should have been enough for the win.

Incredibly, it wasn't. With 10 seconds remaining, Bo fouled Wildcat forward Darryl Winston on a rebound shot, which sailed through the cords. Now, it seemed, all was up for grabs again, since if Winston made his free throw, the game would be tied and perhaps go into overtime.

Instead, Al and his troops got a fantastic break, when the officials ruled "no basket" and instead awarded Winston two free throws—which meant he could not tie the game. Winston made both shots to close to 67-66, but all Marquette had to do was hold the ball for 10 vital seconds. At that point, I thought it was over. Not quite.

For whatever reason, Butch (of all people) suddenly disobeyed orders, letting fly a jump shot that missed, giving Kansas State possession off the rebound and a chance for a final shot with two seconds on the clock. Luckily, Bo was on the spot again, intercepting guard Scott Langton at midcourt and pressuring him enough so that he couldn't get a shot off before the horn had sounded.

I heaved a sigh. The dream was still alive. Al had squeaked through, but barely, 67-66. As I headed for the postgame press conference, my mind was really a jumble. What a game I had seen! A technical foul that shouldn't have been. A basket that turned out not to be a basket. A final shot that shouldn't have been taken. All that, and still, somehow, Al and his troops had survived. For the first time, the word "inevitable" and the phrase "meant to be" entered my mind.

What I didn't know, as I took my seat with the other reporters, was that the best show of the day was yet to come.

Al gave no hint of what was about to happen as he walked calmly into the interview room, followed by Butch and Bo, who took chairs behind him on a small stage. At that point, Al asked if he could talk on his own first, rather than answering questions—after which he suddenly went ballistic, unleashing what later became known as his "St. Patrick's Day Diatribe"—a rambling, nonstop, 10-minute rip of the NCAA that made headlines across the nation.

"I have a tremendous hang-up on that technical foul!" he shouted. "Either I'm sicko or someone else is sicko! I put my hand up to my neck and yelled at my players that the other team is choking and I get slapped with a technical! Now I've been through this bullshit too many times with the NCAA!

"Hey, I coach exactly the same no matter where the hell I am! And every time I come to the NCAA, they keep calling technicals on me! And they're absolutely wrong! And I'm not a crybaby! I kept quiet for the last 10 years! Now either they're taking these officials and brainwashing them before they have my games…"

At this point, I happened to glance up at Bo and Butch, who were seated on the stage behind Al. Butch was petrified. Again and again, he cast a frightened glance over at Bo, as if asking, "Yeah, what the hell is going on here?" To which Bo, who had been through things like this before, just rolled his eyes and shot Butch back a baleful look to "just hang in there, baby."

Meanwhile, Al continued his diatribe, his voice at a fever pitch. "This has nothing to do with Kansas State!" he railed. "Kansas State should have beaten us! We were fortunate to win! We were lucky—that's all! Kansas State outplayed us, they were a lot better prepared than we were, and they should have won the game. It just so happens we had a lot of time left, and we caught them, and we ended up getting a point or two ahead.

"The thing is, I've been quiet about this for years. I've been through this from Athens, Georgia, with Ohio State, with Indiana, with them all. What the hell's going on?! Guy calls a technical foul on me when I'm talking to the team! And the only way a guy can do it is because, subconsciously, he's been told!! And then he won't even come over and tell me!! All I wanted to tell the guy was, 'Hey, I'm talking to the guys, not to you.' Now either everybody's trying to get to Atlanta the wrong way, or let the teams get to Atlanta.

"Now if the NCAA wants equal time, or the officials, I'm 25 years in the business! *Twenty-five years!!* And I've gotta go through that crap again!! And I'm not lying! Take any player who follows me here. I've never said anything about officials. Under no conditions, anywhere, anytime. Now there's too much smoke in back rooms, there's too much whispering, there's too much something going on! We're not that good of a ball club, I admit that! But to call that technical foul, at that time of the game, is a mortal sin!! And it's wrong!! And I'm not a psycho!! The guy makes a call like that! I got one technical foul all year on me!

"Don't you think our Notre Dame and Michigan games, and Creighton and Florida, and all these games are big games? We got three times as many people at the gosh-darned games! I don't do anything different here than I do when I'm at home or on the road. We have big rivalries with the University of Wisconsin and Minnesota, and Northwestern. What happens when I come to the NCAA?!!! What are they trying to prove?!!!

"Now it doesn't make any difference to me; I'm on my way. But I don't want to blow it for these guys! Now I would not say a word here, guys, if we lost. There's no way I could say a word. But I'm just to a point where…Why do you think I made the statement last year?!! Why?!! I'm not an irrational person! I'm not an irresponsible person! But someone has to talk to somebody! What the hell, a man spends 25 years of his life in a profession, and every time he comes to something like this, he has to look like an idiot?!! Who wants to look like an idiot out there?!!

"Now, I'm not looking for any breaks tomorrow night or any night. I never wanted a break from any official. I can't even tell you these guys' names, or any of their names. Some of the guys in the Midwest I can, that I have a lot. But I have never rated an official in my life! I have never blackballed an official in my life! And I have never had a preference list in my life! In 13 years, I've never spoke to the commissioner's office! In 13 years! And I gotta come up here with the NCAA pulling this crap! And that's what it is! Now the guy is a competent official. He wouldn't be here if he wasn't competent. But someone brainwashed him, and they've been brainwashed before!

"And that's the reason I said I wouldn't coach any more in the NCAA. It's, it's been a zoo. Now I'll go by any rules, and I should have gotten it off my chest seven years ago and left seven, nine years ago. It has nothing to do with the official. I'm talking about the subconscious of an official being reached! In some smoke-filled rooms! Somewhere they're prepping them! No official calls a technical foul like that on a guy!

The official had his back to me running down the court! I'm yelling to the guys on my team! I'm saying, 'Hey, they're choking!' And he turns around he blows a technical, and then he won't talk to me!

"So, peace. I'm sorry and so on. I'm not, but I'm glad I got it off my chest. Maybe I hurt some people, I'm sorry. But it's about time some people started realizing that I'm not a bum in a bowery, or a wino in a hallway, or a pimp on a corner! I know my profession! I know it well! And I've worked at it hard! All my life, I've worked at it hard!

"So, peace. Now you should talk to the guys. They won the game. They saved me from not being able to say this. Butch should not have taken that last shot. I gave him hell for taking the last shot. Remember, guys, I do not accept anything in victory that I won't accept in defeat. Butch had no right taking that last shot. The clock was more important. And that was it."

Later, as we were pulling away on the bus, Al turned to me and quietly asked, "Well, Rog, what'd you think?"

"I think you had to tell 'em how you felt, Coach," I replied. I really didn't know what else to say. I had never seen Al that angry before. But we both knew he had barely missed that final bullet this time around. "I do think the call was totally wrong," I added. "Like you said, the guy was looking."

Al nodded. "Yeah. Well, maybe they'll quit looking for a while now," he replied. "Give the kids a break, at least."

That, I knew, was why Al did it. Why he decided to unload like that in public. Given the circumstances, and his total frustration, I think he felt his anger was the only weapon he had left, if he was to somehow nullify the officials' negative feelings toward him. One thing was certain. Buckiewiscz's blatantly prejudiced call had given Al all the soapbox he needed. So what if he came off looking the fool? If it bought his team some time, it was worth it. Three more games, if things worked out right.

I glanced over at Al sitting there next to me, his head back on the seat, eyes closed. Lost in his thoughts. Was he content, I wondered? Regretful? There was no way I could tell. But of one thing I felt certain: that Al had played his hand correctly by going for the zebra's jugular. By doing so, he had gained not just headlines, but an important edge. He had thrown the pressure back on the officials. Exposed them to some of his own brand of "brainwashing" that he hoped would make them take pause, rather than anticipate, in future games. "You're arguing for the next call, not the one you lost," I'd heard him say so many times.

That was why Al had gone ballistic. To hopefully get an edge the next time around. As we rolled along in the darkness, past endless rows of streetlights, the words he had uttered just before the Cincinnati game played back to me again: *"You don't save anything, and you don't look back."*

My earlier question to myself was answered. Al had no regrets.

The NCAA's reaction to Al's postgame diatribe was as expected. Tom Jernstedt, assistant executive director of the NCAA, told reporters in Kansas City that Al was "totally in error" when he claimed the NCAA had brainwashed officials against him and added, "Al has been a credit to the game of basketball, and it's hard to believe he would say something like that. I find it incredible, and I think the basketball committee would resent the remark he made."

Remark? Al's 10-minute tirade had been a remark? Holy shit! It was like saying Noah's flood had been a passing shower. Or that the San Francisco earthquake had been a harmless tremor. Or that World War II had been a misunderstanding. When I first read Jernstedt's remarks, I thought, "What planet is this guy living on?" On second thought, however, I realized what Jernstedt was doing. He was downplaying the whole thing. The last thing he—or the NCAA—wanted in the middle of their "March Madness" showcase was to become involved in any type of full-blown controversy involving the integrity of their officiating. A "no comment" would have been as much as an admission of guilt. Better instead to take the surprised and hurt role, like the father who has been insulted by his tempestuous, if off-the-wall, son.

I smiled to myself. Al had called their bluff...*and won!* From that moment on, I felt confident that any official who worked Marquette's games would think twice before calling a cheap technical on Al. Overnight, he had turned the tables and ceased to be an easy target. What the NCAA was saying, between the lines, to its officials was: No matter what this guy's reputation is, from now on you walk the straight and narrow. Do your job, but don't give him anything he can hang us on. Which was exactly what I believe Al wanted in the first place.

During Marquette's final "Run for the Roses" on the road, when things suddenly started to sparkle and the magic began taking effect, Al had hinted to me a couple of times that reaching the Final Four was, in fact, a realistic possibility. The key, he said, was Bernard. "You know, Rog," he told me, "if we ever get anything out of Bernard, we're a dynamite club. Dynamite. But how the hell do I light his fuse?"

Against Wake Forest in the Midwest Regional final, Al finally got the job done—though I never exactly learned how. A few hours before the game, he and Bernard had a sit-down, and neither one of them would ever tell me what was said. But whatever Al told his proverbial problem child paid off big-time that afternoon—when Bernard played the first great game of his college career to personally guarantee Al a final trip to the Final Four in Atlanta.

Coming off the bench with a minute gone in the second half, Bernard simply exploded. Never before had I seen him play like that or give any indication of the true, pure talent he possessed. To say he took his game a step up is an understatement—he took a whole flight. Quick as a cat, he lofted 14-, 16- and 18-footers that were so true they never touched the rim as they went through. Leaping and battling for position, he grabbed rebounds, created foul situations, and sank six for six from the foul line as calmly and methodically as a butcher cuts meat.

When Bernard walked onto the floor, Marquette was trailing by three. What he did was ignite a four-minute, 14-2 charge that put Marquette in command, 54-45, and all but officially decided who was going to Atlanta. Of those crucial 14 points, Bernard accounted for nine. He scored 16 of his 18 points that second half, but there is one basket I still remember best. With Marquette leading, 68-64, and Al having sent the Warriors into their delay pattern, the 6'9" Bernard suddenly saw daylight and charged for the basket—seeing that only 6'2" guard Frank Johnson was in his way. Soaring like a gull on a sea breeze, Bernard juggled the ball in midair, then sank a herky-jerky shot that brought the crowd to its feet. Overmatched, Johnson fouled Bernard when he tried to stop him, and with 1:23 remaining, Bernard sank the foul shot that made the score 71-64, finishing Wake Forest for good.

With 13 seconds left, the celebration started. Bo and Butch and the other starters, who had come out seconds earlier, stood hugging each other on the sidelines. Marquette fans, knowing it was over, rushed down from their seats to the Marquette bench, reaching out to shake Al's hand. The horn sounded; it was official.

Al was going to the Final Four again!

Was I happy? You bet! Happy for Al, of course, that his merry-go-round hadn't stopped just yet and that he had one last shot at the golden ring. And for the players, because I had watched them claw their way back—out of a black pit that had been DePaul, Detroit, and Wichita State—and knew how much this had to mean to them. And selfishly, of course, for me. Because as any reporter will tell you, the bigger the event, the better the story, the more you like it. No, make that love it. Relish it. That's the demon that drives us hardy denizens of the press. Lord knows, the profession "don't pay squat." But if you are fortunate enough to have the opportunity to cover *the story*—and you do it well—then the respect that comes your way afterwards is the biggest reward of all.

That's what Al and his team had given me that Saturday afternoon in Oklahoma City—a chance to attend a party I'd never been to before: the NCAA Final Four.

The only problem I had after the Wake Forest game was sending my story back to the *Journal* in Milwaukee. We had these quirky machines back then, Tel-e-rams they were called. Heavy, bulky, blue metal things that didn't quite fit under your seat on an airplane and were touchy and temperamental, to say the least. (The great little Radio Shack Tandy computer, durable, reliable, and the size of a library book, was still a year or two away.)

So there I was, back at my motel room, two hours after the game, story and sidebar finished and ready for an evening on the town. Except that my story wouldn't send. Again and again, I tried, with no success. Finally, I called the sports department and got my editor on the line.

Once I had told him my problem, he thought a minute, then asked, "Are you close to any lamps or electrical outlets?" I told him yes. "Then go to the bathroom," he said, "get a glass of water and sprinkle drops of water around the table where you're writing."

If it hadn't been midafternoon, I would have swore Billy Red was speaking from Goolsby's, the *Journal* sports department's late-night haunt, with his fifth or sixth beer in hand. But I did what he said, then tried again—and whoosh! The story, sidebar, box score, everything sailed off into the computer nether-world just like it was supposed to do. Up came the words on the screen I loved to see: Transmission Completed. Once Dwyre confirmed he had it all, I couldn't help but ask, "How in hell did you know to do that?"

"A guy told me, that's all," he replied. "For some reason, if you're too close to a lamp or electric outlet, static electricity builds up and makes a magnetic field around your machine. The water destroys the magnetic field. It happened to me, the last time I was in Los Angeles."

Go figure, I thought. As I packed up the Tel-e-ram, I cursed it heartily in my best newspaperman's vernacular as the piece of crap it was.

What I didn't know then was that the worst was yet to come, that the damned machine would come back to haunt me one more time—and at the worst possible moment imaginable.

From the time we flew into Atlanta on Thursday night, until game time against North Carolina-Charlotte in the NCAA semifinal game at 1:15 p.m. on Saturday, March 26, Al surprised us all by keeping his team in hiding. The players' lone public appearance was at their regularly scheduled practice in the Omni on Friday afternoon. So serious was Al about this that he even kept Hank, who normally handled all the travel details, in the dark about where the team was staying. At the time we flew out, Hank had simply been told to have a bus ready for the team at the airport in Atlanta—destination unknown.

Why the cloak and dagger? Because Al still had not forgotten 1974, when he lost to North Carolina State in the NCAA finals. He still felt, he told me, that all the hoopla created by the fans and friends of the players that first time around was just too much of a distraction.

"It was the first time, and at that time I did not understand the scope of the Final Four," Al explained, when we talked the day before our flight down. "Atlanta is going to be like a tidal wave that engulfs you, just like Greensboro was then. It's not a one-column headline in a newspaper someplace, or merely your name on the marquee. It's a whole city going bananas, and there is no release valve for the players.

"It's not an intentional thing on the part of the fans. They just don't realize, because they're having a good time, when it's past a certain hour. And the first game is an afternoon game, which means the pregame meal is at 9 a.m., and so the guys should be in bed by 11 the night before.

"What happens is that the headquarters [hotel] becomes a rotunda of social functions. And the lobbies become a scalper's heaven. The players' rooms become flophouses for the students going down who can't afford the numbers they're charging for the rooms. Hey, the people don't mean no harm. But these guys are young, and you don't win the NCAA by staying up all night partying."

Al told me he planned to follow the same regimen as what he laid out for the players. Except for scheduled NCAA tournament practices and functions, he planned to be gone, out of touch, out of mind. "I'll get a motorbike and go off somewheres," he said. "That's my release valve.

Nobody else can fit on there with me, and if they do, they don't have a helmet. So I think I'm safe."

When Al told me all this, of course, I didn't believe him. How could the ultimate showman stay away from the biggest show in the world? How could he not be center stage and enjoy the limelight? I just didn't think Al could do it. But he did. With the exception of one dinner I had with him and Pat and a few other close friends on Friday night, I flat-out didn't see the guy that whole weekend, except at press conferences and on the court. And I couldn't fault that. For although I felt we were friends, I realized that I was a reporter, too, and I knew Al wouldn't make any exceptions for me to his rule. He wanted his space, and he made sure he got it.

The shot. That's what I'll always remember about Marquette's thrilling 51-49 squeaker over North Carolina-Charlotte in their NCAA semifinal game that Saturday afternoon at the Omni in Atlanta. *The shot.* That final, agonizing, desperate layup that center Jerome Whitehead threw up just as the clock ran out—and how it put Al into the NCAA finals for the second time in four years. Just one game away from the championship I knew he wanted so badly.

The shot. To this day, I can still see it, how the ball bobbled and hung on the rim for what seemed an eternity, before it finally fell through the net, producing a crowd roar so deafening that the final horn could not be heard.

A white-knuckler? This was it. The white-knuckler of all white-knucklers, in fact. A game that was up for grabs right down to the final second…and then even after, when coaches and players from both teams, not to mention media and fans alike, converged on the scorer's table where the officials were trying—amidst the uproar—to determine whether Jerome's miraculous shot would count or not.

The game didn't start out that way. Far from it. Marquette, thanks to the hot shooting of Jerome and Butch, got out of the gate fast and raced to a 14-point, 23-9 lead with just 6:51 to go before intermission. At that point, I was already thinking Al was home free. But then, to my surprise, Al almost did himself in, sending his team into a delay pattern that did nothing more than kill their momentum and allow Charlotte to regroup and reel off a 13-2 spurt that cut Marquette's lead to 25-22 at halftime.

As Al and the players walked off the floor, I was incredulous. It was the first time I had ever seen Al really hobble his own team with his defensive philosophy. There they were, rolling along, and Jerome playing the game of his life with 10 points and 10 rebounds, and Al had put the skids to them…in the first half! Friendship or no, it was something I knew I would have to ask him about, once this game was over.

"Unfortunately," I scribbled in my play-by-play notebook, "all coaches feel obligated to coach." And then, below it, "McGuire mistake! The delay."

Marquette never did get its head of steam back in the second half, and with 14:22 remaining, things looked grim when Bo was called for his fourth foul and Charlotte edged out to a 35-30 lead. But Jerome (who was coming off two bad games) was on a mission that day, thanks to a pep talk from his father, the Rev. John Whitehead, just before he left for Atlanta, and was not to be denied. Scoring six more points, he ignited a 14-4 spurt that put Marquette up 44-39 with 5:24 left. Unfortunately, three MU turnovers let Charlotte regain the lead by three, 47-44, with 1:41 on the clock.

I have to admit, I thought it was over then. Al's team, frankly, had just not been the same since he handcuffed their offense and ordered them into the delay in the first half. If anything, now, they seemed sluggish and ready to be beaten. But then lightning struck. Butch, who had scored only seven points all day, suddenly sank two long jump shots, after which Gary Rosenberger stole the ball, raced downcourt, and drew a foul when he attempted to try a layup. Rosey missed his first free throw, but made the second, and it was 49-47 Marquette with just 10 seconds on the clock, at which point Charlotte coach Lee Rose called time out.

Al was in his element now. He was back on the streets again, his back to the wall, chin out and pride on the line, playing to the moment…and glad that he was the underdog besides. "When my competitive juices are flowing," he told me later, "I prefer you have Napoleon on your side, because we're going to beat you. When I get in the gutter, I don't care if you're the Amboy Dukes or the Outlaws. My gang's going to win. Or we'll leave a part of ourselves there. It's foolish, I suppose, but that's why a person who can't spell or read can have these moments. It's their instinct."

Even today, I can still see Al in that huddle, holding his hands in the shape of a T as he repeatedly yelled instructions to his players, one by one. "If we get the ball, call time out!" he kept telling them. "Time out, if we get the ball!" Which, as things turned out, is just what happened, when Charlotte's star, "Cornbread" Maxwell, made a jump shot to tie things at 49 with three seconds remaining. As ordered, Al's troops called time out—setting the stage for Al's big gamble and Jerome's unforgettable shot.

This time, while the Warriors huddled, Al paced to the far end of the court, where Marquette would get the ball out of bounds, all the time eyeing the ceiling above, then walked back and began shouting his instructions. "What I wanted to see was the height of the clock," Al explained later, referring to the Omni's huge scoreboard clock that hung above center court. "Because of a long pass, I didn't want the ball to hit the overhang. Butch was to throw the ball to between where Bo and Jerome were standing. The clock doesn't start until it [the ball] hits the man's hands."

From my seat on press row, I could sense what was coming—a long, full-court pass by Butch, followed by a last-second shot by whoever caught it…if indeed anyone caught it at all. Otherwise, it was overtime, and with Bo having four fouls…well, who knew? Most certainly, it was a long shot, I thought, as I waited for the final act to play out. But it was all Al had, and he had done his best to better his odds once the dice were rolled.

And then, in a matter of seconds, it was all over so quickly. With all his strength, Butch threw an arcing, line-drive pass downcourt to where Bo, Maxwell, and Jerome were standing…right in front of the basket. Bo lunged, but the ball sailed past him, and Maxwell grabbed it—but couldn't hold on. In a heartbeat, Jerome picked it up off the bounce, then, leaping high, sent it on its way. Caroming off the backboard, the ball seemed to hang forever on the lip of the rim, and then fell through as the horn sounded.

But was the basket good? For another agonizing 60 seconds, nobody knew. Pandemonium erupted around the scorer's table, as both Al and Lee Rose tried to plead their case, while hundreds of others—assistant coaches, players, media and even fans—rushed up either to join the argument or just to find out what was going on. And in the middle of it all was the diminutive official Paul Galvan, who—while getting an earful from every corner—was trying to determine just what had happened.

Jerome, perhaps because of his quiet nature, kept his distance from the fray. After seeing the ball go through the hoop, he'd first jumped up and down with glee, but then stood like a stone a few feet away from where he'd taken the shot when he realized his basket might not have come in time.

For a few seconds, in fact, he really thought it hadn't.

"I knew it went in, but I didn't know if they'd count it or not," he told me after. "I didn't hear the buzzer, but I knew it had gone off, because everybody came running on the floor. I looked up at the clock and it still said 49-49. I thought, 'If it's good, it should be 51-49.'"

As you would expect, Al was in the middle of the maelstrom around the scorer's table, arguing in his best street-smart vernacular that Jerome's shot was good. "After Jerome's shot, it was an alley," Al told me later. "It was salty, tugboat language. I remember Coach Rose trying to speak the way presidents of universities speak, and I kept slicing and going on like a barracuda."

Amidst it all, Galvan kept his cool. Ordering everybody to back away, he calmly he asked timer Larry Carter: "Where was the ball when the buzzer went off?" Carter paused, then answered, "The ball was in the basket." Galvan asked him to think about it again, and then asked Carter the same question. Again Carter gave him the same answer. That was it! The scoreboard flashed the decision, the Marquette section exploded in cheers, and Al, who had then raced back out on the floor, began hugging and dancing with Butch Lee. "The nicest motion I ever saw in my life," Al said, "was when Paul Galvan, the ref, asked the timer, who said the ball was out of J's hand, and then he turned around and gave the dunk sign."

There was one other question about Jerome's incredible basket that Al argued long and hard to avoid in those hectic seconds after the horn. To Al, it appeared that, after Jerome had tossed up his layup, his hand had been in the cylinder of the basket—which would have been an automatic offensive goaltending call, nullifying the shot. That was why he argued so vehemently about the time factor—to keep everyone's mind off anything else.

"I argued so hard about the clock because I didn't want them to get around to Jerome's hand being in the cylinder," Al admitted.

The problem was, announcers Curt Gowdy and Billy Packer had the luxury of watching the game film over and over—*in slow motion*—and so asked Al about it in their pre-championship game interview that was taped the following day. The slow-motion replay showed that it was close—far too close, Packer opined, for any official to make the call. After which, with that load off his shoulders, Al was off and rambling.

"I think the best thing," he said, "is if they would electrify the rim, and if a ballplayer puts his hand over the rim, that the rim would grab him and hold him until he turns blue. They could release him from the scorer's table, and then the ref knows if his hand went in."

At the end of Al's remarks, all three were smiling and chuckling. But in Al's eyes, as he stared into the camera, I also detected a huge sense of relief…and thankfulness.

Charmed? It was more than that, I felt. This time around, Al had truly been blessed.

I was surprised, and yet I wasn't, when Al's feud with the NCAA went right down to the wire on Sunday, when he showed up for the coaches' final press conference before the championship game at the Omni. Because when Al walked in, he not only found Coach Dean Smith on hand, but three of his players as well. And so, for almost half an hour, Al had to sit and stew, while Smith and his players soaked up tons of national publicity.

When it was finally Al's turn to speak, he made it plain that he was upset.

"It seems there's been some sort of breakdown in communications," Al said, pointedly, before a question could be asked. "We were not told that players were to be here, or we would have had Marquette players here.

"Now, I have a very competent sports information director, Kevin Byrne, and I'm sure, if he had been told, my players would have been here, too, instead of left sitting back at their hotel. So I don't know where the breakdown was, guys, but hey, don't let it happen again, okay?"

More fuel was added to the fire when the NCAA later issued a statement saying that Marquette's practice, like North Carolina's, would be closed to the press. Al, realizing that once again his players had been cut off from the press, protested, but the NCAA said he didn't have the right to open the workout. Al, quite naturally, figured the NCAA was just getting back at him for a statement he'd made earlier, blasting the NCAA for charging $14 a ticket for the final game, which Al felt was far too much for what was billed as "an amateur event."

Dave Cawood, tournament director for the NCAA, said it was Marquette's fault that they had no players on hand for the coaches' press conference. "I tried calling Kevin three times this morning and couldn't reach him," Cawood said. "That's what happens when the sports information director doesn't stay at the assigned hotel so we can get in touch with him."

Bingo. I knew immediately why this had all happened. The NCAA was miffed that Al had dared house his players anywhere else but the

NCAA's assigned hotel in Downtown Atlanta—which I knew Al had done to keep them out of the party atmosphere that prevailed there.

Knowing Al's ego, I was more than a little worried. What the NCAA had done—and very purposely, I felt—was throw Al one final affront that might just be enough to trigger his Hindenburg ego at the last minute…and affect his judgment in the heat of the championship game. It was a cheap trick, to be sure. But I had no doubt that was what had happened, that Cawood and his minions were doing their best to stir Al up—to reach *his* subconscious, since he had neutralized the officials with his diatribe after the Kansas State game in Oklahoma City. The NCAA's strategy was simple: Poke the lion, poke the lion. And hope he reacts, when he roams out under the lights on center stage.

Al knew better. He didn't take the bait. As he told me, when I asked him to comment on Cawood's remarks, "What the hell. I'm getting out. It's not worth making a case about." To me, it seemed, that last time I spoke with him before the championship game, he had his priorities straight. He was ready, he was primed. And he felt he had the team that could win it. He was not about to let the NCAA, or anybody else for that matter, affect his chances this final time around.

"Each game," Al said once, "is like pickup sticks. You hold 'em. You drop 'em, take some away. And every game forms a pattern."

For Al, the final game of his colorful and controversial career— played on a rainy, March Monday night at the Omni in Atlanta—most resembled an emotionally charged play in three distinct acts. Act One saw his team charge out of the box and race to a commanding 12-point lead over North Carolina at intermission. In Act Two, his team faltered and lost that lead, reeling before an inspired Tar Heels charge in the opening eight minutes. After which, in Act Three, Al bested Coach Dean Smith in a tense, nerve-tingling, 12-minute game of cat-and-mouse to finally win that prize that had eluded him for so long—the NCAA national championship.

Act One belonged to Butch. Showing all the quickness, savvy, and shooting accuracy that he possessed, Butch put on an offensive clinic, ripping the Tar Heels with jump shots, free throws, and incredible "shake and bake" drives to the basket. While that was going on, Bo and Jerome combined for 13 rebounds to effectively control the boards. When the horn sounded, it was 39-27, and as the teams were walking off the court, I was amazed.

Who'd have ever thought? I asked myself. God, can it be this easy? If things keep going this way, this'll be a runaway. For a scant second, as I started going over my play-by-play, I dared to hope that it might happen. Maybe it was the Charlotte heart stopper two nights before, I don't know. But the last thing I wanted was any more last-second finishes. All I wanted, I knew, was for Al to win. And the easier, the better.

The other reason I didn't want a last-second finish was because I had been designated the pool reporter for the Omni for the game. This dubious honor fell to me as the Marquette beat man, and to some other poor guy covering North Carolina as well. Our job, as soon as the horn sounded, was to immediately corner the head coaches, get two or three quotes, and give them to the Omni's PR person so that he could run them off and distribute them to the guys who were writing on deadline on press row.

The point was, as long as I had to do it, better after a rout than a "white-knuckler," when there was so much more to ask about and you might miss a great quote while you were doing somebody else's job. As a reporter, I never claimed I wasn't selfish. My job was to get the best story I could. And to that end, the only job I wanted to be doing, at game's end, was mine.

I did have one tense moment early in the first half. With 17:23 on the clock, NC's Walter Davis was called for a foul, but no free throws were awarded. Angrily, Al jumped to his feet...and kicked the scorer's table! My heart sank. Indiana, the year before, flashed into my mind. For a heartbeat, I waited for an official's whistle, for the dreaded T to be called. But for whatever reason, this time, nobody seemed to notice. And to my surprise, Al immediately retreated, a pained expression on his face and limping slightly, to his chair.

Good Lord, I thought. Now what'd he do? Break a toe or something? Marking it down in my notes, I couldn't help but chuckle. Later in the half, Al was up and walking before the bench again, not limping now, so I knew it was nothing serious. Still, I'd have to ask him about it later on.

The second half, North Carolina came out steaming thanks to freshman forward Mike O'Koren. In just three and a half minutes, O'Koren sank two corner jumpers and a pair of layups for eight points, as the Tar Heels outscored Marquette, 10-2, and pulled to within four, 41-37. Al, trying to stem the tide, called time out to settle things down, but to no avail. North Carolina, this time led by Davis, reeled off another 8-4 spurt to tie the score at 45.

At that point, I honestly thought it was over. That it was all about to slip from Al's grasp once again. The game, most certainly, was out of control. How much longer, I wondered, before he reverted to form—before the "monster" reappeared—drawing a technical in a desperate attempt to change the momentum, fire his players up, and shake up the pickup sticks once more? In my mind, it was no longer a question of if Al would explode, only when.

At which point, with 12 minutes remaining, Smith astounded me by playing what he thought was his ace in the hole to start Act Three.

Figuring Marquette was on the ropes and that his team had taken command, Smith ordered the Tar Heels into his fabled Four Corners offense—a delay offense designed to force opponents into a man-to-man defense, after which his quick troops, led by All-American guard Phil Ford—would break the game open with easy, one-on-one baskets designed to draw foul shots as well.

As things turned out, however, Smith's ace turned out to be a joker. It just didn't work, first because Al outfoxed Smith for the next three minutes, and then because Bo—at precisely the right moment—made a great play that turned everything Marquette's way again.

Because Marquette wasn't leading, they could only stay in their zone defense five seconds before they were issued a warning from the officials to initiate action (i.e., move out into a man-to-man). But Al (ever the Fox), used the rule to his advantage, ordering his players to move out into a fake man-to-man defense, then fall back into their zone again, until they got another five-second warning.

Again and again, the maneuvering went on. Stopping action to a standstill on the court, as the clock began to tick down...11 1/2 minutes, 11, 10 1/2, 10. On the sidelines, Smith stood, frowning and frustrated, seeing that Al's tactics were robbing his team of the easy baskets he had hoped for. More importantly, as Al knew, the Tar Heels' momentum was ticking away with the clock, while his players had a chance to rest.

"The clock, I felt, was my friend," he told me later. "They were odds-on favorites and their sweat was drying. They were losing momentum, even though nothing was being done. There was no scoring, but there was something happening. That two minutes was the key to the game. It was like taking a timeout, losing a contact lens, something to ice the other club."

On and on the game went, even to the point where boos began to filter down from the bleachers. The fans, it was clear, wanted some action. How much longer, I wondered, could this go on? At some point, somebody's got to crack.

With 9:43 left, North Carolina did, when Bruce Buckley, the Tar Heels' 6'9" forward, thought he saw daylight and broke for the basket to try a layup. But Bo was there and got a hand on it, giving Marquette not only possession, but the chance to run its own delay game. And what hadn't worked for North Carolina was a (I have to say it) *charm* for Al, when Jimmy Boylan raced in for a layup with 8:28 on the clock to give Marquette the lead, 47-45.

No sooner had the ball swished the net than Al was on his feet. He knew what was happening, that the tide had started to swing his way. The bottle of champagne, he sensed, had finally struck the Queen Mary's bow, and she was starting to turn around. As Boylan ran past, he grabbed him and slapped him on the back.

As Al continued to run down the clock, his troops staying just a basket ahead, two ironic sticks remained to be played in his Grande Finale, before the victory was finally his. The first was played by Jerome—by far the worst free throw shooter on the team—when he was purposely fouled by Buckley with 1:56 remaining. It was then the Big J got a bit of psychological help from Hank, who suddenly jumped up and called him back to the sidelines when he saw the other players weren't ready at the line.

"What do you want?" Jerome asked Hank, expecting some last-second bit of advice.

"I don't want anything," Hank replied, having accomplished what he wanted, that Jerome wouldn't have to stand out there and wait and think about things at the line.

The result? Jerome sank 'em both. And with less than two minutes to play, Marquette had a very big four-point lead.

Smith played the last stick when he ordered his team to foul quickly, in order to gain possession of the ball. O'Koren responded with four fouls in 43 seconds, the last three sending Boylan to the line once, and Bo twice—with Marquette in the bonus! In 26 seconds, the pair sank six straight foul shots, giving Marquette a six-point, 59-53 lead with just 1:02 remaining.

I can't tell you how fast my pulse was beating then. All I could think of was that it was happening...right there, before my eyes. A national championship. Yes, I thought. My God, yes! They're going to do it! Yes!

With 34 seconds left, Rosy stole the ball off Ford, raced downcourt and neatly passed to Butch for the layup. Now it was 63-55, and as I got up from my seat, to go take my place at courtside beside the state troopers, the Marquette section was suddenly up and cheering.

"We're No. 1! We're No. 1! We're No. 1!"

With 19 seconds to go, Boylan was fouled, and he sank them both. Now it was 65-55, and suddenly, out of nowhere, the crowd began a new chant, with 14 seconds remaining. "Al's Last Hurrah! Al's Last Hurrah! Al's Last Hurrah! Al's Last Hurrah!" On and on it echoed down across the floor, and that's when—standing off to the side, ready to follow him to the locker room—I saw Al's reaction. Unable to hold back any longer, Al began to cry.

"Never undress until you die," he'd always said, but he had finally reached a point where he could hold things in no longer, and at that moment, as I saw him wiping away the tears (with Hank hugging him as he cried, too), it really hit me how much it all meant to him, that gutsy dance-hall kid from Rockaway Beach who'd battled so hard all his life and who'd finally made it to the top. Who finally, after 13 years of trying, had plucked the biggest prize of all.

That, to me, was the defining moment of my friendship with Al McGuire. It is how I will remember him all my life. Not just as a colorful, controversial, or legendary coach, but as a friend who, like all of us, struggled upstream against the current in our lives and had finally triumphed. He had done what we all want to do, of course. In our own professions, in our own ways. He had fought the good fight, refused to give up. And he had caught the golden ring!

As I stood there, watching Al cry as the final seconds ticked away, one of those "75-dollar lines" of his came back to me again: "Dream big. Don't be just another guy going down the street and going nowhere."

I had no doubt in my mind, right then, that Al had always dreamed big. Like Fitzgerald's Gatsby, he was the poor boy who had always had his eye on the blue light and the end of Daisy's dock. And now, he finally had it. He was there. He did not have to throw parties any more, or play the clown to thousands. He had finally thrown the "monster" off his back and proven his "respectability" by claiming the ultimate prize.

Today, looking back, that next emotional, hectic hour or two seems pretty much of a blur. Not that I can't remember things, but there was so much happening all at once, and I was trying to be so many places and do so many things. Following Al into the locker room, I got a few quick quotes, then (although I didn't want to) raced back out to the press table to give them to the Omni PR person, and then raced back into the Marquette locker room once again.

What did I ask? Three basics, really. How big a factor was the Four Corners in Marquette's victory? What did it mean to him to finally win the NCAA title after so many years of trying? And Bo's steal, wasn't that the key play that turned things around? Three basic questions that I knew, along with Al's answers, would give the guys now writing some meat to go along with their bare-bones leads.

When I got back to the MU locker room, Al was being interviewed by Billy Red, tears running down his face. "I'm not going to cry," he insisted as he spoke. And then he cried again. "All my life, I've been an alley fighter," he insisted. "And you know, when you've always been one, you began to think you'll never get into the silk lace cuff areas." In spite of his trying to stop, the tears continued to roll down his cheeks. "Everyone says destiny," he continued. "But I don't like to use words from the sandlots, words that television ad men use. I'm just happy for my family. And I'd like to thank God." He paused and glanced up at us. "Yeah, I know I'm a hypocrite. But I just want to thank Him anyway."

And then, Kevin Byrne was at his arm, telling him he had to get back out onto the court for the televised awards ceremony. And so out we went, and I watched them drape the net, cut from the basket, around his neck, and after a long moment of standing there as the photographers flashed away, he was called to center stage, where he received his championship watch and the cheers of the crowd, with his family gathered round.

"I've always been the bridesmaid," he told them, amidst the cheers. "More of the lunch-pail, tin-hat type. I never really thought I'd win." His son Allie, a former Marquette star, hugged him, while his wife, Pat, his daughter, Noreen, and youngest son Robb all shed tears of joy as well.

At that point, I rushed off to the interview room to be sure I got a front row seat for Al's final go-round with the press. Most of what I gathered there later appeared in my next-day game story for the *Journal*, but there are three quotes gathered from that night by Bill Dwyre and me that I must include here, because they accurately describe the depth of the emotion that flowed between all of us who knew Al so well.

First was what Butch told me about those final seconds, when he saw Al unsuccessfully trying to hold back the tears. "When I saw him crying with five seconds left, I elbowed Bo Ellis," Lee said. "I didn't want him to miss it. It was great. He had all those teams with great records, but they didn't go very far. To give him something like this in his last season is a dream."

Quote number two was what Rick told Dwyre in the locker room, when asked about Al and how good a coach he was. Said Rick, "He is just not in this world. He is of another planet."

And finally, it was what Hank told Dwyre, when he found Hank seated on a folding chair outside the Marquette locker room, a basketball resting in his lap.

"It's the game ball," Hank revealed. "I'm waiting for him and making sure I have it for him." Fighting back tears again, Hank added, his lips trembling, "We've been together a long, long time…"

If Al was charmed that night, I was not.

Back at the hotel—somewhere around 1 a.m., as I remember it—that insidious, worthless, unreliable piece of shit we called a Tel-e-ram struck again.

I had finished my main game story and some notes and was relaxing with a beer, while Billy Red, who had completed his sidebar with Al, was finishing up his other sidebar on the other Tel-e-ram he had brought down with him Sunday on the plane. Jerry Karpowicz, another member of our *Journal* staff, was with us to cover the North Carolina locker room, and he had finished his story and was now—before we sent all our stuff back—proofreading my game story on my infernal blue machine.

Suddenly, I heard Karp mutter, "Damn! Shit! Oh, no!" And a few other expletives that you can imagine. What had happened was that as he was scrolling up and down, reading my story, he had suddenly lost graphs seven through 14! Karp was mortified. Dwyre was angry. I was boiling, but trying to keep it under control.

My first thought was that Karp had accidentally hit the kill button and that I should immediately, with or without Dwyre's help, throw him out the window. But since we were 17 stories up and the windows didn't open, I quickly nixed that idea. Besides which, on second thought, I knew Jerry had worked on those machines as much as all of us, and I also knew how touchy they could be. Remembering all the times I had hit a button and had the machine do something else, I figured the stupid machine, for whatever reason, had suddenly gone berserk on me one more time.

Trying to compose myself, I sat down, took a deep breath, and attempted to repair the damage. First I read the first six graphs, trying to mentally regain the flavor I'd had before, then pick up the flow and rewrite (as best I could remember or reinvent) the eight graphs that were lost. After that, I did my best to smoothly blend the new material back in again to the remainder of the story.

Sweat bullets? You bet. Never had I concentrated so hard. Had someone stuck their head in the door and yelled "Fire!" right then, I doubt I would have reacted. This, I knew, was one of the most important stories, as a reporter, that I would ever write. And I felt, when I signed off earlier, that I had written it well. So now, to have to go back and patch it up—like a doctor in an emergency room—was nothing short of mental hell.

Once our stuff was sent, we hit the sheets, but I got little sleep—partly because I was still worried about how my story would read the following day, and partly because of Billy Red's incessant snoring. Nonetheless, we were up with the sun, catching the earliest flight possible back to Milwaukee, during which I napped fitfully, sitting beside my still snoring—and I assumed content—sports editor all the way.

Al was amazingly low key when he and his players were honored upon their return at a luncheon on Wednesday at the Marc Plaza Hotel. In addition to Al, a lot of high-priced speakers were seated on the dais—including Governor Patrick Lucey, Milwaukee mayor Henry Maier, and Milwaukee county chief executive William O'Donnell. But to my delight, it was Kevin Byrne, Marquette's saucy sports information director, who stole the show.

Looking back now, I realize why Al and Kevin fit together like hand and glove—both were dark-haired Irishmen who possessed gifted, street-smart intelligence, remarkable memories, and a quick wit. Not once, in my years covering Al, did I ever hear Kevin tell a McGuire story incorrectly. But I have to tell you, because of his sparkly-eyed, humorous delivery, the stories always came away better for the telling.

On this particular day, Kevin brought down the house by alluding to all the diverse elements in Marquette's success, citing comic descriptions of each player, and then concluding by describing Rick, Hank and Al as "a young assistant who fantasizes about having hair, the soon-to-be-boss who has hair, and the master of it all—the motorcycle gang leader."

After Lucey mentioned that Al should be adequately compensated for his talents, Kevin stepped up and added, "I don't think you have to worry about that. Al always makes about $50,000 more than any of our players. At least, I hope he does. And his salary is about half of Marquette's gross. So good luck, Medalist."

Kevin then went on to list the team's strong points. "We don't have time today to expound on Bo Ellis's defense," he said. "But we do have time to expound on Bill Neary's shooting prowess. On Butch Lee's four passes this season. And Bernard Toone's one rebound. You all remember it. It was against St. Leo's."

Kevin got laughs again, when the Association of Commerce presented MU with a brass etching of the city, the coaches with framed silver reproductions, and the players with walnut boxes with copper reproductions on the lid. "Bernard," Kevin warned, "if you take that thing to a pawnshop, I'll tell Hank."

Kevin went on to explain Jerome Whitehead's late-season slump. "Jerome went on sabbatical in late February and early March," Byrne said. Then he turned toward Butch and added, "Butch, tell Bernard what sabbatical means."

Not even Al was immune to Kevin's needle. Speaking of freshman guard Mark Lavin, Kevin said, "Mark Lavin is quite a success story. From walk-on to NCAA champion in his freshman year. Millions of fans across the nation know Mark Lavin's name…which is more than can be said for his coach."

Al, when he got up to speak, surprised me by throwing out no rejoinders or humorous remarks. Instead, he tritely thanked Father Raynor (the president of Marquette) for "giving me my head. And thanks to the players, for letting us soar like eagles."

Okay. Fine. Well and good. Maybe it was the moment. But that was it? That was *all* Al had to say? Inside, I wondered, what's going on here? Was Al really starting to take himself—and this Medalist thing—way too serious? Was he already slipping inside the corporate coat, where everything you say must be calculated, where what humor does come out is dry as cardboard, and no one really laughs?

That, I knew, was not Al McGuire's world. I knew then that if corporate could not accept his proven bartender's *common-sense logic*, that it would not be long before Al would quickly tip his hat and walk away. Al was a people person; that is why he succeeded. Most corporate types are not. He knew hiring good people and giving them their heads—rather than micromanaging their every move, burying them under starched shirts and endless meetings—was the true route to success. Plus he had a definite dislike for people who spoke just because they like to hear themselves speak.

All of this said—even though I had very little to base it on at the time—I was certain that Al's relationship with Medalist Industries was not long for this world. Because the free spirit, in the long run, will never accept the corporate collar. It does not allow for individual thought or action. And no one was more *individual* than Al. No one.

Two final trivia items.

Just before Al returned to the court following the championship game, he had suggested to Kevin that his "Lucky Suit" should be donated to the annual Channel 10 auction on public television. "I'll bet some Irish guy will pay something for this," he said.

Somebody, Irish or otherwise, did, although to this day I don't know who. As I recall, the bid was something like $115 to $125, which means, after cleaning, the guy probably got it for just a tad under retail.

And Al's toe? Which I thought he must have injured when he kicked the scorer's table early on in the title game? Given the way things turned out, I plumb forgot to ask.

So how did it all happen? Why was Al finally able to grab the brass ring his last time around? Because, I feel, he had finally reached his goal—putting together a team that was truly complementary. Other teams he'd coached certainly had more raw talent. But in this, his final go-round, Al suddenly found himself coaching a team where—in spite of the fact that he had no full-blown superstar—the sum of the parts was more than equal to the whole.

"They all knew their roles," Al told me 10 years later, his eyes sparkling like a child at Christmas when he recalled the members of that championship team. "Jerome stayed close to the iron, Butch was a wild card, a roamer who could do whatever he wanted, with reason. Bo Ellis was the leader, the quiet, unassuming leader with steady performances in all areas.

"Bill Neary was the horse, the hammerer, expendable, the toughest guy on the block who made it happen. Jimmy Boylan was the rock, the tough. He had ice in him. And when Bernard came in, it was talent, an aristocratic talent, not black and blue talent, the talent of a violin player, an artist.

"It was Ulice Payne, the heady player who never turned the ball over. And two guys who played above their heads—Gary Rosenberger, who could be the point guard or the shooter, and Jim Dudley, the Cloud

Piercer, who was the surprise of the tournament. Christ, did he play! He played like a person possessed."

There was one other very important key to Marquette's success that year, Al told me. It was the relationship he had with his two fine assistants, Hank and Rick.

"We worked because we didn't associate socially and our rhythms were different," Al said. "Hank was the encyclopedia, the administrator, the rule book with solid basketball knowledge. Rick was the Cousins sandwich, the guy to bridge the age gap with the players, the recruiter with a flair for modern-day basketball."

And what was your role? I asked him.

Al smiled. "I was the Houdini, who did his disappearing act," he said. "I know that 85 percent of me is buffalo chips, and the other 15 percent is rare talent. I'd say in that 15 percent is the mental toughness, the media, keeping an eye on the elephant, not the mice, and extending the life of the extinct kiwi bird, which is nocturnal."

Al was chuckling as he finished saying this. I could tell by the gleam in his eye that he was pleased. It was another 75-dollar line.

"Now they call me eccentric.
They used to call me nuts.
I haven't changed."

Chapter 8
The Celebrity

J ust because Al McGuire quit coaching, it didn't mean he quit being funny. Far from it. All Al did, the following fall, was step out onto an even bigger stage into "the next stratum" as he called it when he signed on as a college basketball analyst with National Broadcasting Company in October of 1977. Suddenly, his humorous witticisms and off-the-wall assessments were being heard by millions of basketball fans from coast to coast each week, as he shared announcing duties with Billy Packer and Dick Enberg, broadcasting NBC's college basketball *Game of the Week* on Saturdays.

The result was predictable. If Al hadn't been one before, he now became a full-blown celebrity. Right from the start (although initially Al didn't think so), he was a hit. He brought a fresh new approach to the art of broadcasting—an off-the-cuff, humorously insightful, straight-from-the-gut style of analysis that not only rang true, but almost overnight set the profession on its ear. As a coach, he had possessed that keen ability to quickly sense and react to change of tempo during a game. Now, as an announcer, he combined that talent with his concise, inspired use of metaphors to skillfully capture the essence and emotion of the moment for those who were watching.

To put it in a nutshell, Al McGuire and TV were a marriage made in heaven. Why? Because, quite simply, the medium allowed Al to just continue being Al. All his life, he had been a colorful character. He had been a colorful player, a colorful coach, and a colorful speaker. Little wonder, then, that once he became accustomed to some of the technical aspects and logistics of television broadcasting, he quickly evolved into *the* colorful color commentator of his day, setting a style and a standard that would be copied by aspiring broadcasters for years to come.

Al's role on NBC's three-man team was perfect. Week after week, he was the scrappy, unpredictable street kid, never afraid to trade jibes with Packer, the authoritative analyst, but always deferential to Enberg's cool professionalism that kept the ship on course. One other thing also became clear early on: that while Al's title was "commentator," he was the designated "entertainer" as well—the person both Packer and Enberg looked to to supply the "McGuire-isms" that gave their coverage a third dimension no one else could match.

Al, of course, was always equal to the task.

Example: One game I still recall, when Packer observed that North Carolina center Geoff Crompton, who weighed more than 300 pounds, had shed 15 of them. Quipped Al, "That's like the Queen Mary losing a deck chair."

"Billy P is the true analyst," Al told me, later on that first year. "He can explain the passing game, the shuffle, all the Xs and Os. He's the guy who can talk with the chalk on his fingers till two in the morning. What I do is get into the human end of it more, the personal rivalries, the broken fingers and split toenails, the 'Mother in the Stands' or the 'Called Shot' type of thing. The ripple below the water that makes things shimmer and shake. Sometimes it's a sledgehammer, sometimes a light tap. Whatever it takes. But I always try to keep it simple. I try not to use any words a shoeshine kid can't understand."

(Did that last line ring a bell with you, too? As I mentioned earlier, Winifred had indeed done her job well.)

If Al was a little nervous at the start, it was because he was not your typical color commentator, any more than he had been your typical basketball coach. "I've never prepared for anything in my life, so it will just be on the wing," he told me early on. "That's the way I've always done everything. The hang-up, I feel, will be people trying to understand my accent and trying to understand the way I talk and the phrases I use."

In November, when he returned from filming a segment in Cuba for Marquette's nationally televised game against the Cuban National Team at the Arena, he still wasn't certain if this whole TV thing was going to work out. "I think part of it is that NBC and I are still shadow-boxing," he told me as we talked over breakfast at a McDonald's not far from his home. "They're trying to tell me to do things I don't have the ability to do. Like read cue cards, or repeat sentences that are preconceived.

"I mean, if they didn't want me, why did they hire me in the first place? It seems like every time I get involved with something, people try to change me. It just doesn't work. It's like the woman who married the alcoholic and she said she'd change him. So three years later she's an alcoholic and he's going to church every Sunday."

Al needn't have worried. It didn't take NBC long to realize the attraction they had in Al McGuire. He was, by any yardstick, a unique American persona, who had lived his life to a different drummer and who was now was being discovered and enjoyed by more and more new fans every week. In short, Al had arrived. His life story was the stuff that dreams are made of. After clawing his way to the top in the college coaching profession, he'd made a gutsy career change at middle age—and still come out on top. On his last roll of the dice, he had finally bested the "zebras" (and his own personal demons) to walk away with the NCAA's top prize firmly in hand. That Cinderella finish, plus his colorful image and the huge national exposure his NBC job suddenly afforded him, combined to make him more recognizable than many other coaches who had actually been more successful on the court in years past. What they didn't have, of course, was Al's unique personality. As easily as Al had auctioned off his "Lucky Suit," so now he slipped into a role not unakin to that of a modern-day Will Rogers—a humorous, homespun pundit whose off-the-cuff remarks not only tickled the funny bone, but repeatedly struck home.

In a few short years, he would evolve into nothing short of a populist sports philosopher and sage whose colorful opinions were sought on almost every controversial subject.

Seeing all this evolve, I was truly happy for Al. No longer, I felt, could he harbor any doubts as to whether he was merely the dancing jester or the king. For years he had made people laugh, but now he was also making them think. I still remember when he told me about the reporter who asked him if he really felt most athletes deserved their college degrees, given the fact that so many did poorly academically. "I told him what he had to realize was, that half the doctors in the world were in the bottom of their class," Al said. "I thought that was a hell of statement, because I was countering a point from the academic world which [as a coach] will drive you crazy."

Honest, as always, Al admitted that he welcomed (and in fact downright enjoyed) his increased celebrity status immensely. "Being a celebrity," he told me, "is like being rich or poor. Given a choice, you would always prefer to be rich." What amazed me was how, even though he was no longer coaching, the colorful stories and the 75-dollar lines just kept on flowing. Al's mind was a perpetual Fountain of Youth in that regard. Never did I ever see him at a loss for words. And he always had a comeback.

When I asked him once if he ever worried about running out of things to say, he flashed me a look of genuine surprise. Like I had asked if he thought the stars would ever quit shining, or the tides cease to flow. "I guess I never thought about it," he replied. "But no, it doesn't worry me. It never has. Roger, you got to realize, I'm talking about years and years of material here. From behind the bar, from across the street, from everywhere I've ever been, from everything I've ever learned. I don't know what it is, or sometimes where it comes from. But it always seems to be there. It's just how I view my life, I guess."

When Al returned from Cuba—his first big NBC assignment and his first visit to a Communist country—he was at his best, brimming with fresh "material" about his travails on a trip that, while hardly routine to begin with, turned out to be nothing short of bizarre once he got involved. He had envisioned, he said, "a one-hour pop, and then sight-seeing in the mountains." Instead, he got heat, lots of khaki uniforms, and very little usable footage. While sympathetic, I couldn't help but chuckle as I wrote, because—coming from Al—it turned into "An Al McGuire Cuban Vacation" and one of the most humorous interviews we ever did.

His troubles began when he arrived in Miami and was horrified to learn (because his incoming flight had been late) that he and the crew would have to fly to Cuba in a small, chartered plane, a mode of transportation Al avoided at all costs.

"The thing that gets me with small planes," Al said, "is that they always say, 'There's nothing to worry about. This guy is the greatest pilot in the world.' So why isn't he flying a 747 someplace, with 15 stewardesses hanging all over him, instead of being here at some little airport with one flight, taking care of me?

"Anyhow, I was late getting out of Chicago, so I get to Miami and it's nine o'clock at night and dark and here they're jamming all this stuff into this little plane. I'm in the back with Jim Marooney, the producer, and there's two other guys in front.

"So Jim leans forward and says to the one guy, 'Hey, Billy, you want a drink?'

"I said, 'Wait a minute. Pilots don't drink.'

"And Marooney says, 'Oh, he's not a pilot, he's the sound man.'

"And now I'm thinking, 'This is like One Million B.C. or something. What the hell am I doing, flying into a socialist country at night with one pilot?' Hey, that's a no-no."

Once airborne, Al said he spent the next hour sleeping "with my head between my legs. When I woke up, I asked Jim, 'How far to Havana?' He said, 'I don't know.' I said, 'Well, ask the pilot.' He said, 'I don't want to bother him right now. He's praying.'"

Al said when he got off the plane in Cuba, it was like a trip back in time. "I entered the world of 1950 cars," he said. "I think we Americans must be instinctively destructive or something, because the cars are still running down there. Then I got to the Hilton Hotel. It's not called the Hilton any more, but they still call it something that starts with an H so they wouldn't have to change the towels." Al paused, then looked me straight in the eye and added, "Is Conrad Hilton dead? Well, if he isn't, he would be if he saw that hotel."

I couldn't help it. I put down my pen for a moment and roared. Run out of material? Not this guy. Never.

Off and running now, Al allowed how amazed he had been at the prices of things in Cuba—bread, 16 cents a loaf, milk 18 cents a quart. He also noted that he had seen no luxuries and that the clothing styles didn't appeared to have changed in years. "You could tell there had been an embargo," he quipped, "because there was no label on the beer."

During a stop at the legendary Floridita Bar, which Ernest Hemingway had made famous, Al also noted another Cuban custom—no tipping.

"It's a custom a lot of my friends in Milwaukee would like," he said, grinning. "The Cubans just don't allow it. They feel it's degrading. You can't tip anybody—your cabbie, or bellhop, nobody. Hey, we had 14 boxes of films and stuff, enough stuff to give a weightlifter a hernia, and this little guy toted 'em all the way up to our rooms and wouldn't take a cent. And we were on the 15th floor."

I had to ask. Did he meet Castro? "No," Al said, "but I must have met every other soldier on the island. You get very accustomed to drab olive green."

And so, I asked, what did you accomplish in the way of background footage?

"We got a two- or three-minute piece together which I think might have bombed," Al admitted. "The guy I was talking to was named Roberto, and I couldn't say it right, so they said, 'Just think of Ruppert beer.' But you know, I have enough trouble just getting my next-door neighbor to understand me. And he speaks English. Everybody kept saying, 'Go slower. Go slower.' After a while, I felt like I was living in Hattiesburg, Mississippi.

"But I think the job will work out after a while. But see, I was just looking for a weekend takeoff thing, not to replace Dick Enberg or Keith Jackson or anything. I just want to be me. I don't want a lot of restrictions put on me.

"See, I'm not a color man. I'm doing half-time, standup-type things. And I need a pro like Enberg with me. I need a guy with me who put in his seven years at Rice Lake, then four years at Manitowoc, and finally came to Milwaukee. A pro. Hey, I'm just a passing love affair. I mean, if they ever put one of those earphones in my head so somebody's talking in my ear, I'll end up in a padded cell. Man, that's tough. If I'm talking to some guy, and somebody screams in my ear, 'You got 15 seconds!' I'd probably say, 'Forget the commercial!'"

Like I said earlier, Al need not have worried. After a few games of relegating him to halftime spots and brief comments from a sound booth during the games, NBC moved him courtside with Packer and Enberg. Rough he might have been, but the network quickly realized what a diamond it had in Al McGuire.

Al's final comment about his Cuban trip echoed his initial insecurities. "What amazed me was the crew's patience with me," he said. "Like I had three lines and we did it 14 times. They kept putting that stick in front of my face and I'd go blank. And the time we finally get it right, a Russian freighter came by and tooted its horn and drowned us out."

I had to smile. It was probably the only time in his career that Al got upstaged.

When Al had sat down, I noticed he had a plastic shopping bag in his hand. Now, the interview done, he reached down for it and brought out three things—a small metal ashtray with a picture of a Spanish lady, a box of matches, and a trifold cardboard drink menu. They had all come from the "Floridita."

"I brought these back," Al said, almost shyly, handing them to me. "I thought they were something you'd appreciate."

The matchbook was inscribed, "Al McGuire, Cuba, Floridita Bar, 1977." On the front of the menu, Al had written, "Roger J.—We put your name on the wall. Hemingway was asking for you." The menu was signed not only by Al, but Jim Marooney and the rest of the crew.

Al knew how much of a Hemingway fan I was—how much I admired his work, how much he had influenced my writing, and that I even collected first editions of his books. Writing your name on the Floridita's wall was a Hemingway tradition, and now mine was there as well.

Needless to say, I was overwhelmed. As I thanked him and shook his hand, I couldn't help but note that Al seemed genuinely pleased...pleased that I was pleased, as only a friend could be. I was honored that he cared enough about me, and our friendship, to take the time. It was just another of those special moments I was lucky enough to share.

The following April was Awards Month for Al and me, and another very special time for me.

April 23, 1978 was when Al became a doctor.

Not the Marcus Welby kind, of course. (Can you imagine him holding up your first newborn and asking where to apply the clamp?) But at 3 p.m. that afternoon, he became Dr. Al McGuire. Doctor of Humane Letters, to be exact. The honorary degree was conferred upon Al just before he delivered the commencement speech to the graduating class of St. Leo College, in Saint Leo, Florida, a small school located 40 miles north of Tampa.

I caught up with Al at Billy Mitchell Airport, just before he caught his plane south, and when asked how he felt about receiving his doctorate, he was in fine fettle as always. "My mother will be thrilled," he quipped. "She always wanted to be able to say, 'My son, the doctor.'"

But why St. Leo's? I wanted to know. And why the degree?

Al smiled, pointing out that St. Leo was the school Marquette had whipped, 80-39, in December, 1976, at the Arena to start his last season as the Warriors' coach. A season that ended with Marquette winning the NCAA title. "It was a package deal," he joked, referring to the degree. "I agreed to let them out of the second year of the contract in exchange for it."

Despite the jokes, Al said he was pleased to be receiving his doctorate, which (according to a St. Leo press release) honored him for his achievements, not only in coaching, but as a "man who believes in people," and that he did take it seriously.

"I was thrilled with it," he said. "I was pleasantly surprised, pleased. You know, some things that we indirectly slap over the years are the things we want the most. But obviously it wasn't given for my spelling or double negatives."

As Al talked on, I could sense his pride and that he felt this was just another confirmation that he had indeed attained the respectability, the "white cuff" areas that he had always sought. What was happening, of course, was that Al McGuire the person was beginning to transcend his sport, and like a Mickey Mantle or Mario Andretti, he was evolving into a sports personality all his own in the public eye.

"I really think I was fortunate to be honored like this," Al told me. "I've received a lot of awards, but the one I appreciated most was when the coaches made me Coach of the Year in 1974. An award like that is a keeper, one that goes in the den. A denner, if there is such a word. And next to that, this is the most important thing I've ever received." He paused, then shot me a glance. "Uh, that is, except money."

The next thing I asked him was what he planned to tell those graduating students, once he got behind the podium. Al thought a second, with a faraway look in his eye, before he spoke.

"Oh, the refreshingness of the outside world, that they're coming to a time of career changing, the awareness of being human," he said. "You know, to 'live in the moment' type of thing. And that when you learn to treat the parking lot attendant the same way you treat your superior, that is when you've become truly educated."

Seashells and balloons, I thought. I wonder if he'll use that phrase?

It was time for Al to board his plane, and in true McGuire fashion, he got off a fine parting line. "Rog," he quipped, "I think this shows there is still some hope that bartenders will someday rule the world."

Our roles were reversed a week or so later, when I learned the Associated Press sports editors had named me top sportswriter in the nation in the field of Sports News Writing for 1977. The award was based, the AP story said, primarily on my coverage of Marquette in the NCAA finals. Since I happened to be off the day of the announcement, Tracy Dodds, a fellow *Journal* staff member, called to give me the news.

"Roger!" she said happily. "You got it! You got it!"

"Got what?" I responded. And then she told me. And that the story would be in that afternoon's paper.

I was numb. First in the nation. Me?

About three o'clock, Al called.

"Roger!" he said. "Congratulations! I just want you to know how happy I am for you! Jesus!" After I thanked him, Al added in an almost fatherly tone, "You know, Rog, this is a big one. This is a keeper. One you hang on the living room wall. You should be very proud. These are the kind of awards that make careers. I won't keep you, pal. I know your phone is ringing. But I am so very happy for you. Bye."

I got a lot more calls, a lot of handshakes, a lot of letters, and a lot of congratulations over the next few weeks. But none of them meant as much as Al's call. A few days later, I received a Medalist brochure with Al's picture on the front, aptly titled "Portrait of a Winner." Across the picture, he had written, "Rog, Happy for you! Last page interesting. Buy me lunch. See you, Al."

I couldn't help but laugh. It would take me two weeks to pay for that lunch, since the *Journal*, in all its "cheapdom" had rewarded me for being first in the nation with a lousy $5 a week pay raise. That worked out to $260 a year, before taxes. I remember telling someone, "If I won it again, do you think they'd give me ten?"

While I got no big rewards from the *Journal*, Al wasted no time showing me what he thought of my talent. A few weeks later, he called and asked if we could do lunch—and this time, he said with a laugh, he was buying! That, as the Godfather would say, was an offer I couldn't refuse.

"I've got this deal with Miller Brewing Co.," he explained, "and they want me to do a column. It's tied to their 'Hoopla!' promotion, which is point of purchase, Miller merchandise, tickets to the Final Four, that sort of thing. Now, between you and me, it's a very lucrative deal, and I want to do it. But the thing is, they want me to do a column— every week—from November through the Final Four! That's 20-plus columns! Rog, you know me. I can't do 20-plus columns! I mean, I know basketball, but I'm no writer. Christ, I'd be in the looney bin! So here's what I want to do. We meet with them, and I tell them that you and I will write the columns. What we'll do is, I'll call you after the games, we talk, you write the columns, and send 'em off the next day to Miller. What d'ya think?"

My initial reaction was that I was scared to death. What Al was ask-ing me to do was write a national column, written first-person as if *he* were talking, espousing his views, opinions, and predictions once a week. And then I remembered back to that day in the gym, after my article about the clowns appeared, when he had told me, "You know me better than I know me." And, what the hell, after nearly five years, I had his speech pattern and nuances down pat. And so I said, "Let's do it." We shook hands, and that's when I became Al's ghostwriter, a job I would continue to do for nearly eight years.

Unlike the *Journal*, Al was in my corner when it came to money. I will never forget our initial meeting with the Miller execs, how the pleas-antries were observed and the general terms of the deal laid out. After which, Al suddenly turned serious and, looking around the table, said to them, "Now, one thing we must understand here. Roger is a very talent-ed writer. And he must be compensated accordingly." After which, he named a figure that three more years of *Journal* raises couldn't have touched.

At a subsequent meeting, some weeks later, one Miller bean count-er pointedly suggested that it might be better if Al worked with someone in-house and let that person write the column. (In effect, the guy was trying to shortstop me.) Al stiffened and gave the guy his coldest stare. "If Roger does not do the columns, then we do not do the columns," he said, coldly. "Roger must be part of this deal…or there is no deal."

Do I even have to tell you how proud that made me feel? I mean, here was Al McGuire putting a six-figure deal on the line for me. Think about it. How many friends would do that for you? That's loyalty, where it really counts. When the cabbage is on the line.

Being Al's ghostwriter was interesting, to say the least. Sometimes, if it was an article for a newspaper or magazine, it was simply a matter of us sitting down and talking for a while, me hammering out a first draft, and then us sitting down one more time to tweak things. I have to admit that even given how well I knew him and how he'd use certain metaphors and phrases to score points, there were a whole lot of tweaks. Sometimes, just for fun, I'd slip in a totally new line I'd created, and you know what? Al liked 'em! "Hey, that's good, Rog," he'd say. "I like that. You're right. How'd you think of that?"

I know. You want examples. Here's two.

"Always remember, time is money. If you don't believe me, ask a cabbie. Why else does he drive fast when he's empty, slow when he's got a fare?"

"I don't trust first impressions. I don't make a commitment until I know you. I don't start to know you until I've seen you in the same suit twice."

The Miller columns were as scary to me as scrambling on a roof in a rainstorm. We did those, for the most part, by the seat of our pants. I always made sure to watch the games on Saturdays and keep up to the minute on all the top-ranked teams—who was hurt, who was hot, that sort of thing. And I always kept *Street & Smith's Basketball Annual* at my elbow for spellings of names, hometowns, etc. It cut down on the long-distance calls, believe me. And it wasn't just a case of the expense. In most cases, we just flat-out didn't have the time.

Usually, it would go like this. Saturday night or Sunday morning, Al would call. He'd have a subject he wanted to talk about, based on the weekend's results, and a half-dozen or so lines he would rattle off, idea lines I always called them, the bones of the piece. After which, I'd sit down and put things in order, put meat on the bones in Al's vernacular, and then fax the piece off. Early on, I always let Al read 'em first, but after the first year, unless it was on a touchy subject, he never questioned what I sent out.

Looking back now, I realize, man! What trust. But Al knew I would never embarrass him. There's an old newspaper writer's phrase about how, if you don't have a certain fact, you "write around" it. The reader never realizes. Well, I'd gotten pretty good at that after 10-plus years in the business, and so more than once, when I wasn't sure, or I couldn't reach Al to confirm, I just "wrote around" the problem and kept on going. Funny thing, it always worked out okay.

The scariest times were when Al would call from an airport somewhere on Sunday, about to catch his plane…and admit he really didn't know what he wanted to say. "Hey, Rog. Coach here," he'd say, all but drowned out by the noise in the background. "Listen, we're gonna half to punt a little here. I'm, uh, just a little bummed out. I'm flat, something, I don't know. I got some bits and pieces, but you're gonna have to put 'em together, clip and paste, okay?" He'd pause, utter one more "um," and then begin.

After the first time this happened, I learned to be prepared. I always made sure I was ready with four or five topics I could ask him about, get him to voice an opinion or two, and once I had that much, I was home free. It just meant being a little more inventive once I got off the phone. It was amazing how far I could get, given a drop or two of Al's high-test to get me going.

The really rough ones were the times, once or twice a year, when Al was really beat and would one throw out all of four or five one-liners, and that was it! "That's about all I got, Rog," he'd say plaintively. "I'm sorry, but, uh, I'm just tapped out, okay? Just throw it together, like you always do. It'll be fine." Pause. "Um, I got to go now. Call me tomorrow if you really got a problem. I'll be in Philly, but Jeanine [his secretary] will have a number. Thanks, Rog. Bye."

Those were the times I earned my money the hard way, made chicken salad out of chicken shit, as they say. Screwed in at my typewriter (we didn't have computers at home back then), sometimes for three or four hours, I would get down what little grist I had to work with, and then begin phrasing and re-phrasing, trying a line this way and that, tweaking again and again, until I knew I had things just the way Al would say them. The one thing I *never* did, however, was change or alter Al's opinions. Those, the bones I put the meat on, were inviolate.

My biggest disappointment is that I don't have those Miller columns to share with you today. It would have been a stitch going through a few, especially the rough ones, to show just how Al and I worked and how I sometimes had to "clip and paste." (Who knows? A "Ghostwriting 101" course at Marquette, perhaps.) It's strange. Normally I'm a pack rat, and I had them in files, year by year, along with the little four-color "Hoopla!" pamphlets that were put out by Miller at point of purchase. But somewhere along the way, I lost them or tossed them. I even called Miller Brewing Co. before I started writing and asked if they could send me some copies. The people I had dealt with 23 years before were gone, of course. The people there were nice enough to search, but alas nothing was found. C'est la vie.

A short time before, on March 20, 1978, Al had resigned his position as vice chairman of Medalist Industries. I was not surprised. Right from the start, I had had serious doubts that the Showman would be comfortable in a three-piece suit, and within months, it was clear to me that the business world could never replace his passion for athletics…or his ego's natural desire to entertain.

"You know, Rog, I don't know what it is," he had confided to me one day, "but I've tried a lot of my one-liners on these business types, and they just don't go over at all. Instead, they just seem to get upset. Like when they asked me what a vice chairman does, and I said, 'A vice chairman puts gas in the chairman's car.' Well, after a while, I was told not to say that any more. And when I asked why, they said, 'We're a publically owned company, and the stockholders don't like it.'

"So a few months later, a financial guy was doing a magazine piece about me, and he asked me, 'What does the vice chairman do?' And I said, 'He does whatever is distasteful to the Chairman.'" Al smiled wanly. "I thought it was pretty good one-liner, but when the story comes out, they tell me, 'Medalist Industries is on the American Stock Exchange. You can't say things like that.'

"Now, when I'm asked what a vice chairman does, I tell them, 'I improve profits per share,' and everybody is happy. Except me. And my biggest thing now is, I'm trying to learn initials, all these buzz words they have for everything. Like ROI, return on investment. That's all that seems to turn their screw—initials, matrixes, and graphs."

Al frowned. "*Fortune Magazine* has an article on me coming out. I haven't seen it yet, but I don't think I'm going to like it. It was four days of talking, and it was a cardboard-type thing, no humor at all. By the time we got through, everything but the chili we had for lunch was sanitized. Christ, I felt like I was in an operating room, doing surgery.

Everything I said, they wanted to know a reason why, and then a reason why for that. Finally, the one guy got me steamed, and I just told him, 'You want anything else on that, talk to my accountants. I got 17 of 'em. Take your pick."

Looking back, I think that there were two other reasons why Al decided to pull the plug at Medalist, a little over a year after he came on board. One was his newfound success—and national celebrity—at NBC. Given that, Al realized he didn't need a vice chairman's title or key to the executive washroom to gain the "respectability" he'd sought. He already had it. And he was still able to be Al. Secondly, like his father, who had loaned Mr. Brennan just two dollars instead of four, he was smart enough to realize a bad situation that was not going to get any better, so he cut his losses quickly.

The sad part was that during his short tenure at Medalist, Al brought a lot more to the bottom line than he got credit for, as chairman Norm Fischer later admitted. And Jerry Savio, Al's lifelong friend whom Al recruited to be vice president for Medalist's Specialty Sales Division in 1979, described McGuire as a creative "idea guy" who soon became disenchanted when his ideas were repeatedly dismissed by company accountants who claimed "the numbers" (profit margins) just weren't there.

"When they lost him, they lost a fantastic idea guy," Savio recalled. "That's what Al basically was. He would have an idea and pass it on to people in the marketing departments." Unfortunately, Savio explained, Al got discouraged when he was repeatedly told his ideas just wouldn't work. "When you hear that three or four times, you start to think about moving on," Savio said.

My own experience with Medalist Industries at that time was short-lived and hardly rewarding. Enthused about the company when Al had signed on as vice chairman in December of '76, I bought 40 shares, all I could afford. (Memory tells me I bought 40 shares at $20.00 each, something like that.) This was my first—and, as it turned out, only—venture into the world of high finance, but I figured if Al said Medalist was good, it *had* to be good. Why not ride the swell, I figured? Get in now and sell out a few years from now, when the stuff was worth double what it was now. Then reinvest, perhaps with Al's guidance, and make some really big bucks. At least, that was my initial—and, I realized later, naïve—game plan. In my own mind, I saw myself as a crafty robber baron, taking the inside info—the *real gen* as Hemingway always called it—and using it to full advantage.

For the next few months, I sat back happily as I watched the price of Medalist Industries stock rise steadily—if not spectacularly—on the American Exchange. No matter, I thought greedily, if it took a little longer than expected. In the end, I'd still be well ahead.

Then, for reasons I have never understood, Medalist Industries stock suddenly took a downturn, sliding like a snow sled on an icy mountain ridge for three or four days, until it slipped below the price per share that I'd paid originally. Seeing that $800 I had worked so hard to garner from Mother *Journal's* coffers slipping away, I was mortified...and depressed. How could this be happening? Al had told me it was a great investment. Was he losing his shirttail, too? (I dismissed that idea as soon as I thought of it. Al, to my knowledge, *never* took a loss when it came to finances.) The point was, I commiserated to myself, this wasn't the way things were supposed to happen. For the next year, I lived and died with the financial page, watching as Medalist slipped lower, rallied, slipped lower again, rallied again. A couple times, I thought about calling Al and asking his advice, but my pride refused to let me.

Finally, I put a stop to the whole silly business by selling—once Medalist bounced back to about what I had paid for it originally. For a few more weeks, I watched and saw it stay pretty much at the same price. After that, I counted my blessings and took solace in the fact that I had basically broken even. The best thing was that I had learned a good lesson—that the stock market was just too rich and risky for my blood. And besides, now I had back my peace of mind.

I remember that night, after my check from my broker came, and knowing I was out of the woods, I wondered if Al felt that too, though obviously for other, bigger reasons.

Al had mentioned to me his growing frustration over the fact that many of his former fellow coaches were taking offense to remarks he made during NBC's coverage of their games. While I sympathized, I could see that Al didn't seem to realize one very telling point: He was no longer a coach. He was no longer a member of the active fraternity. He now was, in fact, a TV commentator, a member of the media. Those guys whom coaches, for whatever their reasons, love to hate. His perspective was different from theirs now, because of the job he had to do, something neither he nor those who had coached against him for so many years could, at that time, understand. And so they took umbrage. When Al first brought this up, I offered sympathy, but told him in effect, "It goes with the territory. NBC is paying you now. Adapt. Shrug your shoulders and go on."

Al understood what I was saying. But he still thought such criticism was unfair. Until, I think, the second weekend of February in 1981, when NBC covered a Sunday game between UCLA and Notre Dame at South Bend, Indiana. I was there because Al and NBC had allowed me to shadow Al for the weekend, to do a story on what these weekends with Al were like.

Most of my time, riding down by car with Al from Milwaukee, was spent listening to Al read aloud from the Notre Dame press guide. "You never know when you're going to have to fill," he told me, as we sailed along the interstate. "You get a blowout, you got to have something to talk about."

So first, he read to me about Father Theodore M. Hesburgh, president of Notre Dame, and Father Edmund P. Joyce, executive vice president. After that, I got a 10-cent tour as he droned on (yes, Al could drone on!) about the campus, the history of the university and its alumni. And finally, about Moose Krause, Notre Dame's athletic director, who had once been a center on the Irish basketball teams of the early 1930s.

"…so dominant was Krause in the middle," Al read on, "that the three-second lane was conceived as a way to control him." He looked up, pleased, and circled that item in the guide. "That's good," he said. "That's a keeper."

On Al's lap were two 8x12 lineup and fact sheet cards, one for Notre Dame, one for UCLA. Quickly, he scribbled a note about Krause, then paused to explain.

"When I go to places, I try to pick out phrases," he told me. "It's a search-and-record type of thing. You don't know what you're searching for sometimes until you find it. I'm searching for human-ness. Things I can use during the game. Dick has the statistics things, Billy talks about basketball. I search for the human angle. I talk to the $2 bettor, the housewife in the kitchen."

He paused again, a look on his face akin to that of a prospector who's just found a golden nugget. "Here's something: Why have all the assistants who left Notre Dame in recent years not been successful?" Studiously, he noted that on his card. "I think it's because, without exception, they went to programs that were up for grabs, that sort of thing. I mean, why do it? Success in life is job selection. I believe that. Yeah, I've got to ask Digger about that."

Once we got there, however, we found that Digger Phelps, Notre Dame's head coach, was anything but eager to talk to Al about anything. As the Irish practiced, Phelps purposely stayed out in the middle of the court, while Al huddled with assistant coaches, graduate assistants, local radio and TV people, the trainers—anybody who could give him unique little tidbits about the Irish squad.

Following at his side, I was amused at the flurry of notations on his 8x12 Notre Dame card, but only because it was something I, as a seasoned reporter, had been doing at all kinds of sports events for years. The only difference was that I used the background information for later questions for my stories. Al used it for on-air facts to entertain his audience. Although his handwriting wasn't the best, I watched him scribble down things like, "Tempo…'stop at the box'…Tim Andree—got more out of him than expected…Mike Mitchell, two arthroscope operations…" All of a sudden, I knew where Al came up with all his "inside stuff" I'd heard week after week. Like any good Irish cop, he made sure, prior to game time, that he collected up-to-the-minute facts by "walking the beat."

The only problem was, all of a sudden practice was over…and Digger was nowhere to be seen. Al looked stricken.

"Where'd Digger go?" he asked, a plaintive look in his eye. "I want to talk with him." After two or three "I don't knows," he cornered Frank LaGrotta, a graduate assistant, who led us first to Phelps's office, then to the team's locker room, then up and down the halls to other coaches' offices. Still no Digger.

Suddenly, LaGrotta was struck with inspiration. "I know," he said confidently. "He's in the kitchen." And sure enough, there was Digger, sipping at a cup of coffee. When he spied us coming, he glared at the poor assistant.

"Hey, Digger," Al groaned. "I've been walking all over trying to find you."

Digger gave LaGrotta another angry glare. "I'm trying to lose the guy, and you bring him to me," he said.

"I'm just doing my job, Coach," LaGrotta said.

At that instant, the air got tight. I knew it was going to get down and dirty in the kitchen.

"No game tonight?" Phelps asked Al.

"I only do 14 games," Al replied, on the defensive as I'd never seen him. "People think I do a lot of games, but I only do 14."

Phelps gave Al a cold stare. "Fourteen games at $10,000 a game," he said. "That's $140,000. Not bad."

Al stiffened, his pride hurt. "Well, that's a little low..." he began.

"Make sure the IRS gets that," Digger cut in, noticing that I was writing this all down. Digger was at the envelope, I felt, being as abrasive and rude as he could.

Al tried to soften things, offering out his idea about Phelps's former assistants, which Phelps promptly denied.

At this point—perhaps best for all concerned—Roger Valdiserri, Notre Dame's sports information director (a gentleman I had worked with for years before), walked in and announced to us that 96 percent of the country would watch the game next day. Al, still trying to break the ice, brought up the fact that UCLA had not brought its band along.

"I've always said the first 70 tickets shouldn't go to the university president; they should go to the band," he said. "The band is the neutralizer. It's like two cops on horses with billy clubs. They can stop a riot. The band can neutralize 10,000 people on the road, they can make so much noise."

Digger had no comment. Al then asked him what he was going to do. Phelps replied that he had to see some *football* recruits.

Al seemed genuinely hurt by that. "I just wanted to have a beer with you," he said. "You know, I've noticed this lately. You're growing away from me. The coaches seem to be growing away from me. You won't talk to me."

Phelps paused before he spoke. "You don't get the letters I do," he said coldly. "You say something on the air, and I get the letters."

Al, who had been sitting on a table, stood up and threw up his hands.

"Digger! This is what I've been saying. We're in the world of the Beta-max! After the game, all you guys go back home and turn on the Beta-max. I've never heard myself on TV. Never! Digger, we're on the air for two hours. I guarantee anybody in this room, on the air for two hours, you can pick out two lines and say he's an SOB. I'm saying look at the whole program, not just one line."

Phelps seemed unmoved. "You want to see how it's done," he replied, "watch me on the DePaul-Marquette game in two weeks." (Because of a scheduling conflict, Phelps was scheduled to be in Al's chair for that game.)

"That's one game!" Al shot back. "Hell, I can do a First Holy Communion for one game. Talk about everybody giving 400 percent and hustle and desire and all that crap. But you can't do that every week, or you put everybody to sleep. You can do it, but you'll be gone."

"That's fine for you to say," Digger replied. "But we're getting all the heat in the kitchen."

All of sudden, I saw something in Al I had never seen before. Now Digger had gone too far. He refused to understand, and he had, although maybe he didn't realize it, insulted Al by refusing to do so. Al laid down an icy curtain with his eyes. "I'm telling you, Digger, think about it," he said, steel in his voice. "Someday, you'll be in my position, and I'll remember that and call you. Remember I said that. You'll find yourself in the same position five years from now, in the same boat."

Suddenly, Phelps looked uncomfortable. So he threw out a parting card. "For $10,000 a game," he said, "why not?"

Everybody laughed. But I knew, by the looks on both their faces, that the opinions had remained unchanged.

Whether Al ever called Digger years later, when he started doing more broadcasting, I have no idea. But to this day, I think that day was when Al finally began to fully understand what his new role really was.

The subject came up again later that day, during NBC's production meeting, run by producer George Finkel in NBC's suite at the hotel. It was a standard thing, a relaxed briefing during which the directors, producers and analysts went over the telecast timetable from start to finish. For me, it was neat, being on the inside like this, scribbling away while they talked.

"What do we want to talk about when we come on?" Enberg asked. (He and Al were there, but Packer wasn't expected in until Sunday morning.)

"Power vs. mobility, strength vs. svelte, two exact opposites, that sort of thing," Al suggested. "Notre Dame a team that likes to play football, UCLA more like a track meet."

"At noon, we do the voice-over on your halftime feature," Finkel said, referring to Al's one-on-one contest against Lynette Woodard, the women's All-American from Kansas. "What I'd like to do, Dick, you do the intro, then draw Al out with comments while it runs."

Enberg nodded, smiling. "I can kid Al a little; the heavy breathing is funny when she runs him in the ground," he remarked. "You can hear it."

Enberg handed a sheet of paper to Peter Rolfe, the associate producer. "These are the games we need scores on tomorrow," he said.

"Dick, we'll do the halftime feature," Finkel continued, "then you can pretape your billboards [lead-in commercials]."

"You know, rather than talk about a couple players at first, maybe we should point out the crowd," Enberg suggested. "The sixth player, that sort of thing. And we could show what we're talking about. Something showing the crowd screaming and yelling. You know, LaSalle was 0-5 from the free throw line shooting into the student section."

"Maybe somebody could shoot from the free throw line, through the glass, show what it's like looking into all those arms and pompons," Al said.

Harry Coyle, NBC's director, liked the idea immediately. "I can get that shot," he insisted. "No problem. But will they allow my camera out there?"

Finkel shrugged. "Maybe before the introductions," he said, "when everybody's all fired up."

Coyle nodded. "Sure. Just before they leave the floor, we'll catch a guy shooting a free throw out there."

"If the guy stands right on the foul line, we can say, 'This is what a guy sees. This is what it's like,'" Al said.

At this point, Enberg threw in his two cents' worth. "Really, Harry," he said. "I think let's let the crowd tell the story."

Coyle smiled. "We'll play it to the hilt."

That was when Al brought up his conversation with Digger Phelps, an indication, he felt, of a possible problem brewing, that the coaches were shying away from him.

"I can see it," Al told the others. "Dean Smith, Lefty Dreisell, Joe Hall, all of 'em. But where they make their mistake is people look at the line and not the whole picture. Besides, I'm only saying what I would do in that situation. It doesn't make them wrong."

Enberg, always the professional, came up with an answer. "I think sometime soon we've got to take time to explain again to people what we do," he said. "Redefine our roles. Maybe that'll cut down on the second-guessing."

"I don't mind the second-guessing," Al cut in. "I mind the lack of intelligence."

"Coaches aren't noted for understanding what we're trying to do, Al," Enberg said, a wide smile crossing his face. "You were an SOB until you got away from it." At that point, everybody, including Al, broke up.

UCLA practiced that night, and Al continued to fill his 8x12 cards with more notes—nicknames, lines about certain players, their hobbies, that Phelps now owns Knute Rockne's summer cottage. But he mined his most valuable nugget when he talked with UCLA coach Larry Brown.

"Which end of the floor you going to shoot from the first half?" Al asked. Both men knew the visiting team had its choice, and Brown was well aware of the problems of shooting into the maelstrom that was the chanting Irish student section. "We'll take the student end the first half," he replied. Brown chuckled. "I remember last time I asked the kids and they said, 'Let's take the other end, or we'll get hit with all the toilet paper while we're warming up.' I think this time, I'd rather we got hit with the toilet paper and make the free throws."

Al was clearly pleased. And because he was operating on my level now, I knew why. Like any good reporter, he had found his angle.

Covering the game itself was an experience I'll never forget. Thanks to Al, I had a prize seat right behind him at NBC's table courtside, plus an audio plug in my ear so I could hear everything that was said, not only by Al, Dick or Billy, but also Finkel and Coyle, who were coordinating camera coverage from the NBC truck parked outside. Thanks to a tour by Harry the day before, I knew he and George were at that moment seated in front of no less than 19 TV screens, including three that showed slow-motion footage. From those, they would constantly pick and choose throughout the game to capture the action from all the best angles possible.

Was I nervous? You bet. Covering a college basketball game might be routine stuff, but covering *coverage* of a college basketball game, well, that was something new for me. I had not a clue what to expect. So as I sat there—engulfed by the deafening noise of the crowd—I continued to scribble down any impressions, emotions, or conclusions that came to mind, hoping some of it might be of use later on. A few feet away, Al, Dick and Billy stood before the bright lights at courtside, fidgeting like thoroughbreds at the starting gate. Dick in the center, Al to his left, Billy on the right. All three wore earplugs, as well, their audio umbilical cords amidst the howling din.

Suddenly, Ken Finkel's voice burst into my ears: "One minute to air time, guys. Have a good time."

The countdown began. "We have 20 seconds. Twenty seconds to air time," Finkel said. I noticed Al, who had been talking to Larry Brown, was grabbed by Packer and pulled back to his proper spot before the lights. My pulse quickened as the fingers on the director's hand began curling up, ticking off the last seconds to the accompanying drone of Finkel's voice in my ear: "Four, three, two, one…"

At which time, Enberg began.

"From the campus of the University of Notre Dame! A madhouse crowd of 11,345 fans at the Athletic and Convocation Center, on hand for this intersectional match between Notre Dame and UCLA! In the last decade, this has been one of the most highly fought rivalries…" Scribbling furiously, I finally had to give up and just put down a few key words to keep my line of thought. Now that the show was rolling, there just didn't seem to be any letup. Everything just seemed to happen fast. First came the pre-recorded commercials, then they were right back for pregame comments—at which time Al, yelling to be heard above the crowd, hit early on his theme.

"This is the Gipper! The Golden Dome! The sixth man, the crowd! Larry Brown must be aware of it! You must not shoot into the student zoo, or else you blow the game!" While Al talked, the monitors showed Coyle's fine blending of crowd scenes, including the shot of a player shooting a free throw looking into a sea of screaming and waving fans. Then Finkel's voice broke in: "Thirty seconds."

Calmly, Enberg swung round to Packer for his comments. "It's bedlam here, Dick. The key to this game is tempo…" and, as had been discussed in the meeting the day before, he talked about Notre Dame's power and UCLA's speed. Finkel's voice then broke in again. "Commercial! Ten, nine, eight, seven…"

I watched as Enberg, who clearly realized they were a bit behind, but remained unfazed, smoothly interrupted to right things: "…and Billy, we'll be back to see that and more, as NBC college basketball continues!" God, I thought. Al was dead on. Without Enberg, the train would go off the track. What a pro.

The lights faded, the tension dropped, and the three returned to their seats in front of me and put on headsets. "That had to be a great opening," Enberg said. "Magnificent!" Finkel told them. "If that doesn't tell the story…Hey, guys! This is exciting!"

So was the game, which was close throughout the first half. But what caught my attention most were Enberg's off-the-cuff remarks when timeouts were called. No matter that he had a director counting off the seconds in front of his face, or Finkel's voice in his ear. Dick was totally unflappable, smoothly keying to commercials, matching his words perfectly to the seconds remaining.

"…and so, it's time out here, as UCLA jumps out to an early lead!"

In addition, while the game was going on, Enberg amazed me by how he not only kept up with the action on the court, but also handled the constant hammering reminders in his ear from Finkel about what was coming up *on the broadcast* as well—things like replays and slow-motion shots of key plays he had to focus on, or reminders to read previews of certain upcoming NBC shows, including the *Sportsworld* feature.

Example: After one spectacular play, Finkel's voice boomed: "We're showing Tripuka now!" And Enberg, in a heartbeat, calmly blended in with, "Here it is again. You can see Tripuka, grabbing the rebound and going right back up for the shot. Pruitt just a step too late, pushing with the body, getting the foul."

Impressed? You bet. To my mind, Enberg was the epitome of cool, calm and collected. And class.

Al's moment came in the final seconds when, with the score tied at 48, UCLA's Michael Holton was fouled by Orlando Woolridge...and stepped to the line at the end of the court *away* from the student section. Now he was able to repeat the harvest from his pregame talk with Brown.

"You're going to see the crowd go bananas trying to psyche him out!" Al screamed. "But the thing is, he does not have to shoot into the students at the other end! Coach Larry Brown decided to shoot into the zoo the first half, the second half into the season ticket holders! The visitor has the preference of which end, and Larry Brown made a great move, because now the player is not shooting into one million students acting like one million B.C.!"

"That was a thousand-dollar speech, Coach!" Enberg enthused.

"I want an honorarium!" Al replied.

Holton missed his first shot, but made the second to give UCLA the lead, and with five seconds remaining, UCLA's Rod Foster was fouled by Tom Sluby. In my ear, I heard Finkel suggesting: "He's not shooting at the students, guys..." Foster made both shots, but Al passed this time. He had made his point.

Woolridge sank a final basket at the horn, but the three free throws—tossed away from the howling student section—had given UCLA the cushion it needed to win a squeaker, 51-50. As we all stood, and the headsets came off, I watched Al, and I could see he was mighty pleased. He and Enberg exchanged a few remarks, but I couldn't hear what was said because of the noise. My guess, however, was that it had something to do with Al's dead-on anecdote about the student section at the end. Not only was it accurate, it was good, another timely "McGuire-ism" delivered only as Al could.

The best part was that he still had ammunition to spare for the future. He hadn't needed his Moose Krause story to fill, and the fact that

Digger now owned Rockne's summer cottage could always be saved for another day.

"Al McGuire Days." That's what I looked forward to the most, during my last 10 years at the *Journal*, after Al had left Marquette and our paths crossed less frequently than before. Yes, we were doing the ghostwriting thing, but that was mostly by phone, so it wasn't quite the same. Not like when, covering the Marquette beat, I got to sit and talk with him one on one almost daily.

Al was just that kind of person. The times you got to spend with him were special, and I always came away from them feeling just a notch higher in my self-esteem, about who I was and my whole place in the scheme of things. Part of it, I'm sure, was that his energy level was transferable. I mean, he just picked you up, with his zest for life and intellect. And then there was his genuine interest in people. It didn't matter why I was there to talk to him. He always seemed more interested in what I was doing, how my life was going, that sort of thing. He always made me feel important. Like I had talent and worth.

No matter what the reason for our meeting, we always followed a familiar pattern. First, we got "business" out of the way. I'd do my interview on whatever the subject was at the time, and then we'd just sit and enjoy breakfast or lunch, or maybe just a couple beers in the warm sunshine outside somewhere in late afternoon. And that's when we'd talk as friends, Al voicing his concerns on things, me doing the same, and always discussing things that had nothing to do with college basketball—like Hemingway's philosophy, why the Brewers weren't winning, whatever was the latest Hollywood "hit" movie, why ice fishing was the first sign of insanity, or maybe a project he wanted me to collaborate with him on. Whatever. Small talk, we used to call it, back on the farm. But before you knew it, a couple of hours or so had slipped easily by, and then we were saying, "Thanks, and see ya," shaking hands, and I was back in the car and gone.

"Al McGuire Days." I will always be thankful for every one I got. And besides, the great stories just kept coming. Some when we talked "business," others later on. But one thing was certain: If you sat with Al for an hour or two, and couldn't get a damn good, quotable story, then brother (or sister), you'd better hang it up. Toss in your pen and notebook and find another line of work.

Like when Al and I met at a South Side Burger King one time, to talk about Marquette's title run 10 years before. In addition to the stuff he gave me on that, I came away with a great human interest piece we ran in the Sunday magazine. He'd always been known to be as tight with a buck as he was quick with a quip, and I found, to my delight, things hadn't changed.

Al had ordered a bacon croissant. Opening the box, he was dismayed to find the breakfast sandwich contained eggs as well.

"I'm not supposed to eat eggs in the morning because I'm on a low-cholesterol diet," he informed me. He smiled. "I eat 'em in the afternoon and at night."

So Al got up and took the croissant back to the cashier and asked if she would remove the eggs. A few minutes later, she returned to our table with the bacon croissant—minus eggs. Al thanked her, then called her back and said: "Uh, Miss, I assume since I'm not having the eggs that I don't have to pay the full price."

The flustered girl said nothing and left, then returned shortly. "There you go," she said with smile, leaving 41 cents on the table.

I was stunned. But Al, who at that time earned six figures a year as a TV broadcaster for NBC, seemed pleased. "It's not the money," he said, a bit defensively. "It's the principle of the thing."

And then there was the time I was doing a piece on which was better, college or pro basketball? So I got ahold of Al, drove out to see him at his office in Mequon, and in 20 minutes came away with the quotes that made the whole thing golden. What Al pointed out was that college basketball, which had only 27 games a season, compared to the NBA's 82, had an excitement to it that the pros just couldn't match.

"The difference is that college basketball opens up like *South Pacific* or *Annie Get Your Gun*," Al explained. "Fifteen seconds before post time, the countdown starts. Then all of a sudden, the whole place goes bananas. Doctors and dentists are standing in their seats, yelling. It's a happening. The cheerleaders' skirts are pressed, the floors are waxed, and everything else. The pros can't get off on that big a high, because they play too many games."

The problem, Al pointed out, was that the pros were just *too* good.

"They are definitely the best players in the world, without a doubt," he said. "But what happens, they get like the gladiators of the old Roman Empire, in that the gladiators became so proficient that they had to handicap them. Give the other people nets, or tie an arm behind their backs, and so on.

"These guys are so good that the eye just doesn't appreciate. What they do is common. They do it so many times that it takes the thrill off. It doesn't quiver. Things should quiver. There should always be a certain amount of quivering that gets people out of their seats."

Quiver. To this day, whether I'm rating a movie I've watched, or a book I've read, Al's yardstick pops to mind. Did it make me quiver?

Another great source for Al stories was his ongoing travels. Al was sort of a Renaissance Man among modern-day coaches in that he also taught basketball in Greece, Italy, up and down the Mediterranean. And then there were his motorbike trips across the South Island of New Zealand, and South Africa as well. What I think most people didn't realize about Al was that once he was away from the basketball court, Al was basically a loner, a guy who cherished his privacy and always kept his distance. Where his personal life was concerned, crowds were not his idea of fun. And even people he called his "close" friends, like Savio or Norm Fischer, or Herb Kohl, were people who weren't involved in sports and people he didn't see all that often.

"A friend is someone I see every three or four months," he once told me. "I just don't get involved with people, I guess. I don't know, I guess I'm more hit-and-run. I just don't get involved. I tire quickly."

Al's idea of relaxing was to climb on his Harley and go riding— alone. Or when he took a trip, he usually took along one friend to share the experience, as he spent a few weeks riding and observing, soaking up the country's habits and culture. Not only did it make him a more educated man, but it also provided more grist for a healthy number of anecdotes along the way.

I once asked him, when he'd returned from one of his trips, how he convinced Pat to let him go off for weeks at a time like that and not take her with him.

"I time it just right," Al replied. "As I'm going into the bathroom, I say, 'Pat, I'm going to South Africa.' Then I close the door, and she stands outside and pounds on it until she gets tired. 'Don't worry,' I always tell her, 'it won't be for long.'"

He used somewhat the same philosophy when he occasionally came in late. "I walk in at two in the morning, and Pat says, 'Where you been?' And I say, 'Why, did somebody call?'"

I'll never forget how Al's ego took a couple of solid knocks on the New Zealand trip, which he took with Norm Fischer, the president of Medalist. As soon as they arrived in New Zealand, they bought a couple of Suzukis. "We didn't have any choice," Al explained. "There weren't any bikes to rent over there, so we had to buy them, and then sell before we left."

At any rate, all went well until one afternoon when, as they were navigating the tricky, ever-winding roads on South Island, a rainstorm came up, and after they'd both fallen a couple of times, they finally ended up getting their bikes stuck in the mud. At which point, help appeared through the muck and the mire.

"It was raining like hell, and we were tired and trying to get our bikes out of the mud when this guy driving a garbage truck stopped and told us to get in," Al recalled. "I thought he would let us ride with him in the cab, but he told us to get in the back with the bikes and the garbage. I told Norm, as we climbed up, 'Doesn't this guy know we're wealthy people?'"

Even more humbling was the experience that took place the day Al and Norm were leaving. All week long Al had told the lady who ran the inn where they stayed that he was a Canadian, ever fearful that if she knew who he was, he'd never get a minute's privacy. So finally, on the last day, he decided to fess up as he paid his bill.

"I'm not really a Canadian," Al told her. "I'm Al McGuire. I'm an American. I coach basketball."

"Inside or outside?" the woman asked.

Speaking of bikes, I have to tell you about the night Al scared the hell out of his grandson's babysitter. It happened on a warm night in May of 1980, when Martha Van Beckum, who was babysitting for nine-month-old Alfred Joseph McGuire, the son of Allie and Georgia McGuire, was shocked to see a weird-looking stranger pull up on a motorcycle, climb off and walk towards the house.

As the man—a scruffy, unshaven guy with long flowing hair, wearing old blue jeans and tennis shoes—approached, the poor girl panicked. Terrified, she slammed the front door and locked it, then ran through the living room and locked the side door as well. Then she closed the curtains and peeped out, wondering if she should call the police.

As it turned out, there was no need. After standing in the yard for about 15 seconds, Al—who else?—climbed back on his motorcycle and left.

"I guess I can't blame her," he told me, when I called and asked him about the incident. "I do get pretty seedy-looking this time of year. I don't get my hair cut until November, when I have to do it for TV."

Al laughed. "My own grandson, and I can't get into the house. I felt sorry for the girl, though. I'm sure she thought I was some sort of helter-skelter or psycho or something." While Al didn't go to the door, because it was obvious to him that the girl was scared, he did call Allie the next morning.

"Allie, I just want you to know I'm taking A.J. out of the family will," he said.

When I asked Allie about it, he said, "Typical TV star reaction. He was just mad she didn't recognize his face."

If there was a side to Al McGuire that not that many people knew about, it was his mania for collecting toy soldiers. He started in February of '79, when he was in Terre Haute, Indiana, broadcasting the Wichita State-Indiana State game, and during his afternoon wanderings, he walked into a small antique shop...and came away with a lead toy soldier that brought back memories of his youth. After which, collecting them became more an obsession than a hobby. Because after that, wherever Al went and whatever he was doing—telecasting a game, giving a speech or making a guest appearance—he was also always looking for toy soldiers.

What Al was after were what collectors call Manoils, Barclays, and Gray Irons: three-inch, hollow-lead, dime-store soldiers now no longer made—little figures commonly sold from the late 1930s through the mid-1960s for five or 10 cents in Woolworth's and Kresge's stores all over the country. (I had a nice collection of Manoils myself, when I was a kid in the late 1950s, but like so many things, they vanished somewhere along the way.) The point is, by the time Al started collecting them, they were worth up to $40 to $50 apiece, depending on their condition and what they were doing (artillery gunner, ambulance driver, radar operator, etc.).

At any rate, once Al got the bug, he was like a monk on a holy mission, determinedly seeking out lead soldiers all over the country—in antique stores, at flea markets, garage sales, and even the homes of other collectors. He would trade anything for them: money, other soldiers, T-shirts from the Al McGuire-*Milwaukee Journal* Run, his autograph, even his NBC complimentary tickets. Believe it. Al was a serious collector. The *average* price he paid was not cheap—usually $5 to $10 a soldier. And by the early '90s, he had a marvelous collection with hundreds of pieces, even branching out into the area of pre-World War II cardboard soldiers and vehicles that were extremely rare indeed.

When I asked him about his mania, Al admitted it stemmed from his love of toy soldiers as a child. When it came to prices he paid, well, he was philosophical.

"God is punishing me now because I stole once when I was a kid," Al explained, recalling how he had once gone into a store and slipped toy soldiers down his knickers. "See, I went to a Catholic grade school, and we used to wear knickers. I had this hole in my pocket, so the soldiers would fall through into the leg of my knickers. One day, I put two in my pocket, and as I walked out, they fell through and cut my knee."

Over the next two decades, Al continued to expand on his collection—bringing his latest finds back home and wrapping them up in tissue paper and storing them in suitcases, where they would stay until the holidays. "I put 'em all out at Christmastime at the house, and my kids act as if they're interested in them now and then, when they want to hit me for something," Al told me. "Someday when it's all over, I'd like some museum out there to have them, to put on display at Christmastime for children to come and see.

"The thing is, I only trade or buy. I don't sell. I think that if you sell, you're not a true hobbyist. And with me, they get a lot of tender loving care, and I get an awful lot of pleasure out of the collecting. And these are mainly the dime-store soldier, the blue-collar, lunch-pail soldier. They're crude, out of proportion. But maybe that's why the kids liked them so much, because they let you use your imagination."

As more people learned about Al's Manoil mania, he began to get calls at his office in Sussex, and he would frequently find himself driving to people's homes in the Milwaukee area to see what they had to offer. "Most are in a shoe box in the attic or something," Al said. "They're seldom in mint condition. They've been played with, got BB holes in 'em, need some R and R like those Argentine guys who were on the Falklands. But you find some good ones, too, and besides, the fun is in the trading."

The fun for me, as a reporter, of course, were the funny stories I heard and experienced about this particular facet of Al's kaleidoscopic life.

Billy Packer recalled a March day in 1981, when he and Al had some time to fill after Kentucky had defeated Louisiana State in a nationally televised game at Rupp Arena in Lexington.

"The game ended and we were a little short," Packer recalled. "So they sent Al to one end of the floor and me to the other to do a couple interviews to fill time. They go to me, I do my interview and flip to Al…and there's no Al! I mean, nobody knows where he is. He's gone. So they switch back to me and somehow I fill the time for both of us.

"Anyway, a few minutes later, I'm leaving, and here's Al—sitting on the steps of Rupp Arena with some toy soldiers and this little truck in a paper bag. See, the day before he'd been to this flea market, trying to get 'em, but he couldn't make a deal. Now I knew where he'd gone so fast: to meet the guy again. Anyway, he looks up and sees me, and he's happy as hell. Like a little kid at Christmas. 'Look, Billy,' he said to me. 'I got the truck, I got the truck.'"

That same year, Bob Wolf, the *Journal's* sports columnist, and sportswriter Chuck Salituro traveled to Philadelphia to cover the NCAA Final Four. At the airport, they met Al, who offered them a ride to their hotel, and they accepted...not realizing what they were getting into.

"We got in the car, and Al asks, 'Would you mind if we went out of our way a bit to get some soldiers?'" Wolf recalled. "I said, 'Soldiers?' And he said, 'I collect 'em. It's a hobby.' So he gives the driver directions, and it turns out we're heading for some textile plant in the far reaches of Philly to look for toy soldiers.

"Anyway, we kept going and going, and Al kept stopping to ask for directions. We had this street we were looking for, Roosevelt Parkway, where we were supposed to meet a guy waiting for us at a gas station. So finally, we get to the gas station, Al changes cars [gets into the car of the person he was supposed to meet], and we follow him out to this plant. It's an old place, like a warehouse, and it looks deserted. But we found this one office, and here's a guy sitting there with a big box of about 75 soldiers on his desk.

"Al went through them, sorting them out, rejecting a number of them. He kept rejecting some because they were rusted or beat up, but he kept more than he rejected. Out of 75, I bet he took 45 or 50. To make a long story short, we didn't get to the hotel until about two and a half hours after we left the airport! But it was amusing. Here's a guy, a national sports figure, dealing in toy soldiers in a deserted warehouse. It was like a spy movie or something."

Packer's last episode with Al, when it came to finding toy soldiers, occurred in Atlanta, when—like Wolf and Salituro—he let Al talk him into driving out to see a local collector.

"It was the morning of the game, but he had made a deal with the guy to stop out," Packer recalled. "So off we go. We get about halfway there, and I suddenly realize Al didn't know where the guy lived! And he couldn't quite remember the address.

"So now we're driving along, real slow, trying to read the street numbers. It was 1101 Peachtree or something like that, a fashionable neighborhood. Al's checking one side of the street; I'm checking the other. I say, 'The hell with it. Let's go back to the hotel.' He says, 'No, it's got to be there. Let's go a little farther.'

"So we get to the address the guy gave us, and it's a *nuthouse,* a sanitarium! Now I really want to go back, but Al says, 'No, come on. Maybe the guy is a custodian. Maybe he lives in the caretaker's office or something.' So in we go.

"Here we are, in a sanitarium, and Al asking around for some guy who has toy soldiers. And nobody knows anything about it. And Al keeps insisting…We had our NBC blazers on, too, and all of a sudden the guards are kind of looking at us, figuring we probably belonged there, too, and had just got out for a stroll. I mean, I was getting worried. That's when I grabbed Al and we got out of there.

"Anyway, it turns out the guy lived on West Peachtree and we were on *East* Peachtree, way on the wrong side of town. So we go out there, and by the time we got back, we just made the game. Afterwards, I said, 'Al, from now on, you want those damn soldiers, you go alone.'"

The time I remember best was a trading session I attended with Al the following spring, where I saw that generous side of his character shine through again. We'd driven to the home of Chris Olson, a 15-year-old who lived in the Milwaukee suburb of Muskego. Chris was one of Al's "locals"—fellow collectors with whom he traded. After showing Chris what he'd brought along, Al studied the rows of lead Manoils Chris had set up on the dining room table: soldiers marching, firing rifles, manning artillery pieces, climbing telephone poles, peeling potatoes, boxing, carrying the American flag; soldiers, sailors, nurses—65 or so in all, and in good condition. Considering I had never owned more than 30 Manoils in my childhood (most of which were the most common riflemen and marching soldiers), I was impressed.

The format for the trade was simple enough—each of them picked out the soldiers they wanted, and then the bartering began, using McGuire's Manoil price catalog as a guide. In the book every Manoil, Barclay and Gray Iron ever made was listed, plus the going price for fair, good, or mint condition. "You say what you want to trade and what you want; then we'll go to the book," Al said. "That seems the best way. I don't care how the numbers wash. We're not looking to dot every every I or cross every T. Just so we're in the ballpark."

It became quickly evident, however, that while Al had set out some rare pieces, Chris was handicapped a bit in that he did not possess enough figures to trade en masse and wasn't willing to give up his rarer ones in an exchange. His mother, trying to help the cause, had brought out four other cast-iron and lead figures he'd forgotten.

"I know they're common, but they're mint," Chris said hopefully. "See, that's the problem. I don't have anything good to trade with."

Al motioned towards three of the soldiers Chris had picked out. "Pick one of those gunners." he said, "We'll make a trade."

Which they did. And then continued on to make a few more, carefully balancing the prices of the pieces involved out of the catalog. When they called a halt an hour later, Chris had three new pieces—two guys on a rubber raft, a soldier with a map table, and a soldier playing a French horn. Al came away with a soldier jabbing a bayonet, an anti-aircraft gun, a soldier with a shell, and some common marchers.

At which point, Al brought out a tent, rare indeed, and handed it to Chris. "Here, Chris," he said, "we're even. Is that fair?"

Chris's eyes widened, and for more than an instant he couldn't speak. "Yeah, *that's* fair," he said finally, in a quiet voice. He knew what a steal he had. Al smiled. I could tell. Making Chris's day had made his.

As we were driving back, I asked Al why he'd done it, why he'd thrown in that tent at the end. He didn't give me a direct answer. Instead, he asked a question back. Asked if I would like to know his most successful trade. "A doctor from the Veterans Administration Hospital called one day," he said, "And he said, 'I heard you save toy soldiers. You know, my only son died, and I'd like you to have his soldiers. I know you'll take good care of them.'" Al smiled. "He had 55 of them," he added. "I had him come to the DePaul-Marquette game as my guest.

"See, that's another plus in this, Rog. The people you meet; so many nice people. Like I say, the fun I get is in the trading. It wouldn't be any fun if you could just go out and buy everything." He paused, then added, "Besides, I'm cheap."

One of the funniest interviews I ever did with Al was for a Sports Weekend/On the Air piece for the *Journal* in May of 1983. The subject was Al's fledgling TV show, called *Al McGuire on Sports*—which was struggling through its first season, thanks primarily to lack of promotion by the affiliates that were running it.

"You got to be Sherlock Holmes to find it," Al told me, referring to the fact that WTMJ-TV, the local NBC affiliate, was running the show at 5 p.m. on Sundays. "It's on at 5 p.m.—when they don't have on *Tarzan and Jane*. What we learned, you're only as good as the affiliate will promote the show. It's taken so long to build up an audience, because the stations have their own little things they're stroking. They must think I'm located in Ethiopia, but that's part of the game. You pay the price."

In spite of Al's dour words, the half-hour show was also being shown at the time in New York, Chicago, Los Angeles, Cleveland, and Washington, D.C., and its ratings, according to WTMJ, were about average for a new program. The idea for the show, which was developed by Al's son Rob, featured Al talking to different athletes about their sport—Wayne Gretzky on hockey, Rick Mears on auto racing, Ralph Sampson on college basketball—plus some less widely known subjects, such as pro wrestling and the life of black caddies on the pro golf tour.

Now admittedly, this sort of thing had been done before, but what made Al's show unique was his approach, as he put it, "the approach that we don't know anything about it." What that meant was the show played to Al's interest in the human side of sports, and that it would appeal to viewers, who learned right along with Al, who was asking questions they would like to ask.

All well and good. Except that, as Al put it, "the idea is, we're supposed to make money." Which, he went on to say, he hadn't. "This," he said, pointedly, "has been a learning experience…with skyscraper tuition."

What had happened, of course, was that Al—who was a pretty good con man himself—was finding out that swimming with the big fish in the Hollywood pond was a whole new, and costly, experience. When I asked him to elaborate, Al was off and running.

"I found out when you deal with people in Hollywood, you don't get paid," he explained. "Everything is a trade-off. I've been trying to track 'em down for months. The syndicators owe me a talent fee, and then we own the business, but the thing is, there's nothing left of the business. In Hollywood, if someone offers you $1.50 of the gross, or 75 percent of the net, take the $1.50. Because in Hollywood, there is no net. Whatever they make, they use up.

"Now, I'm a pretty good street guy, and I can't even tell the phonies from the street guys. Everybody out there has big wheels, gold around their neck, and sit at front tables. There are no back tables at Hollywood restaurants.

"It goes like this. The sponsors pay the syndicator. The syndicator then pays the expense of the show. He takes his profit, and whatever's left goes into buying toy soldiers [Al's hobby]. Right now, it looks like I'm not buying any toy soldiers for a while."

Still, as you would expect with Al, his 13-show venture into syndication land was not without its lighter moments.

"Like with Calvin Peete," Al said. "We were doing this show, showing why pro black caddies are going the way of the buffalo. I'm talking with some caddies, and this note is slipped under the table that says, 'He's a pro.' It turns out that one of the guys I'm sitting with is Calvin Peete. And the funny thing is, I don't know which one is Calvin Peete.

"And then, when I did the Wayne Gretzky one, I went to the wrong guy and started asking questions. I didn't know what Wayne Gretzky looked like. I knew Gretzky wore No. 99, but it was practice, and they didn't have numbered jerseys on."

By this time, Al had me chuckling, but the best was yet to come, as he described his bizarre experience in filming his look at pro wrestling, which included an interview with a wrestler named Mil Mascaras, whose name translates to "Thousand Masks."

"We go down to this dump where they wrestle in San Bernardino," Al recalled. "This place is a snake pit, an asylum. It's so dark we had to light it. Finally he comes out, he's the last guy on the program, and he has this mask on, so you can't tell what he looks like, and he's wrestling some guy who needs a brassiere.

"Anyway, the mask guy tells Barry Martin, our producer, he won't come out unless I turn the bright lights off. Barry comes over to me and says, 'He won't come out unless we turn the lights off. If we shut them off, it's too dark to shoot.'

"I said, 'Lay a number on him.'

"Barry says, 'A what?'

"I said, 'Lay $500 on him. He'll come out.'

"So Barry comes back and says, 'He wants a thousand.'

"So I say, real loud so everybody can hear, 'Take the lights down! We're leaving!'

"So then the guy comes out, and he says as he walks by, 'I want the $500 in cash.'"

By now, of course, I'm laughing so hard it's tough to write. Even Al is chuckling along with me. We talked a few more minutes, about changes he'd like to make if the show was renewed (which it wasn't), and then I left, simply happy that I had been able to share yet another comic episode in the often zany life of Al McGuire.

There was only one time I know of when, according to Al, he was literally at a loss for words.

That was when, in December of 1978, he was being introduced to Jimmy Carter, then President of the United States, in the Roosevelt Room of the White House, one of 14 people who had recently been named members to Carter's Commission on Physical Fitness.

As Al told me later, if there was ever a time for one his famous "75-dollar lines," that was it. But when actually confronted by Carter's famous Ultra-Brite smile and the presidential aura that it represented, Al just didn't know what to say. Instead, he settled for a smile and a handshake and let his most famous quarry ever get away.

I couldn't believe it (especially since I was a Republican). The Mouth That Roared had been silenced.

"I didn't think I'd ever be awed by anything," Al told me, "because the only thing that impresses a New Yorker is a 50 percent-of-the-check tip. But then he came in the room and started shaking hands, and I was awed. I wanted to say something good. Drop one of my one-liners on him. But then he was in front of me, and I choked. I opened my mouth, and out came nothing. I guess you could say he cornered the conversation. He said, 'Nice to meet you, Coach. Thanks for being on the board.' And that was it."

Al shook his head. "I can't remember that ever happening to me before," he admitted. "Usually, you can always reach into the grab bag and come up with something. But not this time. I admit it. I was impressed."

Al said he thought the president "was slighter than I thought he'd be. I'd pictured him bigger. But you really feel a strength in the room when he comes in. A kinda presence. You realize, there's truly the most powerful person in the world."

Carter spoke to the group for about 15 minutes, thanking them for being part of the Commission—which was supposed to meet four times a year in Washington to advise government officials about what should be done to improve physical fitness in the country. (I never asked Al if it really did. At the time, I felt, like most such Commissions, that it was all ballroom bananas, and Carter, thankfully, was gone two years later anyhow.)

"We were actually only in the White House about a half an hour before he got there, and about 15 minutes after he left," Al recalled. "The rest of the time was spent in the old Executive Building. But it had some nice antiques. I'd like to be left there alone for an hour or two."

Once Al got back to Milwaukee, away from the aura of the president, his unique ability to voice oblique impressions returned.

Of the Commission's $800,000 budget (small by Washington standards), Al quipped, "I knew our budget was small by the size of the hotel room they gave me. I thought I was in an elevator. It had a bathroom, but you couldn't close the door because the knob would knock you off your seat."

On the president's staff: "They all seem to talk the same. Everybody kept saying, 'Y'all come back, now.' What they were really trying to say in a nice way was, 'See you later.'"

Given the subject, I couldn't resist asking Al if he might someday enter politics.

"I'd never do it," he insisted. "I don't want my family tree traced. They might find my brother, Johnny."

My last "Al McGuire Day" took place in August of 1988, and it turned out to be one of the best. Since Al was a just a few weeks shy of turning 60 (his birthday was September 7), I was asked to write an "Al McGuire, Senior Citizen" feature for the Sunday *Journal*, so I called Al and we decided to meet at Westmoor Country Club mid-morning and go from there. And go we did. What followed was a truly enjoyable, day-long sojourn with Al, knocking about in the crisp, warm autumn sunshine, with no planned itinerary, just stopping at antique shops, parks, and little taverns all over Waukesha County along the way.

Al was waiting for me when I pulled into the Westmoor parking lot, sitting on the grass, of all things, under a shade tree, reflecting on God knows what. What a far—and refreshing—cry, I thought, from the brightly dressed peacocks who were popping out of the pro shop, bloated with their self-importance as they headed for the links. "Raa-ger the lodger!" he cried as I walked over. We shook hands. "How ya doin'?" He was, as I expected, dressed in what I had come to know, over the years, as "Al Casual"—a knit shirt, rumpled slacks, white low-cut tennis shoes, no socks. Only a nudist could have been more comfortable.

Given the subject of the story, I eyed Al up a bit as we stood there chitchatting. Yes, his long black hair was grayed and thinning. And there were some wrinkles peeking out from around his vibrant, piercing eyes. But all in all, he looked damn good. And as I found out that day, he was quotable as ever, facing up to Father Time with the same biting, Irish sense of humor that had characterized him all his life.

As we walked to his car, I asked him about getting older, and he smiled and shrugged.

"The first sign the parade is passing me by," he quipped, "is that I'm cheating in my speeches. I've gone from Joe Louis to Rocky

Marciano to Mike Tyson. I started with Shirley Temple and now I'm with Madonna. Because otherwise, I'll lose my audience."

Otherwise, he said, as we climbed in, nothing had really changed. "I'm still cutting deals," he said happily. "Everything I got on is a freebie. Except my underwear. I'm not built well enough for that."

We drove out of the country club and started heading west. Turning this way, turning that. While I had no clue as to where we were going, I assumed Al did and just sat back, enjoyed the ride...and started asking questions.

So how did he feel about turning 60?

"Actually, I'm sort of pleased," he said. "Obviously, there's a worse alternative: not to reach 60. It's like the guy complaining about playing golf, and his buddy says, 'Hey, it's better than being under the grass, right?' It's better to be on top of it."

What was clear to me, right from the start that day, was that Al was on top of life. By that I mean he was controlling his days like he used to control basketball games, getting the most out of each one by doing what he wanted to do, period. For reasons I'll reveal later, I was envious. Al had what I didn't—freedom to dance to his own tune. For $150,000, he was doing 15 or 16 games for NBC, leaving him lots of time to, as he put it, "either come to the day, or let the day come to me."

He admitted, however, before he could climb on his motorbike and do that, he had to take care of what he called "distasteful things," business matters mostly, that had to be done. As we drove along, he told me he always did those things early in the morning, so they wouldn't spoil his whole day.

"Right now, one is to clean out that thing that catches the water in the basement, because my toy soldiers are down there," he explained. I chuckled and told him it was called a dehumidifier. He frowned. "Yeah, a dehumidifier. It's distasteful. So I go down there and I empty that thing out. I've been emptying it out for a number of years now, and I still wonder where the hell the water comes from. It really is remarkable. Where does this water come from?

"And then, if there's any things of trying-ness, delicate, sensitive, I do them right away. Like the poster this company had put up of me, even though our contract ran out two months ago. I mean, either send me the check or take the gosh-darned poster down. Who are we throwing a party for? I expect to be compensated."

All that accomplished, Al told me that once he roars out of his driveway, the modus operandi never varies. He always travels alone, never combs his hair, and never makes appointments. "If you ever see me with more than four people and my hair is combed," he cracked, "then you know I'm getting paid."

On this particular afternoon, Al roamed first to what he called "a great chili and beer place" called Kuhtz's General Store, a small grocery store with a bar and grill in the back, located in Stone Bank, about 20 miles west of Brookfield. When we walked inside, I was leery. The whole place, even where food was sold, was dimly lit, the floors looked dirty and creaked, and from somewhere, I could smell disinfectant. But as usual, Al was right. The chili was hot and tasty, the beers ice cold, and the sandwiches (ham and cheese for me, turkey on rye for Al, as I recall) were great—and so huge they were hard to finish.

As Al spooned down his chili, he opined that it was probably time for him to take another change in his life, sort of, as he put it, "step aside and move into the annex." His original plan last year, he told me, had been to leave NBC when his contract expired and go to New Zealand. Instead, he signed on for three more years because the money was right and he wanted to do something he'd never done—cover the Summer Olympic Games in September in Seoul, South Korea. Now, he admitted, he deeply regretted and felt guilty about making that move, and he was also honest enough to tell me why, for selfish reasons, he did it.

"I should have left NBC last year," he told me. "I like using the Olympics as an excuse, but I think it's because I don't want to give up what I've had the last 10 years. I'm spoiled, Rog. I admit it. Because the contract with NBC has allowed me to live in the moment.

"It was one of the few things I ever did in my life for money. But the dollars were so strong that I was getting paid not to go to ABC or CBS that I sacrificed my career. Because, you see, they're actually paying me *not* to work. I don't get exposure. I do 16 games a year. Billy Packer does that many on his way to the washroom. Dick Vitale does that many for a coffee break. I'm paid not to work, and it's something I've never experienced before. So anyhow, I signed the contract and understood the consequences, but I'm not pleased with myself for doing it."

Our next stop on that sunny, relaxed afternoon was Nashotah Park, for a short, meditative walk among the trees. I'll never forget, once we got out of the car, how Al just sort of took off in his own direction, oblivious, I felt, to my being there, and just strolled on ahead, along the paths among the trees. Glancing up at the dusty rays of sunshine coming down, stopping every so often to touch a tree, or kneeling down to look at a flower. Not once did I call out, or try to catch up with him, or ask him a question. He was in his own world right then, and the last thing I would have wanted to do was spoil it. Finally, we came to an open spot, next to what looked like a small lake, covered with tall brown grass. Al stood there a moment, taking it all in, then turned and said, "Beautiful, isn't it? Well, I suppose we should get back." And so, back we went. But this time, the spell was broken. Al had seen whatever it was he wanted to see, and now he picked up the pace, just marking time with conversation, I felt, until we reached the car.

In Mapleton, Al suddenly turned the car into a farmer's driveway and introduced me to Bob Christenson, a big, hearty fellow who had an antique store and one of the most enormous, well kept gardens I'd ever seen out back. For the next hour, he and Al walked among the endless rows of green beans, lettuce, tomatoes, peppers, yellow beans, sweet corn, carrots, cabbage, onions, rutabagas, potatoes, and some stuff even this Iowa farmboy didn't recognize. Al asking Bob how each crop was faring, Bob telling him what was doing good, what wasn't, and what he expected for a yield that fall. Whether Al had bought some antiques or lots of vegetables from the guy, I didn't know, but I did notice that he didn't mind when, as they were walking along, Al picked and ate green beans raw, right off the plant.

After that, we stopped at Louie's Trading Post in Monterey, another dark little hole in the wall, for some chitchat and a few more beers. The thing was, at Louie's, you could order a lot more beers and still come away OK, because his stock was a bit limited—a tapper of unknown designation at the bar and seven-ounce Pabst "shorties" from the cooler, which Al and I (being thirsty from our walk in the woods), were more than willing to consume, along with some beef jerky sticks and pretzels. The other nice thing was, service was great. The whole time we were there, we were the only two guys in the place.

Louie was a character. An irascible, yet nice, old curmudgeon who loved to sit and talk, it seemed, with anybody about anything. That day, he was especially glad Al had stopped in, because he wanted to show him his new invention that he was sure would make him a million—a specially designed cane for senior citizens. Later on, after a few more "shorties" had been consumed (They were all of a quarter apiece!), Louie also brought out the head of a giant turtle he had preserved. God, what a ghastly thing! All black and green, and withered, and looking like dinosaur remains. As Al and I viewed the pickled skull, Louie roared. "I let the kids take it to school on 'Show and Tell' day," he explained gleefully. "They hand it to the teacher, the teacher faints, and they're sent home, so they get the rest of the day off that way."

A few more "shorties" later, Al and I left Louie with his giant turtle and headed on out once again. Where had the time gone, I wondered?

Glancing at my watch, I noticed it was already half past three. Damn. Although I knew it eventually had to, I didn't want this afternoon to end. I was out there, with Al, no strings, taking things as they came. In fact, we were taking, at our leisure, the best life had to offer—good food, cold beer, and interesting people. What more, I remember thinking, could you ask? It was like being on vacation with a tour guide extraordinaire who also just happened to be your friend. If this wasn't "seashells and balloons," what was?

As we drove along, Al began talking about the upcoming Olympics in Seoul. "I just hope the North Koreans stay above the 38th parallel," he said. "But I think, as long as Russia and China are participating, the North Koreans won't embarrass them."

It didn't sound to me like Al was looking forward to the trip, and when I said as much, he admitted I was right.

"What bothers me is being there a month," he said, "and plus, basketball is not one of the main venues. It's a team sport, very low profile at the Olympics, unless you have a big thing like we did in hockey that time we beat the Russians. So I'm pleased at the experience of it, but not truly looking forward to it, because it seems there's almost too much smorgasbord of nothing, without the potential of good lobster or steak.

"What I'd really like to do, if I'm free, is get up early and get outside Seoul and knock around. I wanted Harley to bring a bike, but they never got back to me, so I've ordered a car, my own car, so I'm not tied in with a pool car with NBC." Al chuckled, then added, "The hardest thing for me to do will be to find where the garage sales are over there."

Our last stop that afternoon turned out to be the house of Tom Snyder, on Lac la Belle. Snyder, a longtime friend and owner of a well known clothing store in Oconomowoc, had not only supplied Al with his suits for years, but given him free rein to use his dock and go for a swim anytime he pleased. Since the temperature was in the 90s, Al decided it was time to cool down, stripping to his blue jockey shorts and diving in. For about 15 minutes, he splashed about while the sun beat down on the sparkling water and an occasional boatload of people roared past.

"I do this a lot here," he said as he treaded water, happy as a clam. "Maybe every couple weeks. Here, or other places. Tom's been a friend since I moved to town. Tom and Herb (Kohl), and Jerry Savio. Herb's running for the Senate now. (Today, 16 years later, he's still there.) I couldn't do that. If they trace my family tree, it'd make Billy Carter look like a Benedictine monk."

After climbing out, Al tugged on his clothes, then we strolled slowly back up the slope from the dock, taking a few moments to savor the cool shade of the trees and the peaceful blue sky as birds chirped merrily about. The time seemed right, I thought, for a few more questions.

About 60, he was asked. Do you feel old? Does getting old bother you?

"No, I feel good," Al said. "I feel I'm coming into the greatest time of my life. Actually, I'm at a point I'm so pleased with Al McGuire that I've stopped trying to stop time. I've found I just can't get a boring day.

"Time just seems to go so fast, Rog. It seems, more so, that every 20 minutes I'm eating breakfast, and every time I do a 180, it's time to empty the dehumidifier again. It seems to fill up every 20 minutes. But I guess it's the lesser of two evils, 'cause it could be like Chinese torture, with water dripping on your head."

And death? Did the thought of it bother him at all? I felt strange, because it was the first time I had talked to him about mortality.

"No," Al replied easily. "I'd like to die alone, is the only thing. I wouldn't like an Italian picnic-type thing. Obviously, we don't have a choice in this because sometimes the gate gets narrow, getting out of life. But I'd prefer to be very private in that." Al grinned. "I guess I'd like just enough time to tell God I didn't mean all the things I did," he said, softly.

Al said his health was good and that mentally he felt fine. But he didn't seem quite sure what he wanted to do next in life. Projects, he said. Something involving kids, something with worth. While he was talking vaguely, he didn't seem truly worried. In fact, he said he felt certain the right thing would come along.

"Look at Churchill," he quipped. "He got his first real pop at 65 when he became prime minister. And I think that aging gracefully, that's the key to life. When life becomes graceful, you have so much more to offer, to put in the kitty, to bring out humor, to bring contentment. You know, I think it's all in your mind, this age stuff. The Chinese have a saying about that, that age is experience, not age."

Before I knew it, we were back at Westmoor, pulling to a halt in the parking lot once again. It was late afternoon, the place was not so crowded now, and as we walked towards the clubhouse, I noted how comfortable it was, now that the heat of the day had passed. Before we said goodbye, I got off one final question, asking Al what meant the most to him over the years, besides his family. His reply was surprising. It was not winning the NCAA championship, or his brilliant TV career, or even Al's Run, although he was very proud of that, as well.

"It's that so many of my ballplayers have stations in life," he said. "That we were able to make sure of that, before it became fashionable, the last eight or nine years. Everybody hits you with numbers [of degrees] today, and you don't know if the numbers are lying.

"I have started to get closer to my players. I remember, a couple months ago, I called Maurice Lucas; I was doing a stand-up in Scottsdale, Arizona. So I get Maurice on the phone, and he says, 'What do you want?' I said, 'I'd like to have a cup of coffee.' And he says, 'No, you don't. You want something. Otherwise, you wouldn't be calling.' So I told him, 'Maurice, I want to touch people. I want to be close.' I find myself doing that more now."

When I told Al what a great day I'd had, he nodded in agreement, noting that most of his days were like this one, where he rose early and let the day develop. "Sometimes, it doesn't develop," he admitted, "because sometimes the guy isn't in the garden. Or nobody's at the bar. But it doesn't matter. It's just a pleasant feeling to be able to move along, and there's always a phone someplace if I want to get something done."

There was one other thing he planned to do, he added as we shook hands. He wanted to take up golf again. He'd given up his golf membership at Westmoor 10 years before, when he got so involved with NBC. Now that the TV commitment was far less involved, he admitted he had a yen to hit the links again.

"I'd like to get back to it again," he told me. "I enjoy the camaraderie, playing some gin in the clubhouse, and using four towels. At home you shower and use half a towel, but at the country club you use four and can spill powder all over yourself."

Smiling, I scribbled down what Al had said, then flipped my notebook closed. As we shook hands, I asked him what he was going to do next. Al motioned towards a nearby bench. "I think I'll just sit and savor a while," he said. "Then go inside, in a little while, and get a sandwich."

It was obvious he wanted to be alone. And as much as I might have wanted to stick around, I would never have dared to impose. "Take care, Al," I said. "Bye, Rog," he replied as I walked away.

If I savored that day perhaps a little more than usual, it was because I was pretty sure it would be the last time I'd get the opportunity. Although I hadn't told Al, I had decided to leave the *Journal* (and the world of newspapers) about a month before. There were a lot of reasons. Over the years, I'd won a lot of writing awards at the *Journal* and received very little in return in the way of recognition or pay increases. The way to the bank there, I had come to realize, was to keep your nose up the boss's fanny, and the toady I was working for then was one of a kind. Luckily, I had a national reputation and had built up a decent freelancing network with six or seven auto racing and bowling magazines. And to top it off, Miller Brewing had contacted me about writing the copy for a lucrative promotional offer that was in the works (thanks, Al). Also, I had some books I wanted to write.

Yes, it was scary when I thought about losing the security of that regular paycheck ("the bi-weekly insult" as we in the sports department called it). But thank God, I had a wife with more courage than me, who insisted I make the move. "You're too damn good for them. They'll never pay you what you're worth. You're just burning yourself out at that place. I can see it."

I also got a great piece of advice from Michael Knight, a former auto racing writer who had left the business and gone into racing PR, and who at the time I was considering leaving the *Journal* was the PR person for Newman/Haas Racing, handling Mario and Michael Andretti. A few months earlier, during a quiet moment on the CART Indy car race weekend at Milwaukee, we'd had a few minutes to talk.

"Roger," he told me, "at least now, I call the shots in my life. I've had some bad days since I left the newspaper business, but I'll tell you what. The worst day I've had was still better than the best day I ever had in newspapers." (Now, 16 years later, I can happily say thanks to them both.)

Which is not to say that, once I made the move that September, I didn't miss those occasional "Al McGuire Days" a whole lot. I did. And unfortunately, our paths after that seemed to cross less and less.

"I wanted to put something back into the kitty here. My family grew up here, and I've done well in this city of my choice."

Chapter 9
A Special "Thank You"

"I come from New York," Al McGuire liked to say, when, like a strutting cock in the barnyard, he was intent on showing his toughness. "You fall down, someone will always pick you up...by your wallet."

Not that Al wasn't proud of his New York City roots. He was. Growing up in Rockaway Beach, in the shadow of the Big Apple, he had learned many valuable lessons at an early age, lessons in life that forever shaped his personality and gave him the unique, street-smart, "don't con a con man" philosophy by which he lived...and ultimately found great success.

The point to be made, however, is that it was in Milwaukee—a uniquely Midwest, German "beer and bratwurst" burg on the shores of Lake Michigan—where Al finally found it. Where, after paying his dues in places like Dartmouth and Belmont Abbey, he was finally able to find his niche. An adopted home in heartland America where he was able to take root, settle in, raise a family, carve out a memorable career, and enjoy what he would have labeled a "Park Avenue" existence for the remainder of his life.

There were lots of things Al loved about Milwaukee (besides the fact that, next to Christmas, St. Patrick's Day was probably the most celebrated holiday around). Given his behind-the-bar upbringing, he genuinely understood Milwaukee's no-nonsense, down-to-earth people, and their unabashed "work hard, play hard" life ethic. He enjoyed the fanfare of the Great Circus Parade, the picnic-like atmosphere of the many cultural "Fests" held on the lake front every summer, and that Old World feeling of "gemuetlichkeit"—a German phrase that stood for "a general sense of good will and well-being" not unlike the "seashells and balloons" philosophy Al so much believed in. Most of all, however, he admired the die-hard support Milwaukee sports fans gave to their professional and college teams—the Packers, Bucks, Brewers, Marquette and the University of Wisconsin—no matter if they were winning or losing.

"There's something about this city," Al told me once. "It's big enough it doesn't need a winner. A pro team here can SRO [standing room only] as long as you dive for the ball. You don't have to get the ball, but you must come up with Spalding on your forehead. But if an athlete is willing to give the effort here, the numbers will turn out.

"Maybe it's because the winters are long. That might create it. But it seems that anything put on in this part of the state, if it's done in a Park Avenue way, it breaks through the sound barrier. It's top shelf. Because the people are that way."

Little wonder, then, that during the fall of 1977, shortly after he had left Marquette, Al was already trying to think of some way he could give something back to the community—a sort of special "thank you," if you will, for all the support Milwaukee had given him during his years at the university.

And wouldn't you know? The catalyst turned out to be another Irishman—my boss, Bill Dwyre, the sports editor at the *Journal*. As Al explained it to me, "Bill had a special son, and we talked once, and that's how the concept came about."

The "concept" was the *Milwaukee Journal*/Al McGuire Run—an annual five-mile charity race that would benefit Children's Hospital, which was located on the Marquette campus in downtown Milwaukee. "Al's Run," as it quickly came to be known, took place each year on the final Saturday in September, when weather conditions were normally gorgeous, the low 80s and bright sunshine. And because of the *Journal's* sponsorship, front-page headlines were guaranteed.

I have to admit, as a guy who had two arthritis-encased knees (from old football injuries) and was just past 30, I wasn't overly enthused about "Al's Run" at the start (although once I visited the Intensive Care Unit at Children's Hospital and saw what a great job those people were doing there, my feelings took a quick 180). But the public was—and big time. The running and jogging fad was sweeping the nation like wildfire back then, with events like the Boston Marathon gaining national attention by drawing thousands of runners from all over the nation. What Al and Billy Red were smart enough to do was take advantage of that phenomenon and turn it into nothing short of a miracle for the children of Milwaukee and southern Wisconsin.

Talk about a win-win situation. For just six dollars, the participants got what they wanted—a healthy stretch of the legs from 15th and Wisconsin (two blocks west of Children's Hospital) all the way east to Lincoln Memorial Drive on the Lakefront, where they would turn left to make a U-Turn, first north, then back south down to the finish line on the Summerfest Grounds. There, the winners of the various classes (including wheelchair participants), would receive their awards, after which a huge open-air "brats and beer" party (with band) would get under way.

Year after year, I saw the same thing. All those thousands of runners, coming away with smiles on their faces, happy that they got their five miles in, happy that they enjoyed a good party, and knowing that they had raised hundreds of thousands of dollars for Children's Hospital in the process. For the *Journal,* it was the ultimate "feel-good" community public relations event, which also generated national publicity for the newspaper and the city.

And for Al? For him, I think, it was a genuine "Day in the Sun"— a thoroughly enjoyable happening he had helped create and of which he could feel justly proud. To this day, I can still remember standing there with him on the Lakefront, just after "Al's Run" was over one year, as the people, hundreds and hundreds of them, came over to express their thanks. Some wanted pictures, some wanted autographs. But most just wanted to experience that special moment of warmth and shake his hand.

"God bless you, Al," one man said.

"My son was in Children's nine weeks ago," another chimed in. "Thanks for giving something back to the community."

Al smiled gamely. Although not a man to show his emotions easily, he was close to fighting back tears just then.

What saved him, at that moment, was a 10-member kazoo band in green shirts that walked up beside Al and played a hearty rendition of "When Irish Eyes Are Smiling." When they finished, Al was in control again. "Remember, whatever whisky or butter can't cure can't be cured!" he roared.

And then he was engulfed by the crowd again, as more and more people came up to say hello, shake his hand, or have their picture taken.

Quipped Al at one point, "I feel like Proxmire." (Wisconsin's U.S. Senator, William Proxmire, who was probably running for re-election that year.) In fact, Al did resemble a politician as he kept up a steady banter with the people as they came past.

"Every time a young lady comes up to me, they always say, 'My mother said to say hello,'" he told one woman, who shook his hand. Laughing, he added, "It's terrible. I get all puckered up, and they say that, and it just crushes me."

One guy who looked really exhausted gasped, "Are we in Chicago yet?"

"No, just about to Racine," Al replied.

Because of the huge numbers, lots of people walked past and had to settle for a wave because Al just couldn't reach them all. "Be sure to stick around!" he shouted once, as he returned a wave to a group that was cheering him as it walked past. "Stick around, will ya? I'm going to need someone to buy me a beer later. I got no money."

Finally, after about an hour, the crowd began to thin a bit, and we turned and walked on in to enjoy the fun. Al looked at the people all around, obviously very pleased. "Can you believe this, Rog?" he said. "Can you believe I did all this? I have to say, I'm very humble, and very proud. This really turned out nice. Just super. Sometimes, you really don't realize how visible you are, I guess. But you know, it always seems that things that are successful are successful because of the people you don't know. The invisible ones of the 29,000, the common guy who makes it happen."

Happen? "Al's Run" didn't just happen. It exploded. After a modest first year (4,100 participants and $20,000 raised), it took off like a skyrocket on the Fourth of July. The second year, it doubled in size, raising $42,000, and by 1987—the last year I covered the event—it had attracted nearly 190,000 entrants and raised over $1 million for Children's Hospital (It would be $2 million by the time Al left in 1994.) Al had good reason to be proud. His was a very "special" gift indeed.

For me, of course, "Al's Run" was yet another chance to experience just that many more "Al McGuire Days" every year—although I usually only saw him for a half-hour or so just prior to the start, and then for maybe another hour at the Lakefront after the race had ended. Still, I always looked forward to that special Saturday in September each fall—and the three or four times in the weeks prior when I'd get sent out to do a preview story of some kind with Al.

To this day, I still don't know which I personally enjoyed the most—watching him touch and interact with all those people "who make it happen" on the day of Al's Run, or listening to his humorous anecdotes when I did those interviews with him for the advances. One thing, however, was certain: Whether he was running, walking, stooping, or sitting, Al was still the master of the colorful phrase.

In August, 1981, for example, I caught up with Al one morning at Children's Hospital, where he'd confiscated a small, out-of-the-way office about the size of cloakroom to serve as his "headquarters" prior to that year's Run. I mean, it was barren. Just a table, two chairs, and a phone. But that, I found out as I sat down to interview Al for an upcoming Sunday feature, was all he really needed.

When I walked in the door, there sat Al, "McGuire casual" in red-checked slacks, a Carmen red sweater and white shirt, and white tennis shoes (no socks), chatting merrily away on the phone. Good God! I thought. Where was Marquette's blue and gold? You'd think he was a UW alumnus or something.

As he continued talking, Al motioned me to sit. After a minute or so, he hung up and explained to me that what he was doing was con-ducting his own phone solicitation scheme to sign up members of the newly created "400 Club," his latest gimmick to add members and raise funds for that year's Run.

"This is how it works," Al quickly filled me in. "You get in a run, and you call until you milk it dry. You talk to one guy, and he gives you a couple more names to call, and they give you a few more, and so on…a pyramid type thing. But you always ask permission to use the guy's name as an intro.

"See, every year I like to have some type of twist to the thing, but what's happening, it's like reinventing the wheel each year, you're start-ing out from zero level, no equity. I've gone through betting on myself, having people pledge bets on each minute I better my time, and last year it was how much weight Rick [Majerus] and [Milwaukee Bucks vice president] Wayne Embry could lose.

"This year, I formed the 400 Club, where an individual or a busi-ness gets to wear a gold number at the Run if they contribute $100 to the Intensive Care Unit. It's tax-deductible, and they get a different color T-shirt to wear, and some perks, like having coffee and donuts with me before the race, that sort of thing.

"Of course, a lot of people don't run, but we send them the gold number for their office or den," he continued. "And then we send a black and white number to a young person who can't afford to run. We feel these are people who will renew each year, if nothing changes in their area." Al smiled. "So it gives us a base, some equity."

When asked, Al told me he had arrived at his little office early each morning, and after a cup of coffee and roll, started dialing on the phone. He admitted, in spite of his famous name and the growing popularity of "Al's Run," that reaching people wasn't easy, especially on Thursdays (which this just happened to be).

"Anything I get today, I get before noon," Al told me. "After noon, forget it. Thursday afternoon is a real Dunkirk. You can't get a tooth pulled, you'd better not get sick or need a lawyer on Thursday afternoon, because the men are always at the country clubs. It wouldn't be a bad day for the Russians to invade us. The world is run by secretaries on Thursday afternoons."

Al admitted to me that he felt soliciting by phone was more than a little demeaning—"an experience," as he called it, not unlike recruiting when he was at Marquette. But he quickly added that he was more than willing to do it, if it "increased the chances for all those kids over at Children's Hospital."

"Jesus, Rog," he asked, "you been there? You see the things they do?" I told him that I had. "Then you know what I mean," he said.

There was a moment of somber silence. But once again, Al rescued things with his sense of humor. "You know, when I was in Rockaway Beach, we had a summer business," he said, "and in the summertime, there was this Mrs. Weiss who came around, and she was always collecting bottles or selling chances for St. Carmila's or something. She was a real pain in the rear end. So when my father would see her, he'd go downstairs. He'd always tap a barrel of beer or anything—just to get away from her." Al was laughing now. "So now, here it is 30 years later, and I'm Mrs. Weiss.

"You know that country song? Where the wife calls, and 10 guys say, 'No, he's not here.' Well, I can tell by the secretary's voice that he is there, but he's motioning, 'No! I'm not here!' He knows I'm calling for a hit."

Al said he had one rule he followed religiously—never call anybody he thought truly couldn't afford the $100 "hit." When I asked, he admitted that he'd called some of his former players who he knew now were doing well in the business world. "There was Guy Lam, who used to play for me," Al said, letting me know by the look on his face that a story was coming on. "I catch Guy, and I said, 'What number do you want?' And he said, 'No. 30.' I said, 'Why?' He said, 'That's the number I wore.' And I said, 'Oh, well. I never seen you with your jacket off.' See, he never got off the bench. But he was so hurt, he almost took the $100 back."

Al admitted that the phone solicitation gig could, at times, get awfully frustrating. "One guy, the other day, while I'm waiting for him, the Muzak comes on," Al said, "and when he finally gets on the phone, I said, 'I want to get a seat on flight 202 for Dubuque, Iowa.' For Christ's sake, I thought it was Republic Airlines!"

When I brought up training for the upcoming Run, Al said he was training with Rick, but that it hadn't been easy. "The other day, we went to a Mexican restaurant after we ran, and I swear, Rick ate like he was going to the electric chair," Al exclaimed. "I told him, 'Rick, what good does it do us to run if we're going to eat like this afterward?'"

This particular Thursday, Al decided before he ate lunch to just sip at his coffee and try the phone some more, before his self-imposed noon deadline applied (it was then about 11:30). His first three calls failed because *already* people weren't in, but then he tied up with another one of his longtime friends, Dick Podell. At which point, his best Used Car Salesman demeanor took over as he tried to start another run.

"Dick? How are you? You got a minute I can talk to you? I'm calling on the hospital thing, the Run, so I want to lay somethin' on you. Another thing [he was laughing now, and I wished I could hear the other end of the conversation]. You must be an easy touch. You're on everybody's list…

"Anyhow, I gotta give you my pitch. We have gold numbers this year, the gold numbers count $100, tax-deductible, no hanky-panky. And the money goes to the Intensive Care Ward at Children's Hospital. You get the gold number, a different color shirt, coffee and donuts with me before the race, that sort of thing.

"So I can put you down? Oh, $100! I thought I told you earlier. Okay. Give me your address. We get everything to you. Are there two people you know I can use your name to call? Uh-huh. Jerry Bloch. Can I use your name? You have a number for him? Okay. One more will do it. Ken Phillips? How do you spell the name? Same number. Okay.

"The number I'd like to give you is 106, for your son to run in, okay? [For some reason I didn't understand, that was a special number

for either Dick or his son.] You got it. Whatever you want. Can I do anything for you? Okay. Fine. Thanks, pal."

Al, I could see, was on a run now. "See, this is what you call pyra-
miding," he explained quickly. "He gives me numbers, and so on. You
need someone to feed you names. But it has to be human, every call. No
form letters, nothing like that."

And with that, Al was back on the phone, taking care of business.

"Yes…is Jerry Bloch there? Coach Al McGuire. Jerry? Al McGuire.
You got a moment?"

I knew it was time to leave. I had more than enough for my story.
And so, with a quick wave, I left Al talking on the phone, using his per-
sonalized, repeated referral system to make his pitch and do whatever he
could to help those kids at Children's out. How successful was he? I never
did find out if he actually got 400 pledges, but my guess is he came close.
All I know is, in the 45 minutes I was there that day, Al signed up five
new members for his "400 Club" at $100 per, bringing total member-
ship to 110. What that meant, on the bottom line, was that with a
month yet to go, he'd already secured another $11,000 for the kids.

In front of the cameras for NBC (and later, CBS), Al always
remained the colorful Showman, but there was something about "Al's
Run" that brought out his philosopher's side each fall as well. As sure as
the leaves began to turn, and the afternoons grew shorter, Al always
seemed to be more introspective at that time of year, more reflective
about life and why it was the way it was, and how he saw his particular
role in things, just as he had beneath the pictures of the clowns in his
dimly lit office years before.

The reason, I think, was that Al realized—after visiting the
Intensive Care Unit at Children's Hospital—that the Run *was* serious
business. This was no game. The future of those gutsy kids, many of
whom were battling incurable illness, was at stake. Winning, Al had
often said, was only important in war and surgery. And now, he found
himself a participant in that arena, leading an army of thousands just to
try to give some of those kids another month, another week, another day.
Al told me once, he never looked up as he passed Children's Hospital,
just three blocks after the start. Because he felt the sight of those kids—
waving gamely from their windows as the runners went past—would
have been too much for him to take. This, he knew, was by far the most

important game he'd ever coached, and he was determined to give it nothing less than his best.

If the truth be known, however, running was not Al's favorite form of exercise. Walking. That was his thing. Walking, he told me one fall day in 1981, was one of the oldest, easiest, least expensive, and yet most overlooked ways of exercising there is.

"I've always walked," Al said, launching into one of his familiar discourses. "See, I've always believed the key to being comfortable with yourself is getting off your duff. No matter how great your mind is, you'll never use it to the fullest without a trained body.

"I've always kept in shape by walking. I never let a day go by that I don't walk. It's great exercise, and a quiet time, when you can be by yourself, when you can retool. The running end is not that much enjoyment for me. I've yet to see a person smile when they jog." He laughed. "What I'm thinking about while I'm jogging is the cold beer at the Last Chance Saloon."

Unfortunately, Al believed, walking had become a thing of the past—a "turn of the century sort of thing" that he felt most people today could use more of in their busy, modern-day lives. "I feel if a person's office is in a high-rise, he should walk up and down the stairs, not take the elevator," Al intoned. "For years at Marquette, when I was coaching, I always walked for exercise. We used to stop the bus for something to eat, and I'd always get out and walk. Lots of times going from the hotel to the arena, I'd start out walking 10 minutes ahead, and the bus would stop and pick me up on the way."

Al didn't change his habits once he'd quit coaching and started broadcasting games for NBC. "I have a rule, I never sit down at an airport," he insisted. "I'm in them a lot. So every time I can, I stretch. I walk around. I hate to sit and wait. That way, I can push the walking end of it and get my walking in for the day.

"Walking is a major thing. It seemed most of the constructive things I've come up with, I thought of them while I was walking. It's my favorite type exercise. Nothing else comes close for me. I don't know why people don't walk. I like to do my business walking, talk to friends walking. I don't know of anything I don't like to do walking. But you say to people, 'Let's take a walk,' and they look at you like you're a Neanderthal man or something. They want to know the reason. I say, 'No reason; I just love to walk.'

"Like, the biggest sin in golf is golf carts. They shouldn't have 'em. Have 'em for people who have physical problems, but to go play golf in a golf cart, you may as well go ice fishing. It doesn't make sense."

As was always the case, when Al got off on one of these tangents, I didn't interrupt with questions. I just kept writing, not sure quite where he was going, or what his point was finally going to be, but enjoying the ride along the way.

"Walking is a pleasant thing," Al continued. "There's an aesthetic touch to it. It's a shame we don't do more of it. It's almost like the porch, which is left off homes now. That's a mortal sin. Walking has gone the way of the porch swing, the rumble seat in the back of cars. It's a shame.

"See, most people think they must meet in a tavern, or a restaurant. The nicest thing, I believe, is a park. If I ever was in a position to leave something, I'd like to leave a park. So people would have a means to enjoy that. It's something for all ages. And it stands the test of time."

Two years later, Al's favorite exercise was incorporated as the latest "gimmick" into "Al's Run" with the addition of the three-mile "walk" for, as Al put it, "people whose knees can't take the jogging...but would like to take part. It's for the young people who want to bring their children." Al was particularly pleased that Pat—who else?—led the walking contingent, which assembled four blocks east of the starting line, then swung out onto Wisconsin Ave. and headed for the Lake Front once the runners had passed.

I always wondered why Al hadn't brought up the "walkers" idea the year before, because in '82 he really had no new "gimmick"—as he always put it—to help keep increasing the numbers. Early on, in August, he'd talked about really targeting women at the college level, remarking, "If you get the girls to run, the guys will come along, too." But nothing came of that.

What I remember most about that year was when I caught up with Al for a pre-Run interview and got a whole lot more story than I'd ever dreamed of. Three stories, in fact, for the price of one. First I learned that he had landed a weekly sports spot on *Entertainment Tonight* (whose audience was 30 million).

Second, I got some great quotes on how pleased he was with the success of "Al's Run." "Five years," Al mused. "You know, it just doesn't seem like this will be the fifth year. And it's still special to me, because it's a nice happening, and the whole thing's up front. All the money collected goes to Children's Hospital. No hanky-panky."

A smile of satisfaction crossed Al's face.

"The run gives me the feeling of being of worth as far as being human in a lot of ways," he admitted. "Like, I usually get there early, two hours before the start. I get there at 8:30; post time is at 10:30. Those two hours are the most pleasing two hours of my life, walking around before the run, seeing all of those people, knee-high to early 70s. All shapes and forms. Enjoying. That is a very pleasing thing.

"What's happening, it's gotten to the size that other people are picking up the pieces. It's not my little postage-stamp happening anymore. One that excites me is people are inviting friends in from the outside area. They're house guests, runners for a weekend. They invite them in, cook out, do their scene, and it's all part of the Run.

"You know, the real promoters now are the people who have run in Al's Run. They're the ones who push it. They're the catalysts. Because they keep getting more friends to run, making their intimate circle larger."

The third and unexpected bonus, however, was when I asked Al about his problems training for the Run (after all, he was 52, and he admitted it wasn't getting any easier), and we suddenly branched off into why his colorful, multifaceted career (from coach to exec to TV analyst to sports personality) just seemed to keep on evolving like topsy, even as he got older. Al admitted he wasn't quite sure. But it was all the opening he needed, and I found myself treated to yet another of his philosophic, introspective, and thoroughly enjoyable ruminations—delivered only as Al could, in his colorful, insightful way.

"I know I'm a character, but I don't work at being a character," he insisted. "I just be myself. I don't change what I do. I prefer to eat in the rundown places, or a McDonald's or something. If a guy wants to meet me on business, I meet him at Arthur Treacher's. He thinks I'm wacky, but I don't think I'm wacky.

"My wife Pat laughs at me. She'll say, 'You put your sweater on inside out.' I say, 'Okay, next time I pull it on, it'll be right then.' Hey, I haven't changed. The only time I comb my hair is when I go out to get a check. And if I'm with more than four people, I feel I should be paid. I think what it is, my lifestyle, while it is not acceptable in business, the seersucker-suit world, it seems to be acceptable to the rank and file. I seem to be able to touch the two-dollar bettor, be acceptable to the apron and blue-collar workers.

"The incomes still seem to come in. And I seem to have a license for some reason that is acceptable. But it puzzles me why I am a personality, because I don't do things that aren't pleasing to me."

Al paused a second, then took off again, while I, feeling like a psychiatrist sitting next to the couch, continued scribbling down his words as fast as I could. Having been down this road many times before, I knew we were about to get into that "75-dollar line" and "$10,000 interview" territory pretty quick.

"A very strong key in my life is my inability to spell and that I have a difficult time reading," Al went on. "Once I admitted that to myself in my late 20s, I cleared the trees a lot. After that, everything was simple. If I hired a secretary, she had to be able to spell well, or she didn't get the job." He chuckled. "And maybe that's why I don't like memos much.

"What I try to do is let the day come to me. Then it's a piece of cake. I like new things. New things keep you new, keep you young. And I always felt if it took six hours a day to do your job, then you weren't qualified.

"I still think a lot of people feel I prepare for everything I'm doing," Al continued. "I don't. I don't watch TV, I don't go to sporting events. It's just a style, an evolution, and end result. I'm a guy on a motorbike, collecting toy soldiers.

"I have no office. My secretary, Wanda, is in Sussex, 12 miles the other way. I catch her every two weeks. I think I'm the same person. I don't talk in bars as much as I used to. And I don't think I'd ever take a job, because of the style of life I lead. It's a style that's non-negotiable, a style nobody can have. It's not for sale."

Al paused again, and this time he looked me in the eye.

"You know, I really like myself. But Hitler and Mussolini liked themselves, too, I guess. Roger, I've always felt, something was out there. You know what I mean? I don't know what it is. It could be my older brother Johnny beating me out of my mother's will.

"I don't know. But I do know a person must perform, must have a reason somewhere in their day, a reason for your life."

Boy, I thought, talk about a lesson in life. Could this get any better? It did. Because Al went one step further, with that uncanny ability he had, to tell me in his own particular way how he handled the darkness we all must one day face.

"I never go to wakes," he told me. "You know, a good friend of mine, Bill Hughes, died recently, and I called his daughter and told her, 'I didn't go to your father's wake. But I bought him a drink once.' See, so many times, everyone brings tons of flowers, but when the guy was alive, they didn't do anything for the person. I'd rather buy you a drink while we're living than flowers when you're dead." Al shrugged. "'Cause what I've always said, Rog, is what it all boils down to, the crowd at your funeral is always governed by the weather."

The part Al liked least about the Run was the start. Those first dramatic seconds after the gun went off, when the crowd of runners surged forward, and the first couple hundred yards after that—when it was all he could do to keep from getting knocked down and trampled by the one or more of the elite group of serious and well trained college and high school runners from all over the country who were competing. For the TV cameras, he knew, it was necessary that he be at the front for the start, but he also knew, if he got bumped and went down, he could be seriously injured. So as a precaution, a cordon of four or five good-sized runners were positioned around him, members of the Badgerland Striders Club, whose sole job it was to make sure nobody ran him down.

"I do need somebody with me then, because they really come out of there at the start," Al explained to me one year, as we stood talking on the sidewalk near 17th and Wisconsin, a short time before the start. "Believe me, you can get bumped and go down. Having all those rubberbacks going past you at the start is scary.

"The thing I try to do, when I'm in front of the starting line and they go off, is be like Carl Lewis in the Olympics for a while, and let them go by gradually." Al chuckled. "There are a few phonies in the front, though," he insisted. "I had one guy, before the race last year, who was going through all the muscle-flexing routine, and when he took off, he led the pack for 300 yards. Then 300 yards later, he was standing on the corner, throwing up. He just wanted his picture in the *Journal*."

One thing I didn't realize was that, during the run, a lot of the runners would talk to him as they passed him by. "All the runners have six-second conversations with me," Al explained. "They say something, and I just nod back. That's all I do for five miles is nod. I look like one of those little dogs in the back of the car, with his head going up and down." He paused a bit, then added, "You know, people think I don't say anything 'cause I'm acting macho. I'm not macho. I'm afraid of dying, especially now that I have money."

One other thing Al didn't like (and it happened only once) was when the Striders decided that for safety's sake, they needed to keep track of where Al was. So they put a guy right next to him, running along with a walkie-talkie in hand to report on where he was and how he was holding up.

It drove Al crazy.

"Every so often, this guy would say something like, 'Coach at the two-mile mark! Feeling good!' Except that when I looked up, the two-mile mark was still 200 or so yards away," Al exclaimed. "Christ! It was aggravating. So I told him, 'Hey, fella, don't say that, will ya? The two-mile mark is still 200 yards away. Wait until we get there!

"See, I don't want to know the distance. I'm better off that way. I just know that when I get to the downhill run by the Yacht Club, I've got it licked. Hey, when I go into a hill, I've got my head down because I don't want to see that hill. It's too much. Like a tidal wave, like having a blanket over me. I don't know why they had that guy with me. I guess to notify the paramedics if I went down. Everybody's worrying about me, and all I'm worrying about is the $20 I got in my sock."

Even training for the Run, which Al admitted got harder every year, occasionally had its hazards. Like the afternoon Al got locked inside the football field at Brookfield East High School. "I went over to Brookfield East and started to jog," he told me. "I wanted to do two miles, and there was a track in back. So while I'm jogging around, the groundskeeper locked the fence. And after I finished my two miles, I couldn't get out.

"My legs were so tired, I was afraid to try and crawl over the fence. Finally, I saw a couple of kids in the parking lot, and they showed me a hole in the fence, where they would sneak into football games. So I said, 'Can you hold up the bottom of this thing?' And they did, and I went right under it."

To this day, I still can't help but laugh about the year (1986, to be exact), when Al almost did himself in...thanks to his own forgetfulness.

It was an unusually hot, muggy day that year, 76 degrees, blazing sun, and 80 percent humidity as the 11 o'clock start time rolled around. For some reason, I was late getting to the start area, and just as I walked up, the gun went off, and I saw Al taking off at the head of the pack...clad in heavy blue jogging pants!

Holy Christ, I thought. What's he up to now? As I retreated to my car, to drive down to the finish line on the Lakefront, I wondered if it was some gimmick he'd devised, but then I thought, 'No, he can't be that stupid.' This was no day to be running a five-mile race in jogging pants.

At any rate, it was over an hour later (about 20 minutes longer than his normal finishing time) when Al finally came slowly loping into the chute, and I could see he was really hurting, sweaty and wilted and gasping for breath. And the first thing he did, after he left the chute, was to walk over to where the Milwaukee Fire Department's fireboat was hosing down the runners and allow himself to be showered from head to foot.

After which, he collapsed in the shade of a tree on the lakefront grass.

So what happened? I asked him. And why did you wear those heavy pants?

Al gave me an embarrassed smile.

"The truth of the matter is, I forgot to put on my shorts," he said, still panting heavily. "There I am at the starting line, and I go to take off my sweat pants, and all I've got underneath is my skivs. And so there I was, up against the gun...but there was nothing else I could do."

Even though I knew Al was beat, I couldn't help but laugh. Why was it, I wondered, that things like this always seemed to happen to him? Zaniness and lunacy. It was the story of his life. Peter Sellers reincarnate.

"The funny thing is, people are going to think I did it for attention," Al rambled on, "but little do they know it was a matter of 'No ticky, no shirty.'" But how, I pressed, could you not know you didn't have your running shorts on? "Maybe it was because my skivs are blue like my shorts; I don't know," Al replied wearily.

Al said he gave it his best at the start, but that just after the one-mile mark, he knew he was in trouble.

"Right after I got over the river and was starting to go up Pfister Hill—where you go past the Pfister Hotel to the Northwest Mutual Building—that's where I hit the wall. A mile and a tenth out," Al said. "I tried to jog a couple more times, but it was no go. And the sirens and ambulances were enough warning to me to slow up, just walk it out and finish, have some suds, listen to the Booze Brothers...and thank Mom for the good weather."

Al shook his head wearily. "You know, I really am beat," he admitted. "Sweating feels nice, but not as much as it used to a few years ago. When we had shade from the buildings for a while, it wasn't bad. But that last mile and a half was like Humphrey Bogart's *Sahara*."

For a minute, the two of us just sat there, not saying anything, while Al continued to enjoy the cooling shade. Then, out of nowhere, he said, "You know what was going through my mind that last mile? That poem I heard once:

Oh, God, take the sun from
    the sky,
It's torturing me, burning
    me up.
Oh, God, can't you hear
    my cry?
Water. Pour a little cup.

Al smiled. "It's from a poem about a guy caught on the wire in the First World War," he told me. "Funny, isn't it, what goes through your head?"

"It's time. Every carnival has an end. Circuses close. Honeymoons come to an end sooner or later. It's been super, but now it's time."

Chapter 10
Farewell

When I first heard that Al was sick, in the spring of 2000, I honestly didn't think that it was all that serious. From what I read in the papers, he had simply decided to skip the NCAA tournament for CBS this year because he was worn out and suffering from anemia. It sounded to me like all he needed was a good rest before he took up his play-by-play duties once again in the fall.

Sounds logical to me, I thought. "March Madness," I knew, was one of the hardest grinds there was for play-by-play announcers, especially in the early rounds, where—because of the tournament's ever-expanding field—there were often four games played a day. In addition to which, Al, I knew, was 71—and we all have to cut back a little sometimes, right? Even Al, who was one of the most vital and energetic people I had ever known.

You have to realize, our paths had gone separate ways during the 1990s. While Al continued covering college basketball for CBS, I had become even more involved with auto racing, signing on as public relations director at Road America in Elkhart Lake, Wisconsin, which hosted five major race weekends each summer, including the CART Indy car series. That, plus working on a number of books and freelancing for various racing magazines, had kept me pretty busy…to the point that I really didn't have time to keep up with college basketball like I had before.

Not that Al and I were completely out of touch. We exchanged cards at Christmastime and phone calls three or four times a year, but my life had gone a different direction now, so unfortunately, what we had in common became less and less. What touched me was that the first thing Al always asked about when we talked was how I was doing. It was sort of like I was one of his players and he wanted to be sure my life was going okay.

"Roger!" he ask, enthused. "How ya doing? Are you making money?"

After which, I'd jokingly reassure him that I was doing fine. That I could still afford the essentials, like food and electric and dog food for my two black Scotties, and then we'd get down to talking about whatever was on his mind. His biggest worry for me was that, as a writer, I wasn't doing more, although in addition to my Road America job, I was still freelancing regularly for *Auto Racing Digest*, a Chicago-based publication.

"I don't know, Rog," he'd say, like a concerned parent talking to his son. "I just don't think that it's enough, you know? You need to get out there more. You got the gosh-darned talent. But you need to keep your name out front."

At which point, I'd bring up the book. The one he'd always promised we'd do, but which we still hadn't done. "I've got my winters free now," I'd remind him. "You know, Al, it'd be a knockout. And tell me, honestly. Who could tell it better than you and I?"

At which point, Al always got defensive, skitterish almost, like a horse unsure of his footing. "Yeah, well, it's just not something I want to do," he'd always say, uneasily. "Let me think about it, OK? The timing just doesn't seem right. But don't worry. If I do, you'll get the call." And then, quickly, he'd switch the subject to some other project he had in mind, with something like, "Hey, a guy asked me last week about a piece for this airlines magazine. What'd ya think?"

"If you want to, let's do it," I said.

"Okay. We could have some fun with it, I think. I'll be in touch."

In 1998, Harley-Davidson was celebrating its 95th Anniversary, and we had a huge ride-in planned on our AMA Super Cycle Sunday at Road America, where more than 2,700 Harley riders, led by Willie G. and Bill Davidson, would take an honorary tour of the four-mile track. Naturally, I called Al and asked if he would like to be in the front row, with the Davidsons…but to my surprise, he declined.

"Nah, Rog, I think I'll take a pass," he said. "I don't ride as much as I used to, and never in groups like that. Christ, if the damn thing goes down on me, I'd never get out from under."

That should have signaled something to me—if nothing else, that Al, like all of us, was indeed getting older. It was about a year later, I found out, that Al had given up riding his Harley altogether.

The last time I saw Al was in the summer of '99. Road America had a vacancy on its board of directors and was in hopes that Tom Poberezny, the president of the Experimental Aircraft Association in Oshkosh, would decide to come on board. Tom, I knew, was a big Al McGuire fan. So I called Al, and we set a date for lunch so I could get a picture signed for Tom.

It took a bit of looking to find Al's office, tucked away on the ground floor of a nondescript-looking building on a small side street in Pewaukee. At first, I didn't think I had the right place, but no sooner had I walked through the door than I heard Al's familiar rousing welcome as he came towards me, "Rog-ah the lodg-ah! How you doing?"

For 71, Al looked great. Slim and trim as always, his tousled hair was a little grayer, but his handshake was firm and his smile still easy and infectious. Al introduced me to his assistant, Jeannie Busalacchi, and then we sat down at a table and exchanged small talk for a bit, catching up on what each other was doing and asking about what various people we both knew were up to now, that sort of thing. "I'm hungry; let's have some lunch," Al suggested at one point. "You like Chinese, Rog?" When I nodded, he called to Jeannie. "Hey, Jeannie, why don't you get us some Chinese, OK? The three of us can mix and match."

Al, it was good to see, hadn't changed a bit. The food was good, the mood informal and relaxed. While we were eating, Al signed the picture for Tom, and another one for me, and then I turned on the cassette recorder I'd brought along and played for Al the tape of his famous "diatribe" after the Kansas State game once again. Al enjoyed it from start to finish, smiling and making amused faces as he listened, shaking his head from side to side. "Can you get me a copy, Rog?" he asked, when it was finished. He was being honored at a dinner that was coming up, and he thought it would be a hoot to play it for the audience that night so that, as he put it, "they'll know what a calm, level-headed guy I used to be."

Before I left, Al led me into another room, where part of his vast collection of toy soldiers was spread out on a couple of tables. "I'm trying to find a place for them," he mentioned, "somewhere the kids can come to look at them, and press their nose against the glass." I asked him if he was still actively collecting. "Sometimes. Not that much," he said.

"Sometimes I think I've cornered the market. There's not that much around. Not that's rare, something I don't have, and that's in good condition. And when I do find something, I think because it's me, the price goes up like the gosh-darned stock market, and so I take a pass."

There was a pause. Then, after a bit more small talk, I was on my way. Sadly, I realized as I walked to the car, that as much as I loved the guy, Al and I just didn't have that much in common anymore. What cemented us together now were our pasts.

That fall was a sea change again for me. After 11 seasons, I left Road America to become vice president of corporate communications at EAA, exchanging the world of motor sports for the world of aviation. For me, the job offered a fresh challenge, one with a pretty steep learning curve, to be sure. And so, I admit, Al and his world were pretty much "out of sight, out of mind"…until I read about his decision to skip the NCAA tournament the following spring.

Summer is the busiest time of year at EAA, preparing for our annual weeklong AirVenture convention and fly-in in late July, which attracts 675,000 people and 10,000 planes annually. It was my first "big show"—an event that for a newcomer can be overwhelming to the point of being scary. Plus, EAA had scheduled a national press conference in September at the Smithsonian Museum in Washington, D.C., to announce our "Countdown to Kitty Hawk" initiative—a two and a half-year program commemorating the 100th anniversary of powered flight, which would culminate with a two-day celebration at Kitty Hawk, North Carolina, on December 17, 2003. Since it was my job to stage and coordinate the announcement, for a "first-timer" I had an awful lot on my plate.

From the papers, I kept up with how Al was doing as best I could. From what I read, he had good days and bad days and was taking blood transfusions for what many suspected was leukemia. That's all I knew. Then, the last week of July, in the midst of the convention, I was shocked when I read he had gone into the hospital and then been transferred to the Franciscan Woods, a hospice-like managed care facility in Brookfield.

A chill went down my spine. From personal experience, I knew what the word hospice meant. My father had checked into a hospice at the end. It was a place you went to die.

My first instinct was to call. But then I remembered how fiercely Al regarded his privacy and how he'd told me years before that when he died, he wanted to die alone. He didn't want his death to be "an Italian picnic-type thing." And so, more than once, I put my feelings aside out of respect for his and put the phone down instead.

Until, in mid-August, I decided to call Pat one night. At first, she seemed surprised to hear my voice, then thanked me profusely for calling. How's Al doing? I asked. "Oh, I think he's doing okay," Pat said. "He has his good days and his bad days. But Roger, he's just so tired sometimes. You know, all my life I've known him, Al has always been a very energetic person. And now, it's like he just doesn't have any energy."

Hesitantly, I asked if she thought I should call him.

"Oh, sure," she replied. "I know he'd like to hear from you. Just a minute, I'll get the number..."

"You sure it's not too late?" I asked, noticing it was 8:30.

"No, I don't think so," she replied. "In fact, it might be a good time, because there won't be any people around."

We talked a few more minutes, and I told her to be sure to get her rest, to keep herself strong. That it was the best thing she could do for both herself and Al. And that Mary and I would be praying for them both. "Thanks so much," she said. "Thanks for calling, Roger. Good night."

And so there I sat for another five minutes. Yes or no. Call or don't. And then I finally did.

"Hello?" Al's voice seemed faint.

"Al, this is Roger."

"Oh, hello, Rog," he said. This time, there was no hearty greeting. "I'm glad you called, Rog. I really am. It's good to hear from you. How you doing? OK? You making any money?"

I didn't know whether to laugh or cry. "I'm making money, Al," I said. "Don't worry, I'm making money." I had told myself I wouldn't break down, but right then I almost did. "The thing I need to know is, how about you?"

"OK, I guess. Given the circumstances."

"Pat says you get pretty tired sometimes."

"Yeah, I do. But after I get a transfusion, I'm dynamite for a while. It's just like I told the reporter who called yesterday, 'I think my white blood cells all went south.'" He chuckled. "Not too bad, huh? You might want to write that down."

For a moment, I didn't know what to say. I just knew if I voiced my true feelings, I would start crying.

"We had a great run, Al," I finally said.

"Yeah, we did. By the way, I want to thank you, Rog. For all the nice articles that you wrote about me. All those years. Even after I left Marquette. You know, in all those years, you never misquoted me once. And there were times you made me sound better than me."

I couldn't help it. The tears were coming. "That's because it was you," I said. "With all those 75-dollar lines, I couldn't miss."

I could almost feel his smile on the other end of the line.

"Yeah, those 75-dollar lines," he said. "Funny, isn't it, how they always just seemed to be there."

At that point, I heard other voices in the background. "Uh, Rog, I'm sorry, but I got to go, OK? They want to give me my transfusion now."

"No problem, Al. I was just glad to talk to you again. Take care, my friend. We're praying for you. God bless."

"You, too, Rog. And thanks again. Good night."

Two days later, I sent Al a final letter. In it, I was able to say a lot of things I couldn't have in person, about why I so treasured our friendship over the years.

"Covering Marquette when you were there was great!" I wrote. "It was like covering the president! Exciting, always something new, and of course, the best quote provider in the world! I still feel the ultimate highlight of my years in journalism was that night in Atlanta, the national championship win. God, you deserved that so much, because you worked so hard to get there. I was just glad to be along for the ride."

After describing some of the things I had learned from Al, I concluded, "But what I really want to say, Al, is that you have always been a very special person, not only to me, but to thousands like me who were so fortunate to share YOUR life. Stop reading this a minute and listen. You must feel our love flooding into your heart."

Ernest Hemingway, Mickey Mantle, John Wayne, my father, and now Al McGuire. The last of my heroes was dying.

A few weeks later, Karl Svatek, assistant sports editor at the *Milwaukee Journal Sentinel*, called and asked if I would write a remembrance to Al, which would be published at the time of his death. Naturally, I said yes. I was honored that Karl had thought of me and told him I'd get it off soon. I was due to go in for knee replacement surgery mid-September, and I knew—given the long recuperative period—that I'd better get it done before then.

Besides, who knew how long Al would last? And I definitely wanted to be able to be at least a part of the last hurrah he truly deserved.

Al was coaching his last Big Game, and like the pro he was, he milked the clock and kept his sense of humor right up until the end.

When reporters called, he told them how he was "heading for the dancing lights," how he "hoped for a soft landing," and joked about how he was planning "to have a cash bar" at his wake.

He knew he was living his final days, but that didn't mean he couldn't do it on his terms. "There's this big gray elephant in my room, and nobody will admit it's there," he said. When Digger Phelps called and asked how he was doing, Al replied, "I'm on my third undertaker. I've had two guys die, waiting for me to die."

A week before he died, when he was drifting in and out of consciousness, he suddenly started talking to his son, Allie, about the University of Wisconsin, where the team was being run by an interim coach while they searched for a successor. "I want you to call the athletic director," Al told his son, "and I want you to tell him to take my name off the short list."

At 2 a.m. on Friday, January 26, 2001, Al McGuire died at the age of 72. His wife Pat, his children, and the grandchildren were at his side.

As Mary and I got out of the car, Gesu Catholic Church on 12th and Wisconsin loomed before us, its windows and spires as dark and gloomy as the skies overhead. Freezing rain fell lightly, making the sidewalks slick with ice. I had seriously considered not coming at first—and not just because of the hour and a half drive in threatening weather. Al's rule was still in my mind: You don't attend the wake of a friend. Better that you bought him a drink when he was living. And, Lord knows, I'd bought him plenty during our years together, and he the same for me.

And yet, when it finally came down to it, I could not stay away. In my heart, I knew I had to be there. First of all, out of respect for Pat and Allie and the rest of the family. But most of all, just to say goodbye to a special friend one final time.

"The crowd at your funeral is always governed by the weather," Al had always said. But this time, I knew, as we climbed the wide steps of the church and went inside, he had been wrong. For although it was only midafternoon (the funeral was scheduled to start at 7 p.m.), a large crowd had gathered in the entryway, as a steady stream of people stopped by to pay their last respects. The celebrities, like Governor Thompson and Herb Kohl, Hank and Rick, Al's former players, Billy Packer and

Dick Enberg, I knew would all arrive later for the funeral. What touched me then were all the everyday people—"the $2 bettors" as Al called them—who were stopping by now. Ordinary people, businessmen and fans, who had been there at the Arena way back when, when Al made his mark in life and forever left his mark on them. Scanning the crowd, I saw a wide diversity of people—young and old, black and white, some well-to-do and some who weren't. All coming now, to pay their last respects. Always the reporter, I couldn't help but wonder just how Al had touched each one. There was, I knew, a special story behind each face.

Off to the left of Al's coffin stood a 4x5-foot picture of Al triumphant—his arms raised, beaming in the glow of one of his more famous victories. Passing that, I came to where he lay, quiet now, at peace. Looking so small, so wasted after his final fight. Dying had taken a lot out of Al McGuire, because he was so full of life.

Reaching down, I touched his hand.

Goodbye, Al, I said silently. Go in peace. God bless.

My biggest regret was that Pat was not there, that I did not get to see her. That quiet, lovely lady who had been at Al's side all those years. But we were able to talk with Allie and his wife, and Robbie, and meet Al's grandson A.J., and spend a bit of time with an old friend, Mike Kupper of the *Los Angeles Times*, who had covered Al's early years at Marquette when he was with the *Journal*.

The afternoon was fading into darkness, and I knew it was time to leave. We had a long drive ahead of us, and I had done what I wanted—said goodbye to Al that final time. That night, I knew, Al would be in good hands, that the eulogies would flow, and that there would be laughter in addition to the tears. Just as Al would have liked.

And so, we left, making our way back out into the sleet and growing darkness, which would accompany us on our return. Before I made the trek down those long stairs again, however, I turned back one more time and took one last look at the lines of people who were filing past Al's coffin.

I felt not only sad, but empty. Another chapter of my life had closed as well.

My remembrance of Al had appeared in the *Journal Sentinel* that morning. At the wake, I felt warmed when a number of people told me how much they had enjoyed it, because it had been truly written from the heart.

This is the story I thought I would never have to write, because Al McGuire was a person so full of life that I just never imagined that someday he would not be with us.

As my life and career changed over the years, he remained a constant to me, a reminder of a time in my life I thoroughly enjoyed: covering Marquette University's basketball team, and most of all, the man who coached it.

Never, in my 33-year involvement in the world of sports, both in writing and public relations, did I ever meet a sports personality who was so vibrant, so colorful, so full of the joy of the moment, on stage and off, and frankly, just so darned much fun to be around.

That was Al. One of college basketball's finest coaches—most certainly. One of the sport's most flamboyant characters—without a doubt. But most important to me, he was not only coach of the team I covered for *The Milwaukee Journal* back in the 1970s, but a person who later became a good friend through the years. Already, I miss him greatly.

The story recalled many incidents from our years together, some of the more famous Al McGuire stories, how he cried when he won the national championship, and things we did together. And then I summed it up with the following tribute, words that I wrote the day after he retired from Marquette.

"He gave his profession an eloquence and a sense of humor that probably will not be seen again. Blessed with the gift of gab and a crackling Irish wit, he could bring down the house one moment, dazzle and hush it with philosophical phrases the next…The McGuire legend, made up of the hundreds of funny, tragic, idiotic stories, is what will be remembered long after the numbers—the victories and the national rankings—are forgotten. For the numbers are only the sand. But the stories, the reflections of the man himself, are the best, the seashells gathered from the sand.

"That's my last hurrah to you, Al. And this time, I'm the one who's crying."

Over the next few weeks, I wished many things. That we'd done the book together. That I'd stayed in closer touch during his final years. That I'd gone to see him in person, although I'm not sure I could have handled it, during his last days. That I'd have been able to say to him in person things I could only write on paper.

And then, a familiar phrase came back to me, a bit of Irish wisdom Mary's mother told me once. "If wishes were horses," she said, "beggars would ride."

At which point, I quit my second-guessing for good, where Al and I were concerned, and instead, remained thankful for my ride.

Appendix A:
Al's First International Dictionary

Aircraft carrier: A dominant big man; center.

Back-room lawyers: Professional agents.

Barracuda: To cut a player down; to chew a player out.

Battleship: A slow aircraft carrier.

Belly: An opponent's weak spot.

Berry-eating period: When things get tight; when a team or a coach could choke.

Big Apple: New York City.

Black Byrd: Nickname for Robert Byrd.

Black Jerry West: Nickname for Earl Tatum.

Blue chipper: A great high school recruit.

Checkerboard: Black-white relationships.

Cloud Piercer: Nickname for James Dudley.

Cupcake: An easy opponent.

Curtain time: Game time.

Curtains: The point at which a game has been decided.

Dance hall player: Player short on talent, but big on effort.

Diving points: Tricks players do to get fancy when they shoot.

Dousman: Nickname for guard Dave Delsman.

Dr. Evil Blackheart: Nickname for Pat Smith, who successfully threw a basketball into Lake Michigan.

Dunkirk: A disaster; poorly played game.

Dynamite: A great player or game.

Emmy game: A game that has great fan attraction (Example: Marquette vs. Notre Dame), no matter where the teams are in the rankings.

French pastry: A player or a game with style.

Going uptown: Getting a postseason tournament bid.

Hail Mary shot: A low-percentage shot, usually taken in the final seconds of a game, which would take a miracle to make.

Heavyweight: A tough opponent or player; opposite of a cupcake.

Keeper: A player who has a big future; as in fishing, a fish good enough to keep.

Knockout punch: The ability to knock an opponent out of a game with a sustained scoring spurt.

Lights out: The same as "curtains."

Memos and pipes: University administrators.

Merry-go-round: The world of sports.

Nose bleeder: A super jumper, or rebounder, who goes amazingly high.

Out of the gate: The start of a season.

Park Avenue: Anything first class.

Play above the rim: To rebound well.

Push: An even game; a tossup; no team favored.

Run for the roses: A successful late-season drive that lands a team a post-season tournament bid.

Sandfight: A hard-played game by both teams.

Seashells and balloons: The best of everything; everything's cool.

Secretariat of college forwards: Nickname for Bo Ellis during his senior year.

Short strokes: The final minutes of a game, where every basket counts.

Tap city: Beaten and going nowhere.

Tenth Avenue: In the dumps; opposite of Park Avenue.

The Dream: Nickname for Dean Meminger.

The Enforcer: Nickname for George Thompson.

The Real Thing: Marquette's season opener. Also described as "the moment of truth," "the tide's up," "pop time," and "the point of no return."

Thoroughbred: A gifted athlete; the best of his class.

Three o'Clock shooter: A player who shoots well in practice, but can't hit anything during the game.

Trickster: Nickname for Jackie Burke.

Uptick: Momentum; when a team is playing almost up to its capacity.

Uptown: A postseason tournament bid.

Whistle blower: A coach who uses a lot of drills and makes his players wear look-alike sports coats.

Whitehorse: Nickname for Jerome Whitehead.

White knuckler: A close game; down to the wire.

Zebras: Referees.

Appendix B:

The Record: McGuire at Marquette

Regular Season

Season	Home			Overall		
	W	L	Pct.	W	L	Pct.
1964-65	7	7	.500	8	18	.307
1965-66	11	4	.733	14	12	.538
1966-67	13	2	.867	21	9	.700
1967-68	14	1	.933	23	6	.793
1968-69	15	0	1.000	24	5	.827
1969-70	16	0	1.000	26	3	.896
1970-71	15	0	1.000	28	1	.965
1971-72	16	0	1.000	25	4	.862
1972-73	14	1	.933	25	4	.862
1973-74	14	1	.933	26	5	.838
1974-75	13	2	.867	23	4	.851
1975-76	15	0	1.000	27	2	.931
1976-77	11	5	.688	25	7	.781
MU Totals	174	23	**.883**	295	80	.787
Belmont Abbey				109	64	.635
Overall				404	144	.737

Postseason

Season	W	L	Pct.
1966-67	3	1	.750
1967-68	2	1	.667
1968-69	2	1	.667
1969-70	4	0	1.000
1970-71	2	1	.667
1971-72	1	2	.333
1972-73	2	1	.667
1973-74	4	1	.800
1974-75	0	1	.000
1975-76	2	1	.667
1976-77	5	0	1.000
Career	**27**	**10**	**.730**

"The Run for the Roses" NCAA National Championship (1976-77)

Marquette 66, Cincinnati 51
Marquette 67, Kansas State 66
Marquette 82, Wake Forest 68
Marquette 51, North Carolina-Charlotte 49
Marquette 67, North Carolina 59

Appendix C:
Al McGuire (1928-2001)

September 7, 1928: Born in New York.

1948: As sophomore at St. John's University, joins brother Dick on basketball squad. Becomes team captain in 1951.

1951: Drafted by the NBA Eastern Conference champion New York Knicks with their sixth draft choice, again joining brother Dick on roster.

July, 1954: After three seasons with the Knicks (4.1 points on 38.4 pecent shooting, 2.0 assists per game), traded to Baltimore Bullets.

November 27, 1954: NBA playing career ends when Bullets are disbanded after 14 games.

1955: Hired as assistant basketball coach at Dartmouth University.

1957: Hired as head basketball coach at Belmont Abbey.

April 11, 1964: Hired as head basketball coach at Marquette University, succeeding Ed Hickey, after compiling a 109-64 record at Belmont Abbey.

1966-67: With first big-time star, George Thompson, leads Warriors to 21-9 record and gains first national acclaim with runner-up finish in the National Invitation Tournament. Lost to Southern Illinois and star Walt Frazier, 71-56, in title game at Madison Square Garden.

1967-68: Earns Marquette's first NCAA tournament bid since 1961 and finishes with a 23-6 record.

June 7, 1969: Medalist Industries, a Milwaukee-based manufacturer of industrial and recreational products and athletic apparel, buys McGuire's Hall of Fame Sports Camps Inc. and begins longtime business relationship with McGuire.

1969-70: Angered that his 22-3 squad is placed outside the preferred Mideast Regional for the NCAA tournament, turns down the Warriors' invitation and takes team to the NIT. Warriors beat St. John's for the title and finish 26-3.

1970-71: One-point loss to No. 10-ranked Ohio State in the NCAA tournament, after late-season departure of star Jim Chones for pro basketball, is only blemish on 28-1 record.

1971: Named College Coach of the Year by Associated Press, United Press International, *The Sporting News* and U.S. Basketball Writers Association.

November 29, 1972: Named athletic director at Marquette, succeeding Sam Sauceda, on September 1, 1973.

1973-74: Advances to NCAA championship game, which Warriors lose, 76-64, to David Thompson and North Carolina State in Greensboro, North Carolina.

March 24, 1974: Named Coach of the Year in university division by the National Association of Basketball Coaches.

March 19, 1975: With his team a first-round victim in the NCAA tournament, is hired by NBC to do television commentary and analysis for the tournament.

December 17, 1976: Stuns fans by announcing he will retire as coach after season to become vice chairman of Medalist Industries, effective May 1, 1977.

March 28, 1977: In last game as coach, leads Warriors to a 67-59 victory over Dean Smith's North Carolina squad for the NCAA championship. McGuire's record is 295-80 at Marquette, with 27-10 mark in 11 postseason tournaments. Overall, his record was 404-144.

October 10, 1977: Hired by NBC as college basketball broadcaster and analyst.

March 20, 1978: Quits as vice chairman of Medalist Industries. Lends name and support to Al's Run, a charitable five-mile run that raises $2 million for Children's Hospital of Wisconsin through his final year of involvement, 1994.

March, 1992: Hired by CBS as college basketball analyst.

May 11, 1992: Inducted into Basketball Hall of Fame.

March 5, 2000: Works final game as broadcaster, between Wisconsin and Indiana at the Kohl Center in Madison. Announces that he is suffering from some form of anemia.

July 27, 2000: Hospitalized for undisclosed illness. Transferred to Franciscan Woods hospice some days later.

January 26, 2001: Dies at age 72.

A Final Remembrance

Leaning against my computer, this picture of Al has watched me all through the months I wrote this book. It was taken during a photo shoot in a greasy little South Side Milwaukee bar for a "20 Questions" interview for *Playboy Magazine* in April, 1983. For nearly an hour, Al sat there, his elbow on the rail, a bottle of Miller High Life at his side, while the producer and her cameraman took literally hundreds of Polaroids of Al in that one position, smiling and frowning, looking happy or looking angry, moving the lights and screens and reflectors this way and that, until everything was just right to shoot real film. "Now I know why those babes look so good," Al muttered during one break. "And here I thought it was the airbrush."

This picture is the one the producer folded up a couple times, trying to decide how much more to crop where. After which, it went on the floor with the rest. Quickly, I retrieved it and kept it as a souvenir. To this day, I can't remember which picture Playboy finally used, but this to me is the Al I will always remember—with his piercing eyes, no-nonsense demeanor, and Irish tough-guy stare. A person who wasn't afraid to fight, but always enjoyed a laugh.

One final wish. That someday, instead of a building or a statue, the powers that be at Marquette find and name that park after Al that he so wanted. A place where, as he put it, "Poor kids can come and play."

Okay. I can't help it. Here's one final story, as only Al could tell it.

"I went into a restaurant one night and ordered lobster, and the waiter brought me one with a claw missing. I called him over and told him about it. He told me that in the back there's a tank they keep the lobsters in and while they're in there, they fight and sometimes one loses a claw. I told him, 'Then bring me the winner.'"